Multilingualism in European Bilingual Contexts

MULTILINGUAL MATTERS SERIES
Series Editor: Professor John Edwards, *St. Francis Xavier University, Antigonish,*
Nova Scotia, Canada

Other Books in the Series
Language Planning in Nepal, Taiwan and Sweden
  Richard B. Baldauf, Jr. and Robert B. Kaplan (eds)
Can Threatened Languages be Saved?
  Joshua Fishman (ed.)
Language and Society in a Changing Italy
  Arturo Tosi
The Other Languages of Europe
  Guus Extra and Durk Gorter (eds)
Motivation in Language Planning and Language Policy
  Dennis Ager
Multilingualism in Spain
  M. Teresa Turell (ed.)
A Dynamic Model of Multilingualism
  Philip Herdina and Ulrike Jessner
Beyond Boundaries: Language and Identity in Contemporary Europe
  Paul Gubbins and Mike Holt (eds)
Bilingualism: Beyond Basic Principles
  Jean-Marc Dewaele, Alex Housen and Li Wei (eds)
Ideology and Image: Britain and Language
  Dennis Ager
Where East Looks West: Success in English in Goa and on the Konkan Coast
  Dennis Kurzon
English in Africa: After the Cold War
  Alamin M. Mazrui
Politeness in Europe
  Leo Hickey and Miranda Stewart (eds)
Language in Jewish Society: Towards a New Understanding
  John Myhill
Maintaining a Minority Language
  John Gibbons and Elizabeth Ramirez
Urban Multilingualism in Europe
  Guus Extra and Kutlay Yagmur (eds)
Cultural and Linguistic Policy Abroad: The Italian Experience
  Mariella Totaro-Genevois
Language Decline and Death in Africa: Causes, Consequences and Challenges
  Herman M. Batibo
Directions in Applied Linguistics
  Paul Bruthiaux, Dwight Atkinson, William G. Eggington, William Grabe and
  Vaidehi Ramanathan (eds)
Language Diversity in the Pacific: Endangerment and Survival
  Denis Cunningham, D. E. Ingram and Kenneth Sumbuk (eds)

For more details of these or any other of our publications, please contact:
Multilingual Matters, Frankfurt Lodge, Clevedon Hall,
Victoria Road, Clevedon, BS21 7HH, England
http://www.multilingual-matters.com

MULTILINGUAL MATTERS 135
Series Editor: John Edwards

Multilingualism in European Bilingual Contexts
Language Use and Attitudes

Edited by
David Lasagabaster and Ángel Huguet

MULTILINGUAL MATTERS LTD
Clevedon • Buffalo • Toronto

Library of Congress Cataloging in Publication Data
Multilingualism in European Bilingual Contexts: Language Use and Attitudes/Edited by David Lasagabaster and Angel Huguet.
Multilingual Matters: 135
Includes bibliographical references.
1. Multilingualism–Europe. 2. Bilingualism–Europe. 3. Language awareness–Europe.
I. Lasagabaster, David. II. Huguet, Ángel.
P115.5.E85M87 2007
404'.2094–dc22   2006022425
A catalog record for this book is available from the Library of Congress.

British Library Cataloguing in Publication Data
A catalogue entry for this book is available from the British Library.

ISBN 1-85359-930-1 / EAN 978-1-85359-930-9 (hbk)
ISBN 1-85359-929-8 / EAN 978-1-85359-929-3 (pbk)

Multilingual Matters Ltd
UK: Frankfurt Lodge, Clevedon Hall, Victoria Road, Clevedon BS21 7HH.
USA: UTP, 2250 Military Road, Tonawanda, NY 14150, USA.
Canada: UTP, 5201 Dufferin Street, North York, Ontario M3H 5T8, Canada.

The policy of Multilingual Matters/Channel View Publications is to use papers that are natural, renewable and recyclable products, made from wood grown in sustainable forests. In the manufacturing process of our books, and to further support our policy, preference is given to printers that have FSC and PEFC Chain of Custody accreditation. The FSC and/or PEFC logos will appear on those books where full accreditation has been granted to the printer concerned.

Typeset by Datapage Ltd.
Printed and bound in Great Britain by the Cromwell Press Ltd.

In memoriam

Jehannes Ytsma (1957-2005)

One of the contributors to this volume, Jehannes Ytsma, died while the manuscript was being reviewed. It was a shock, first of all because this kind of news is always unexpected, but the impact is even greater when the person concerned is young, healthy and seemingly full of energy. Yet, on December 9, 2005 Jehannes died of a heart attack at the age of 48.

I had first met Jehannes many years ago at one of the conferences where we happened to coincide and we shared a meal and a couple of drinks. He was a specialist on bilingualism and trilingual education, which are also my fields of research, and therefore we had many scientific interests in common. In fact, the week before his passing away he had just sent me an email asking for some data about the Basque educational system.

When I talked to him about the project put forward in this volume he immediately wanted to contribute, as he was always ready to work and share his knowledge and new experiences with his colleagues. Unfortunately, he could not see the final product and we, as editors, did not have time to congratulate him on his work nor thank him properly for his cooperation.

I would like to dedicate this volume to his memory and to his family.

David Lasagabaster
University of the Basque Country

Contents

The Contributors

Sandro Caruana is Senior Lecturer at the Department of Arts and Languages, Faculty of Education, University of Malta. He coordinates Italian language and teaching methodology courses and also lectures on sociolinguistics and on the language of the media. His main areas of interest regard teaching Italian L2 and the effects of the media on language acquisition. His works have been published in a number of international journals and also include *Mezzi di comunicazione e input linguistico. L'acquisizione dell'italiano L2 a Malta* (2003, Franco Angeli, Milano).

Håkan Casares Berg is coordinator of the Language Section of the Galician Culture Council. He has worked as a researcher at the universities of Vigo and Santiago de Compostela and at the Socio-linguistics Seminar of the Galician Academy of Language. He is a member of the editorial board of *Estudios de Sociolingüística* and is one of the four commissioners for the monitoring and fostering of the Plan for Linguistic Normalisation driven by the Galician government. He has published *Galician among the Youth* (2003) and *The Galician Society and its Language* (2005).

Antonio Fernández Salgado completed a MA in Romance Philology and Hispanic Philology (Galician–Portuguese) and studied at the University of Santiago de Compostela. He specialises in sociolinguistics and has been a researcher of the Seminar of Sociolinguistics of the Galician Academy of Language since 1999. He is also a member of several research projects like 'A draft of measures to improve attitudes towards the Galician language and the extension of its use' and 'Evaluation of Bilingual Competence at the End of Compulsory Education', among others. He is also the co-author of the volume *Galician among the Youth* (2003). At the moment he is working on the review of the *Sociolinguistic Map of Galicia*.

Ángel Huguet is Lecturer at the Faculty of Educational Sciences of the University of Lleida, Catalonia, Spain. His research line during the last ten years has been focused on multilingualism and bilingual education. His current interests are oriented towards equal opportunities at school in contexts of immigration. His latest publications include the volumes

El conocimiento de la lengua castellana en alumnado inmigrante escolarizado en 1° de ESO. Un estudio empírico (2005), co-authored with José Luis Navarro and published in Madrid by the Spanish Ministry of Education and Science, and *Fundamentos en educación bilingüe* (2006), co-authored with José María Madariaga and published in Bilbao by the University of the Basque Country.

Rudi Janssens studied sociology at the Vrije Universiteit Brussels (Belgium), receiving his doctorate in 1995 based on the dissertation 'A Boolean Approach to Attitude Measurement'. He was formerly attached to the Centre of Statistics and Operational Research and is currently working in the 'Centre of the Multidisciplinary Study of Brussels' at the same university. He works as a researcher on different aspects of language use in a multilingual urban environment, especially on economic, educational, political and migration aspects. He is currently also participating in projects on the applicability of the Belgian language policy in former Yugoslavia and the relation between migration and language use.

David Lasagabaster is Associate Professor of English Studies at the University of the Basque Country. He has published on second-language acquisition, foreign-language teaching methodology, bilingualism and multilingualism. His latest publications include the volume *Trilingüismo en la enseñanza. Actitudes hacia la lengua minoritaria, la mayoritaria y la extranjera* (2003) published in Lleida by Milenio Educación and the co-edited (together with Juan Manuel Sierra) volumes *Multilingüismo y multiculturalismo en la escuela* (2005) and *Multilingüismo, competencia lingüística y nuevas tecnologías* (2005), both published in Barcelona by Horsori.

Janet Laugharne is a Reader in the Cardiff School of Education, University of Wales Institute Cardiff and the school's Director of Research. She is a highly experienced teacher and currently supervises masters and research degree students. She is an independent inspector for Estyn, the Welsh inspectorate. Her research specialism is bilingualism and bilingual education, particularly in relation to Welsh, English and other languages in the UK. Janet Laugharne is one of the principal investigators for a Welsh Assembly Government research project, MEEIFP (Monitoring and Evaluation of the Effective Implementation of the Foundation Phase), in collaboration with the London Institute of Education.

Xaquín Loredo Gutiérrez completed a MA in Educational Psychology at Santiago de Compostela University. He is currently a researcher of the

Seminar of Sociolinguistics of the Galician Academy of Language. He has taken part in several projects such as 'A draft of measures to improve attitudes towards the Galician language and the extension of its use', 'Evaluation of Bilingual Competence at the End of Compulsory Education', the review of the *Sociolinguistic Map of Galicia* and 'The State of the Art in the Teaching of Galician Language and Literature in Secondary Education'. He is the co-author of publications like *Galician among the youth* (2003) and *The Galician Society and its Language* (2005).

Laurence Mettewie teaches Dutch language and linguistics at the University of Namur (Belgium). Her research focuses on the socio-psychological factors interfering in second-language acquisition processes, such as attitudes and motivation. She also studied the situation of Dutch-medium schools in Brussels, hosting many Francophone pupils and the impact of that Francophone population on language competence and attitudes. Moreover, she is involved in the development of bilingual education programmes in Belgium.

Muiris Ó Laoire works as a senior lecturer in undergraduate language, communication and culture courses at the Institute of Technology Tralee and works on a consultative basis on the Review of Languages at the NCCA (National Council for Curriculum and Assessment) Dublin. He is co-editor of *Teagasc na Gaeilge* (Ireland) and *The Celtic Journal of Language Learning* (USA). He is the author of textbooks, academic books and several papers on sociolinguistics, language regeneration and language pedagogy.

Maria Pilar Safont Jordà is Associate Professor of Sociolinguistics and ELT Methodology at the Universitat Jaume I in Castelló (Spain). Her research interests involve the development of pragmatic competence by third-language learners of English, as well as factors influencing third-language use. She has carried out various studies on the acquisition and use of specific speech acts by third-language learners of English, and she has published part of her work in international journals like *The International Journal of Multilingualism* and *The International Journal of Bilingualism*, and has recently authored the book *Third Language Learners. Pragmatic Production and Awareness* (2005).

Isabel Suárez Fernández is a sociologist with training in both socio-linguistic research and language planning. She received her MA in Sociology at the Faculty of Sociology at A Coruña University. Since 1999 she has taught at the Sociolinguistic Seminars of the Galician Academy of Language, where she has done research and published on language attitudes and bilingual competence in Galicia. Some of her published works, which she has co-authored, are *Situation of Galician Language in Santiago de Compostela* (2001), *Galician among the Youth* (2003) and *The Galician Society and its Language* (2005).

Jehannes Ytsma (1957–2005) was senior researcher at the Fryske Akademy. He was a specialist in the study of bilingual and trilingual education and published on many topics, such as Frisian in education, models of trilingual education, bilingualism in early childhood, interaction in multilingual families, the sociology of language in Friesland, migration and the integration of newcomers or language attitudes. He was the co-author of *Frisian: The Frisian Language in Education in the Netherlands* (2001) and co-editor of *Trilingualism in Family, School and Community* (2003). He died on 9 December 2005.

Introduction: A Transnational Study in European Bilingual Contexts

DAVID LASAGABASTER and ÁNGEL HUGUET

In the last decades there has been increasing interest in the maintenance of minority languages and a greater awareness of the need to speak foreign languages. As a result, the presence of more than two languages in the curriculum is commonplace in many European bilingual contexts. Although this is an expanding phenomenon in Europe, the number of research studies tackling the analysis of language use and language attitudes towards multilingualism is very limited. This volume intends to examine language use and language attitudes towards three languages (the minority, the majority and the foreign languages) in different European bilingual contexts.

Language attitudes are learnt and, therefore, educators play a paramount role in their formation, to such an extent that attitudes formed under educator influence may be extremely difficult to change. Students who face a situation in which different languages are in contact realise in early schooling that society, family and school all place importance on these languages. The students' own assessment, together with the information and the knowledge they gain, will lead to the establishment of their attitudes towards the different languages, the speakers of these languages and to the learning process itself.

The teacher's role with regards to the formation of language attitudes can thus be crucial in the students' future language attitudes. All the papers included in this volume, therefore, elicit information from university students whose degrees are geared towards teaching. The sample consisted of more than 1800 undergraduates. This has a twofold objective. Firstly, all the participants were enrolled in similar degrees and thus the possible effect of the specialisation variable could be controlled. Secondly, our different research studies focus on the analysis of the language use and the language attitudes held by those who are going to become teachers in the short run and whose influence on future generations' attitudes is beyond any doubt.

The book consists of nine chapters on language use and attitudes in nine different bilingual areas/states: the Basque Country, Catalonia,

Galicia, and the Valencian Community in Spain, plus Belgium, Friesland, Ireland, Malta and Wales. The book is divided into two main sections: the Spanish context and other European contexts. It is worth pointing out that in Spain 40% of the population live in bilingual areas, as Galician is spoken in Galicia, Catalan in Catalonia, the Valencian Community and the Balearic islands, and Basque in the Basque Autonomous Community and Navarre. This makes it one of the most interesting contexts to carry out research on language use and language attitudes (see Table I.1). The bilingual communities with the largest populations (Catalonia, the Valencian Community, Galicia and the Basque Country) are included in this volume.

In the different chapters that make up the volume each author briefly describes each particular sociolinguistic context and educational system (paying special attention to the presence of the different languages in contact), followed by a brief summary of the results obtained in previous studies on language attitudes carried out in the context concerned. Language use and language attitudes towards the minority language (L1 and/or L2), the majority language (L1 and/or L2) and the foreign language (L3) have been examined by analysing the results obtained from an essentially identical questionnaire completed in the nine different bilingual settings. A final chapter compares and discusses the results.

In every single case the researchers used the same questionnaire to gather the data and the same methodology was applied in each setting, allowing comparison of the results obtained in bilingual areas notable for their singularities. The instrument used was based on Baker's (1992) and

Table I.1 Population and percentage of Spain's officially bilingual communities

Autonomous community	Population	% of overall Spanish population
Catalonia	6,343,818	15.53
Valencian Community	4,163,161	10.19
Balearic Islands	842,029	2.06
Galicia	2,693,747	6.59
Basque Autonomous Community	2,082,253	5.10
Navarre	555,898	1.36
Total	16,680,906	40.83

Source: Huguet (2004: 401)

was translated into different languages: Basque, Catalan, Dutch, English, French, Flemish, Frisian, Galician, Irish and Spanish. The reliability tests carried out before its implementation showed that all the translations of the instrument gave consistent results when tested on different occasions, a fact underlined by the high correlation indexes obtained after having passed the test twice (all the correlations above 0.88), leaving at least a month between the first trial and the second. The results of the test–retest are apportioned in Table I.2.

The questionnaire (see the Appendix) utilised to gather the data can be divided into three main parts. The first one deals with personal information, such as age, sex, parental occupation or L1. In the second section the participants were invited to answer questions concerning the use of the two official languages with regards to: (i) their closest relations (family, friends, classmates or neighbours) and (ii) the means of communication (television, newspapers and journals, music, and radio). They were also asked about the importance attached to the minority language to do everyday activities such as going shopping, making friends, reading, writing, getting a job or bringing up children. The final section focused on language attitudes by means of the same ten items on a five-point Likert scale for each of the three languages.

Table I.2 Results of the test – retest

Context	Language	Observations	Correlation	p-value
1. Catalonia	Catalan	48	0.943	0.0001
2. Galicia	Galician	104	0.963	0.0001
2. Galicia	Spanish	92	0.873	0.0001
3. Basque Country	Basque	108	0.976	0.0001
3. Basque Country	Spanish	132	0.948	0.0001
4. Valencian Community	Catalan	92	0.980	0.0001
5. Belgium	Dutch	36	0.965	0.0001
5. Belgium	French	60	0.967	0.0001
6. Friesland				
7. Ireland	English	84	0.970	0.0001
8. Malta	English	80	0.963	0.0001
9. Wales	English	72	0.883	0.0001

It has to be stressed that there were some minimal variations in some of the items used. For example, item 18 (first part) was added in those contexts where different linguistic models are available (such as the Basque Country), but was not included in those where there is no opportunity to choose between different models (as is the case in Malta). Similarly, we will take advantage of this introductory chapter to explain the recoding of some of the items in order to avoid repetition later on in the individual chapters. Thus, as for the *parental occupation* (item 6) or socioprofessional status, the highest answer (irrespective of whether it belonged to the father or mother) was chosen and then all the answers were codified in three categories: High (which corresponded to answers 'a' and 'b'), Medium (answers 'c' and 'd') and Low status (the rest of the answers, that is to say, 'e', 'f' and 'g').

Similarly, the attitudes towards each of the three languages in contact were codified in the following way: the option *Strongly Agree* (SA) was recoded as 100, the option *Agree* (A) as 75, *Neither Agree Nor Disagree* (NAND) as 50, *Disagree* (D) as 25 and *Strongly Disagree* (SD) as 0. Once the results were codified, the *average* for the ten items related to each language was obtained, which allowed us to distinguish three categories: (i) the first one was made up of *Unfavourable attitudes*, that is to say, those between 0.000 and 33.333; (ii) the second category comprised *Neutral attitudes*, for those whose scores were between 33.334 and 66.666; (iii) the third one consisted of those students who held *Favourable attitudes*, i.e. those between 66.667 and 100.000. In this way, we had at our disposal a *quantitative* variable (the average score for the ten items) which could also be used as *qualitative* (depending on their favourable, neutral or unfavourable attitudes).

There are four main reasons why this publication can make a contribution to this area of research, and which differentiate it from earlier works. Firstly, this is a transnational study involving nine different bilingual areas/states. While reviewing studies in this field, we noticed that there is a dearth of studies directed at comparing the language attitudes of different European contexts (Lasagabaster, 2003). There are studies wherein the language attitudes of inhabitants from different bilingual settings within the same country are examined, but very few transnational studies (and none involving so many different contexts) such as the one this volume puts forward. Moreover, it includes bilingual contexts (such as Galicia, the Valencian Community or Malta) that have received very little attention so far.

Secondly, it involves not only the minority and the majority languages concerned in the different bilingual areas, as is usually the case in the vast majority of studies, but also the foreign language. Therefore, it goes beyond bilingualism and into multilingualism.

Thirdly, the instrument (as seen above supported by very high reliability indexes) and the methodology are the same in all cases, which allows us to compare contexts that share some similarities, while at the same time retaining their own sociolinguistic features.

And finally, the sample is made up of a specific group of university students (would-be teachers), whose influence on the language attitudes of their future pupils may be very relevant. Thus we strongly believe that the possible impact of this new generation of teachers on the different educational systems under analysis, both in the short and the long run, is worth considering and examining in detail.

As stated before, the book is divided into two parts. It is worth remembering that, although the first part deals with the three minority languages officially recognised in Spain – Basque, Catalan and Galician – there are other minority languages (Aragonese, Asturian or Bable and Aranese) spoken in the Spanish context which unfortunately are more often than not ignored (Turell, 2001: 2). Having said this, the first contribution by Ángel Huguet, carried out in Catalonia, is focused on Catalan, Spanish and English as the foreign language; Xaquín Loredo *et al.*'s contribution deals with Galician, Spanish and English as L3 in Galicia; whereas the third contribution by David Lasagabaster analyses the language use and language attitudes towards Basque, Spanish and English in the Basque Country. The languages considered by Maria Pilar Safont in the fourth Spanish contribution are Catalan, Spanish and once again English as a foreign language, a reflection of the languages in contact in the Valencian Community's educational context.

Chapters 5–9 tackle other European contexts. Thus, the fifth one, Mettewie and Janssens', is set in the bilingual region of Brussels and the languages under examination are Dutch, French and a range of foreign languages, due to the complex sociolinguistic features of this particular context (30% of its inhabitants are not Belgian). In Chapter 6 Jehannes Ytsma covers Frisian, Dutch and English in Friesland, whereas in the following chapter Ó Laoire takes into consideration the linguistic situation in Ireland and deals with Irish and English with French, German or Spanish as L3. In the next chapter Sandro Caruana puts forward the results obtained in Malta with respect to Maltese, English and the L3 (predominantly Italian), and in the ninth chapter Janet Laugharne introduces the sociolinguistic situation in Wales by presenting her data with regards to Welsh, English and the L3. The book is rounded off with a final contribution by Ángel Huguet and David Lasagabaster in which a comparison of the nine different bilingual settings is completed and some final considerations are presented.

Last but not least, it has to be pointed out that this publication is aimed at a diverse readership. Not only can it be of interest to preservice and in-service teachers, researchers, scholars, students and all those involved in education departments and ministries, but could also prove useful to those working and studying in a wide range of fields, such as sociology, sociolinguistics, psychology, second-language acquisition, education, bilingualism, multilingualism and even politics.

References

Baker, C. (1992) *Attitudes and Language*. Clevedon: Multilingual Matters.
Huguet, A. (2004) La educación bilingüe en el Estado español: situación actual y perspectivas. *Cultura y Educación* 16, 399–418.
Lasagabaster, D. (2003) *Trilingüismo en la enseñanza. Actitudes hacia la lengua minoritaria, la mayoritaria y la extranjera*. Lleida: Milenio.
Turell, M.T. (2001) *Multilingualism in Spain*. Clevedon: Multilingual Matters.

Appendix A

The instrument underwent some minimal changes depending on the context. L1 refers to the minority language, L2 to the majority language and L3 corresponds to the foreign language. For example, in the case of the Basque Country, the L1 would be Basque, the L2 Spanish and the L3 English, whereas in the case of Ireland, the L1 would be Irish, the L2 English and the L3 Spanish, German or French.

Attitudes towards three languages in contact

We would like to ask you to help us by answering the following questions. This is not a test so there are no 'right' or 'wrong' answers and you don't even have to write your name on it. We are interested in your personal opinion. Please give your answers sincerely as only this will guarantee the success of the investigation. Thank you very much for your help.

1. Age (in years and months):

2. Specialisation (degree to be obtained):

3. Course:

   In the following please put an 'X' in the right place.

4. Gender: Male __ Female __

5. Mother Tongue:__ Basque
   __ Spanish
   __ Basque & Spanish

6. Parental occupation   Father   Mother

a/ Manager, director or owner of a business/company with more than 25 workers   ☐   ☐

b/ Bachelor's degree (lawyer, architect, chemist, engineer, doctor, lecturer, economist, etc.)   ☐   ☐

c/ Degree or HND (*Higher National Diploma) (school teacher, technical engineer, social worker, etc.), or middle management without a bachelor's degree (commercial head, production head, administrative head, etc.)   ☐   ☐

d/ Owner of a business or company with less than 25 staff, health worker, clerical worker, salesperson, etc.   ☐   ☐

e/ Specialised worker (mechanic, chauffeur, policeman, plumber, waiter mason, electrician, etc.), farmer or cattle breeder.   ☐   ☐

f/ Labourer, seasonal worker, watchman, etc.   ☐   ☐

g/ Housework   ☐   ☐

h/ Others (please specify) ....   ☐   ☐

7. In the following section we would like you to answer some questions by simply giving marks from 1 to 4.

    1 = None, 2 = A little, 3 = Good, 4 = Very good

For example, if your Chinese is 'very good', your Japanese 'good' and you can speak no Arabic ('None'), write this:

	Chinese	Japanese	Arabic
General proficiency	4	3	1

Please put one (and only one) whole number in each box and don't leave out any of them in the first three columns (L1, L2 and L3). If you know another language, please put numbers in the 'Other' columns after specifying the language concerned.

In your opinion, what is your language proficiency in...?

	L1	L2	L3 Other (Specify:)	Other (Specify:)
General proficiency				
Reading				
Writing				
Speaking				
Listening				

8. I started learning L1 at the age of _____

9. I started learning L2 at the age of _____

10. I started learning L3 at the age of _____

11. Have you ever been to an L3 speaking country?:   Yes __ No __

12. Hometown: a) More than 100,000 inhabitants __
              b) Less than 100,000 inhabitants __

13. Province: _ Araba
              _ Bizkaia
              _ Gipuzkoa
              _ Nafarroa

14. My hometown is mainly a: __ L2-speaking community
                             __ L1-speaking community

15. I studied at a: __ public school
                    __ private school

16. How often do you watch TV in L3?
__ Never __ Hardly ever   __ Once/twice a week
__ 3 to 5 times a week   __ Daily

17. What type of High School studies did you complete before entering university?
__ Technical-Scientific   __ Humanities and Social Sciences
__ Artistic   __ Other (specify): ....

18. In which linguistic model did you predominantly complete your preuniversity studies?

__ Model A __ Model B __ Model D

Now we would like to know which language you speak to the following people. Please put an 'X' in the box which best expresses your situation. For example, if you always speak in L2 with your father, put an 'X' in the last box:

	Always in L1	In L1 more often than L2	In L1 and L2 about equally	In L2 more often than L1	Always in L2
1. Father					x

In which language do **YOU** speak to the following people? Choose one of these answers:

	Always in L1	In L1 more often than L2	In L1 and L2 about equally	In L2 more often than L1	Always in L2
1. Father					
2. Mother					
3. Brothers & sisters					
4. Friends in the classroom					
5. Friends outside school					
6. Teachers (except with language teachers)					
7. Neighbours (near my house)					

Which language do **YOU** use with the following?

	Always in L1	In L1 more often than L2	In L1 and L2 about equally	In L2 more often than L1	Always in L2
1. Watching TV					
2. The press					
3. Music					
4. Radio					

How **important** or **unimportant** do you think that the **L1 language** is for people to do the following?
There are no right or wrong answers.

For people to:	Important	A little important	A little unimportant	Unimportant
1. To make friends				
2. Read				
3. Write				
4. Watch TV				
5. Get a job				
6. Be liked				
7. Live in the L1 country				
8. Bring up children				
9. Go shopping				
10. Make phone calls				

11. Pass exams				
12. Be accepted in the community				
13. Talk to friends at university				
14. Talk to teachers at university				
15. Talk to people out of university				

Here are some statements about the **L1** language. Please say whether you agree or disagree with these statements. There are no right or wrong answers. Please be as honest as possible. Answer with ONE of the following:

SA = Strongly **A**gree (circle **SA**)
A = **A**gree (circle **A**)
NAND = **N**either **A**gree **N**or **D**isagree (circle **NAND**)
D = **D**isagree (circle **D**)
SD = Strongly **D**isagree (circle **SD**)

1. I like hearing L1 spoken... SA A NAND D SD
2. L1 should be taught to all pupils in the
   Basque Country.. SA A NAND D SD
3. I like speaking L1.. SA A NAND D SD
4. L1 is an easy language to learn.................................... SA A NAND D SD
5. There are not more useful languages to learn
   than L1... SA A NAND D SD
6. I prefer to be taught in L1... SA A NAND D SD
7. Learning L1 enriches my cultural knowledge.......... SA A NAND D SD
8. I would not mind marrying a L1 speaker.................. SA A NAND D SD
9. L1 is a language worth learning.................................. SA A NAND D SD
10. If I have children, I would like them to be L1 speakers regardless of
    other languages they may know................................ SA A NAND D SD

Here are some statements about the **L2** language. Please say whether you agree or disagree with these statements. There are no right or wrong answers. Please be as honest as possible. Answer with ONE of the following:

SA = Strongly Agree (circle **SA**)
A = Agree (circle **A**)
NAND = Neither Agree Nor Disagree (circle **NAND**)
D = Disagree (circle **D**)
SD = Strongly Disagree (circle **SD**)

1. I like hearing L2 spoken.. SA A NAND D SD
2. L2 should be taught to all pupils in the Basque
   Country.. SA A NAND D SD
3. I like speaking L2.. SA A NAND D SD
4. L2 is an easy language to learn.................................... SA A NAND D SD
5. There are not more useful languages to learn
   than L2.. SA A NAND D SD
6. I prefer to be taught in L2.. SA A NAND D SD
7. Learning L2 enriches my cultural knowledge........... SA A NAND D SD
8. I would not mind marrying a L2 speaker.................. SA A NAND D SD
9. L2 is a language worth learning................................. SA A NAND D SD
10. If I have children, I would like them to be L2
    speakers regardless of other languages they
    may know... SA A NAND D SD

Here are some statements about the **L3** language. Please say whether you agree or disagree with these statements. There are no right or wrong answers. Please be as honest as possible. Answer with ONE of the following:

SA = Strongly Agree (circle **SA**)
A = Agree (circle **A**)
NAND = Neither Agree Nor Disagree (circle **NAND**)
D = Disagree (circle **D**)
SD = Strongly Disagree (circle **SD**)

1. I like hearing L3 spoken.. SA A NAND D SD
2. L3 should be taught to all pupils in the
   Basque Country... SA A NAND D SD
3. I like speaking L3.. SA A NAND D SD
4. L3 is an easy language to learn.................................... SA A NAND D SD
5. There are not more useful languages to learn
   than L3.. SA A NAND D SD

6. I prefer to be taught in L3.. SA A NAND D SD

7. Learning L3 enriches my cultural knowledge.......... SA A NAND D SD

8. I would not mind marrying an L3 speaker................ SA A NAND D SD

9. L3 is a language worth learning................................. SA A NAND D SD

10. If I have children, I would like them to be L3
    speakers regardless of other languages they
    may know.. SA A NAND D SD

Thank you very much for your cooperation

Part 1
The Spanish Context

Chapter 1

Language Use and Language Attitudes in Catalonia

ÁNGEL HUGUET

Introduction

Catalonia, together with the Valencian and Balearic Communities, is one of the three autonomous communities in Spain where part of its inhabitants speak Catalan as the common language for their social relations. Although it is usually not mentioned, this also happens in the narrow strip in Aragon. These areas can be seen in Figure 1.1.[1] Catalan, unlike Basque, also present in this volume, is a Romance language that is a small distance from Castilian or French. This is one of the reasons why its comprehension is well extended among the population in Catalonia, and only about 4% claim not to understand the Catalan language (see Table 1.1).

The above percentages have been obtained from a macro review made in the bilingual communities of the State in 1993, and another one made in 1998, which showed little difference. But the data from the comparative exploitation of the 1991 and 1996 census are probably even more interesting. The latter show a remarkable evolution with regard to the population's linguistic abilities in the Catalan language: the rate of comprehension has moved from 93.76% to 94.97% of individuals; the rate of expression has moved from 68.34% to 75.30%; and the rate of writing has moved from 39.94% to 45.84% (Institut d'Estadística de Catalunya, 1998).

When this evolution is analysed according to age groups, significant variations can be observed. The knowledge of Catalan is at its maximum among the young generations that have attended school in Catalan.[2] It decreases as age increases, to reach its minimum levels among mature generations of ages between 55 and 64 (these generations have been marked by noteworthy events: they are the generations of important immigration in the 1960s and they attended school in the post-war period). Finally, there is a recovery in the level of language knowledge among the population who attended school during the Republic with the *Generalitat de Catalunya* (the Catalan Government) in the 1930s (Institut d'Estadística de Catalunya, 1998; Farràs *et al.*, 2001).

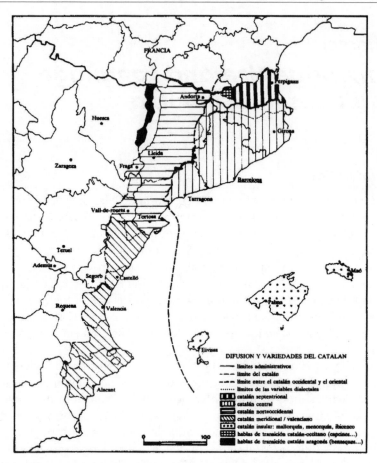

Figure 1.1 Spreading and variants of the Catalan language (reproduced from Siguan, 1992)

Table 1.1 Percentage of individuals that consider Catalan as their main language and linguistic competence acquired

Do not understand Catalan	4%
Understand, but don't talk	22%
Can talk, but not as the main language	23%
Talk as a main language	50%
Talk Catalan and Spanish equally	1%
Totals	100%

Source: Siguan (1994)

Catalan language underwent a process of normalisation in the beginning of the last century; therefore, it has not been a problem to use it as a language of instruction at school at all levels over the years. But its use was not widespread until recent years when *La Generalitat* (the Catalan Government) was restored and Catalan education has become something totally normalised. The presence of Catalan in preuniversity education was limited to the *Escola Catalana* (Catalan school, similar to the Basque *ikastola*) that belonged to the private network of education through cooperatives, quota, etc. The integration of an important number of these schools into the public system during the 1980s is a key to understanding the presence of Catalan nowadays in education and, consequently, the models of bilingual education.

The Catalan Educational System

After the Language Planning Act was passed in 1983 and was later developed, it can be said that all pupils in Catalonia are in contact with the Catalan language as a language of learning. In other words, it can be affirmed with no hesitation that nowadays most of the educational system in Catalonia is bilingual, like, for instance, the systems in Luxemburg or in francophone Canada (Huguet, 2004).

As far as legislation is concerned, the Department of Education of *Generalitat de Catalunya* published a few decrees in the beginning of the 1980s, in which the presence of Catalan in preuniversity education and the degrees required for teaching Catalan or in Catalan were regulated. But not until the Language Planning Act was made public did the current regulation come into force.

The 1983 Language Planning Act, and its more recent version of 1998, coincides in that pupils absolutely need to be able to use Catalan and Castilian normally and correctly at the end of their compulsory education, whichever language they use at the beginning of their education. In order to achieve this aim, according to the law, it is up to the families to decide which type of education they want their children to follow, i.e. Catalan curricula with Castilian as the second language, or the other way round. The law does not introduce the concept of 'mother tongue' or 'family language' but uses the term 'usual language' and leaves it to the families to choose the language in which their children will be educated. Regarding the teaching staff, the law gives preference to the population linguistic rights over the teaching staff rights; Article 18 reads: 'according to the requirements of the teaching task, teachers need to know both official languages', and the *Generalitat* regulates the mechanisms for teachers to access the educational system.

On 30 August 1983, a decree completing an Order dated 8 September of the same year was published in the *Diari Oficial de la Generalitat*

(Catalan Government's Official Journal) where the presence of Catalan in preuniversity education was regulated. As a general rule, the election of the language of instruction was free in Nursery Education and the first cycle of Primary School, and the *Departament d'Ensenyament* (Autonomous Department of Education) undertook to ensure that all teaching staff at these levels would know both languages. Both in Catalan and Castilian education, the other language needed to be studied as a subject. The organisation and didactics taken by the school were left to the board of teaching staff that, together with the families, had the last word about the presence of each language at these levels of education. It was also established that regardless of the learning language in the first cycle of Primary School, all schools were supposed to introduce either Social or Natural Science in Catalan during the second cycle; and both Sciences during the third cycle. In Secondary Education two subjects out of four (Natural Science, Design, History and Mathematics) had to be taught in Catalan. The same criterion was applied for Vocational Training, one of the subjects having to belong to the area of Applied or Training sciences and the other one to the Technological–Practical Area. Obviously, Catalan and Spanish as subjects were taught in all courses, in all cycles of preuniversity education.

This pattern, as has been mentioned already, abolished any educational model where Catalan was only a subject. Teaching is organised in Catalan, with Spanish as a language, or as a bilingual programme where both languages progressively reach the same position in the curriculum, regardless of which one is used for learning how to read and write. This pattern made it possible for many Catalan educational programmes to be extended to children from Spanish-speaking families, i.e. linguistic immersion programmes, partly thanks to the positive attitude toward education in Catalan of an important part of the Spanish-speaking population (Areny & Van der Shaaf, 2000; Huguet & Llurda 2001; Huguet & Suïls, 1998).

With regard to linguistic models, when the Language Planning Act was passed, bilingual education was limited. About 40% of private schools used Catalan and Spanish as teaching languages. The percentage was lower in public schools, although 25% of these centres had started Catalan programmes in Nursery Education, many of which were programmes of home/school language change (Vila, 1992, 1998). But things changed a great deal in a few years and nowadays most schoolchildren in Catalonia follow educational programmes with Catalan as the main language regardless of their family language, either for keeping their family language or as linguistic immersion programmes. In the first case the family language coincides with the school language, whereas in the second case there is a change in the family/school language. But although these are roughly the bilingual education models developed in Catalonia, from the development of the *Proyectos Lingüís-ticos de Centro* (Centre Linguistic Projects)[3] their accomplishment in practice is very diverse, especially the treatment of languages with curricular presence. In fact, we find that programmes that can be very different from each other are labelled altogether as immersion programmes.

In Nursery and Primary Education, 73% of schools carry out all teaching in Catalan (58% of private schools), 25% are in the process of implementing new courses totally in Catalan (29% of private schools) and the remaining 2% can be considered at a standstill, as a number of subjects are regularly taught in Catalan (13% of private schools). Regarding Secondary Education, 30% of schools carry out all teaching in Catalan (66% of private schools) and 70% in both languages, with different levels of presence of each language in them (34% among private schools). This information regarding Nursery and Primary Education can be seen in Table 1.2.

Eighty-one percent of schoolchildren had their education in Catalan in Nursery and Primary School, and 19% in Catalan and Spanish. If we look only to immersion linguistic programmes, taking into consideration the classrooms that met the requirements for this type of programme (about 70% were not from Catalan-speaking families), 84% of pupils participated in them (91% in public schools and 65% in private schools) (Servei d'Ensenyament del Català, 2001).

A relevant part of bilingual education in Catalonia is made up of immersion programmes that enjoy a specific treatment (Bel, 1991; Comet, 1992; Serra, 1997). In general their features comply with the psychopedagogical requisites of linguistic immersion: voluntariness, bilingual teaching staff, specific methodology, initial ignorance of the teaching language of most of the schoolchildren, etc., and they have received special support and treatment from the *Departament d'Ensenyament*. It must be stated that the Catalan immersion linguistic programme had a clear referent in this type of programme carried out in Canada. The

Table 1.2 Percentage of educational centres according to the level of presence of Catalan language

	Public schools	*Private schools*
Teaching in Catalan (%)	73	58
Evolutive bilingual (%)	25	29
Stationary bilingual (%)	2	13
Totals (%)	100	100

Source: Servei d'Ensenyament del Català (2001)

Canadian model, backed up by quick, increasing and reliable results, helped to realise that the acquisition of a second language by its use as a school language was possible (Lambert, 1974; Ouellet, 1990). But the features of these programmes, as they have been implemented in Catalonia, have some differences with the Canadian model.

The modality of immersion developed in Catalonia is total early immersion. Two fundamental features define the programme as total early immersion: early, because schoolchildren are immersed in the second language from the beginning of their schooling and because during the first years the teaching time of the new language is about 90–100%. But, while in Canada immersion programmes go from the ages of 5 to 16 years old, in Catalonia immersion starts at 3–4 years old and finished, until recently, at the age of 7 (end of the initial cycle, when children have usually learnt how to read and write). Not until the academic year 1993/94 did the Catalan immersion programme extend to the end of Primary Education. Although this restriction in the programme duration never totally happened in practice, it encompassed serious limits in its development. On top of this, the results of the first evaluations of these programmes left it clear that, although a good competence of Catalan and Spanish was promoted, such competence never reached the levels obtained by their monolingual peers that had been schooled in their mother language.

Another different feature of the Catalan model from the original model deals with the time of instruction of the second language. While in Canada the programmes include one daily hour of instruction in the students' language from the very beginning, this happens very seldom in Catalonia.

The institutionalisation of linguistic immersion programmes has been a very important support and there has been a spectacular increase in the number of this type of programme during the last years. Thus, in the academic year 1992/93, 154,317 out of 309,210 Nursery and Primary School children in Catalonia (almost 50%) were following an immersion programme. Equally, 77,011 out of 279,785 (27.5%) did the same in private centres. Therefore, nearly 40% of all Nursery and Primary School children in Catalonia, (231,328 out of 588,995) followed linguistic immersion programmes (Servei d'Ensenyament del Català, 1994). Arnau and Artigal (1995) provide very similar figures, and they add that such figures place the immersion programme in Catalonia second in the world rank for its extension, only surpassed by the nearly 300,000 pupils in immersion programmes in Canada. The percentage of schools applying linguistic immersion programmes is very high in areas with a higher presence of Spanish-speaking immigrants.

Remarkable efforts were made in the 1990s in order to assess linguistic competence in Catalan and Castilian of schoolchildren in Catalonia, and to establish the factors that determine this competence. Results of this research (Arnau *et al.*, 1994; Bel *et al.*, 1993, 1994; Vila, 1995) reveal that the most significant factors in explaining the difference in level of Catalan are the family's socioprofessional level, the family language and the degree of presence of Catalan at school. For Spanish, the only significant factor is the family's socioprofessional level.

Also, the level of Catalan acquired by children from Spanish-speaking families in linguistic immersion programmes is that required in order to follow without problems the learning activities in the curriculum (Sanuy *et al.*, 2002; Serra & Vila, 1996). After revising the different assessments carried out on the linguistic immersion programme in Catalonia, Vila (1995) concludes that there are no differences in the knowledge of Spanish but, on the contrary, Spanish-speaking children have a significantly higher knowledge of Catalan than their Spanish-speaking peers attending programmes in their language.

Finally, the results of more global research carried out at country level need to be mentioned (Instituto Nacional de Calidad y Evaluación, 1998). This study was carried out with 14- and 16-year-old children and shows that the results of the proof of reading comprehension in Spanish, which can be marked between 0 and 500, were similar among children in Catalonia to those among children from the rest of the country (218 versus 220 at 14 years of age, and 266 versus 271 at 16 years of age). This would be a clear indicator that including Catalan as a teaching language, through programmes of maintenance of the family language or through linguistic immersion programmes, does not entail a lower level of knowledge of Spanish.

Recently published data from the international survey PISA 2003, carried out in 41 countries among 276,165 schoolchildren, point in the same direction. Some of the knowledge and abilities that could be expected in 15-years-old students, ready to finish their compulsory education, were assessed. Spain participated in this review in a global way and Catalonia, together with the Basque country and the Community of Castile-Leon, produced an enlarged sample, providing higher precision to the contrast of results. Results place the Catalan community above the state average in reading comprehension (483 versus 481) and in mathematics performance (494 versus 485), thus proving that the bilingual educational system has not hindered in any way other school abilities considered as basic (Consell Superior d'Avaluació del Sistema Educatiu, 2004).

As for the teaching of foreign languages, and as in most Western countries, English has become the hegemonic foreign language. The desire to achieve a good level of competence in this language has led to the development of some bilingual experiences where English is used as a means of instruction or to the presence of this foreign language in the curriculum from nursery education onwards, with a view to improving the low command of English that pupils have traditionally achieved in Catalonia. A recent survey carried out in 2004 on a representative sample of 1935 pupils in 100 different centres in the Community (Consell Superior d'Avaluació del Sistema Educatiu, 2005) concludes that although oral comprehension has improved, oral production and grammar competence have not, whereas written production and comprehension have even worsened.

This survey was the continuation of a previous one undertaken in the year 2000 on a sample of 2004 pupils within a plan implemented to improve the teaching and learning of foreign languages at preuniversity level (Consell Superior d'Avaluació del Sistema Educatiu, 2003). In both surveys participants were in their 5th year of Secondary Education and had chosen English as their first foreign language. The evaluation was based on validated tests used at the Official School of Languages in Catalonia, tests that are equivalent to the B1 level of competence of the European Council common framework of reference. These tests consisted of five parts: oral comprehension (15%), written comprehension (15%) oral expression (40%), written expression (15%) and grammar competence (15%).

The authors of the survey remark that pupils perform better in oral and written comprehension when the texts are short, and that their literal comprehension is better than their inferential comprehension, a finding also confirmed in the grammar test. Whereas students feel more at ease when it comes to speaking (in spite of vocabulary and coherence problems), written production represents the language skill that they find more complex. Finally, it is important to point out that parents' academic background and the use of audiovisual materials in the English classroom are the variables that exert a more significant effect on the results. The following also turned out to be influential variables: perseverance and academic expectations, motivation towards the learning of English and the presence of a teacher who is good at motivating students and at fostering work in small groups.

Studies on Language Attitudes Carried Out in Catalonia

Although this is only a brief summary of some reviews carried out in Catalonia about linguistic attitudes, there is a vast tradition of research about this subject in this community.

Considering the book's scope and in the line of Lasagabaster (2003) we wish to point out three types of research: (1) the research emphasising the evolution of the attitude towards Catalan and Spanish during the last 25 years, (2) the research emphasising attitudes towards English and (3) the research analysing attitudes within university environments.

As regards the first one, Woolard and Gahng (1990) analysed, using the match-guise technique, the variation in the beginning of the 1980s. They gathered two samples of secondary school pupils of ages between 16 and 17, one made up of 240 students and the other one made up of 276 students.

In both the 1980 and the 1987 reviews, Catalan seemed to have a higher status than Spanish and every language group had a better attitude toward their own L1, but while in the first group there was a very strong relationship between language and Catalan identity, there was a weakening in the second group, as it wasn't so important who spoke Catalan but rather which language was actually used.

Data yielded by Huguet and Llurda's (2001) survey in Catalonia and Aragon bilingual contexts should be interpreted in a similar way. Attitudes towards Catalan and Spanish by 94 students in their second year of secondary school were analysed in this study carried out in Catalonia. Although attitudes towards both languages were positive in general, Catalan tended to take priority over Spanish. The family linguistic condition happened to be a determining factor to explain these attitudes in the case of Spanish, but not in the case of Catalan. Therefore, attitudes towards Catalan were positive regardless of the family language, while attitudes towards Spanish were significantly better the more the family spoke the language.

Among the reviews that have given priority to the analysis of attitudes towards English, Tragant and Muñoz (2000) studied the relationship between attitudes and success in this language. For this purpose they had two sample groups: the members of one of the groups had started studying English at the age of 8, the members of other group had started studying English at the age of 11, and they were tested in three consecutive academic years. Although the attitude content was based on only one question, which yielded information about types of motivation, a more positive attitude was perceived among those who had received more tuition, and a high instrumental component in the manifested attitudes.

In another review by the same authors (Muñoz & Tragant, 2001) attitudes towards English as a foreign language of about one thousand 10–18-year-old pupils were analysed at two different times: after 200 h and after 416 h of tuition. The questionnaire was completed with a test of language knowledge in English, which, in contrast with the question-naire data, found a clear relationship between attitude and success. Furthermore, those who had received more intense tuition in English had better attitudes towards this language.

Finally, we refer to two reviews done at universities. The first was carried out by Mateu and Vila (1994) at the Polytechnic University of Catalonia with the participation of 800 students, 500 teachers and 400 administrative staff. The results were: knowledge of Spanish was general at all levels, but there was still a small percentage with difficulties with Catalan, especially at the written level. English was the best known foreign language, followed by French, at a long distance. Besides, all groups pointed out that Catalan was the most important language for the development of university life, although a good knowledge of English was seen as a need amongst teaching staff for research purposes.

To finish this short review of different research studies done on linguistic attitudes, and still within the ones done at universities, we mention a work in which the linguistic attitudes of the University of Barcelona students were analysed (Vicerectorat de Relacions Institucionals i Política Lingüística, 1998). This research was done on a sample of over 1000 students selected at random, and was carried out through questionnaires where data were analysed according to variables such as family language, age and gender. The results pointed out very positive attitudes towards the Catalan language, but these were mainly influenced by the family language, that is, attitudes were significantly better when Catalan was L1 than among bilingual or Spanish-speaking individuals. Age or gender did not produce significant differences.

The Catalan Study

The sample

The participants in the research were 309 university students. They were all in their first academic year at the Universities of Girona (54%) and Lleida (46%). Twelve percent were men and 88% women. Their age average was 20 years and 2 months. Twenty percent studied Psychology, 29% studied Social Education, 26% studied Teacher Training for Nursery School, 12.5% studied Teacher Training for Primary Education, 7% studied Teacher Training for Special Education and 5.5% studied Music Teacher Training.

Their distribution according to L1 was as shown in Figure 1.2.

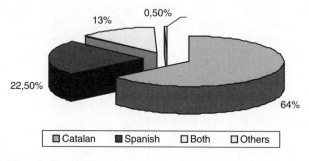

Figure 1.2 The students' L1

Most students have Catalan as L1, almost 23% have Spanish and about 13% are Catalan–Spanish bilingual.[4] With regard to the families' socioprofessional background, 16.8% (52 individuals) belonged to the high class, 44.7% (138) belonged to the middle class and 38.5% (119) belonged to the lower class. Twenty-six percent lived in a city of over 100,000 inhabitants, and 74% lived in smaller towns or villages. Nearly 85% lived in places where the predominant language was Catalan.

With regard to the foreign language, 31% had started learning English before the age of 8 and the remaining 69% at the age of 8 or older. With regard to their contact with the English language, 33% had visited an English-speaking country, but 95% never (63%) or very rarely (32%) watched TV in English.

Finally, over 90% had attended school following totally Catalan education models, and 5% had followed Catalan–Spanish bilingual education models or Spanish-only education models.

The instrument and the procedure

The research instruments and procedures used for the rest of the research studies contained in this volume coincide with ours, as explained in the introductory chapter. Given the sociolinguistic situation in Catalonia and the level of competence in Catalan of the population in the ages we work with, the questionnaire was always used in Catalan. The questionnaires were handed out in September 2004, right at the beginning of the academic year.

Results

The level of competence in the three languages in the school curriculum that participants in our research claim to have is a clear reflection of the process of linguistic recovery of Catalan started 25 years ago (Huguet, 2004; Vila, 1995). As represented in Figure 1.3, about 99% of individuals have a good or a very good knowledge of Catalan and

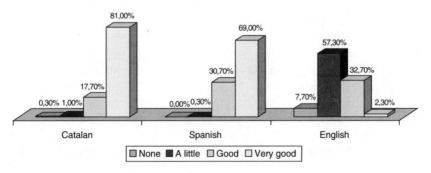

Figure 1.3 Level of competence in the three languages

Spanish; although only one third say they have an equivalent knowledge of English. Equally, over a third of those interviewed affirmed to know another foreign language with a good or very good level of competence.

According to the data yielded, the most used language within the family (70% of cases) is Catalan, but as we get away from the individual's family unit, the presence of Catalan is reduced by up to 50%, sharing the space with Spanish (see Table 1.3). This gives us an idea of how important this language is in a bilingual society such as the Catalan society.

The social bilingualism mentioned above can be clearly seen in Table 1.4, which shows how the subjects of the sample use communication media in each of the official languages. A remarkable balance can be observed between watching TV, listening to the radio or to music, or reading the press, both in Catalan and Spanish.

With respect to the importance given to Catalan (see Table 1.5), the higher percentages refer to 'being popular', followed by 'being accepted by the community'. At the other extreme, Catalan is not perceived as something absolutely necessary for 'reading', 'bringing up the children', 'getting a job', 'writing' or, in particular, 'living in Catalonia'. This reveals that, in spite of the progress made with regard to the Catalan language's social presence and knowledge, there's still a long way to go, as there is still a big imbalance in favour of Spanish.

When analysing the attitudes towards the three languages in the school curriculum (see Figure 1.4), we observed that the percentage of more favourable attitudes is in the case of Catalan, well away from Spanish and English. In both cases neutral attitudes and around a third of positive attitudes prevailed. Unfavourable attitudes were very low in percentage, and there weren't any in the case of Catalan.

The variables that seem to have a bigger impact in determining the attitudes towards the three languages (Catalan, Spanish and English) in this study are analysed in the following paragraphs (see Table 1.6). First, it is worth mentioning that the variable gender, significant in most works about this subject (Huguet & Llurda, 2001; Lasagabaster, 2003), did not appear relevant in this case. A majority of women among teacher training students and its influence may affect our results, but in order to state this, further reviews should be carried out in this regard.

The family language, on the contrary, was significant and, as expected according to previous reviews (Huguet & Llurda, 2001), individuals with Catalan as L1 showed more favourable attitudes towards this language than Spanish speakers [F 3, 299 = 48.920 ($p < 0.001$)] or Catalan–Spanish bilingual speakers [F 3, 299 = 48.920 ($p < 0.001$)]. Catalan–Spanish bilingual speakers, moreover, have more favourable attitudes towards Catalan than Spanish speakers [F 3, 299 = 48.920 ($p < 0.011$)]. Just the opposite happens to speakers with Spanish as L1 towards this language compared

Table 1.3 Language used when talking to the following people

	Always in Catalan (%)	In Catalan more often than Spanish (%)	In Catalan and Spanish about equally (%)	In Spanish more often than Catalan (%)	Always in Spanish (%)
Father	68.7	2.0	1.1	3.0	25.2
Mother	69.7	1.0	1.6	3.6	24.1
Brothers and sisters	73.5	0.7	1.9	2.6	21.3
Friends in the classroom	52.1	27.8	15.2	4.2	0.7
Friends outside school	44.7	20.7	20.4	8.4	5.8
Teachers	66.0	23.3	7.5	1.6	1.6
Neighbours	54.7	16.1	15.9	6.8	6.5

Table 1.4 Means of communication and language used

	Always in Catalan (%)	In Catalan more often than Spanish (%)	In Catalan and Spanish about equally (%)	In Spanish more often than Catalan (%)	Always in Spanish (%)
Watching TV	6.8	26.2	47.2	17.5	2.3
The press	16.8	28.2	37.6	14.2	3.2
Music	4.2	7.8	46.6	30.6	10.8
Listening to the radio	15.4	17.3	44.1	16.0	7.2

Table 1.5 Importance attached to the Catalan language to do the following activities

For people to:	Important (%)	A little important (%)	A little unimportant (%)	Unimportant (%)
Make friends	27.7	28.3	21.8	22.2
Read	8.1	11.4	29.2	51.3
Write	6.5	8.8	25.7	59.0
Watch TV	17.0	32.6	34.8	15.6
Get a job	4.5	9.8	29.9	55.8
Be liked	45.0	36.3	9.5	9.2
Live in Catalonia	4.2	4.9	21.4	69.5
Bring up children	7.8	12.0	25.6	54.6
Go shopping	26.9	43.0	17.0	13.1
Make phone calls	21.8	36.7	23.4	18.1
Pass exams	18.0	20.3	22.5	39.2
Be accepted in the community	30.9	34.2	17.6	17.3
Talk to friends at university	18.2	29.6	30.8	21.4
Talk to teachers at university	15.6	25.3	33.1	26.0
Talk to people out of university	20.5	36.0	24.3	19.2

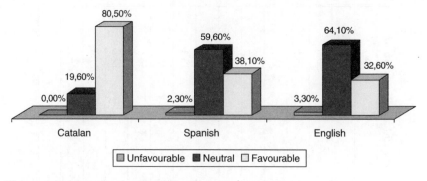

Figure 1.4 Attitudes towards the three languages

to Catalan speakers [F 3, 298 = 53.417 ($p < 0.001$)] or Catalan–Spanish bilingual speakers [F 3, 298 = 53.417 ($p < 0.001$)], as also Catalan–Spanish bilingual speakers have better attitudes towards Spanish than Catalan speakers [F 3, 298 = 53.417 ($p < 0.001$)]. No differences were observed regarding attitudes towards English according to L1.

The families' socioprofessional level did not appear to make any difference to attitudes towards Catalan, Spanish or English. Regardless of this variable, attitudes kept the same percentages as explained above. The same can be affirmed about the age at which individuals started to learn English and its influence over the attitudes towards this language: the role of English as an international lingua franca can perfectly explain these results. But having visited an English-speaking country and having encountered the language and the culture accounted for the attitudes towards the English language [F 1, 299 = 12.855 ($p < 0.001$)].

The linguistic model followed in Primary and Secondary Education was also significant. Therefore, those who were educated in Catalan showed better attitudes towards this language than those who were educated in Spanish [F 2, 298 = 10.308 ($p < 0.001$)] or bilingual Catalan–Spanish [F 2, 298 = 10.308 ($p < 0.003$)]. It also happens the other way round: those who were educated in Spanish showed better attitudes towards this language than those who were educated in Catalan [F 2, 297 = 10.003 ($p < 0.001$)] or bilingual Catalan–Spanish [F 2, 297 = 10.003 ($p < 0.003$)]. No differences were observed in attitudes towards English according to the school linguistic model.

The size of the city where they lived was only significant with regard to attitudes towards Spanish, as those living in cities with over 100,000 inhabitants showed better attitudes towards the Spanish language than those living in smaller towns or villages [F 1, 298 = 7.089 ($p < 0.008$)]. This fact is, of course, related to the migration flows from rural to urban areas and the bigger presence in cities of Spanish speakers coming from other parts of Spain.

Table 1.6 Summary of the most influential variables on language attitudes

Independent variable	Attitudes towards Catalan	Attitudes towards Spanish	Attitudes towards English	Competence in English
Gender	n.s.	n.s.	n.s.	
L1	Catalan > Spanish/both, Both > Spanish	Spanish > Catalan/both, Both > Catalan	n.s.	
Socioprofessional status	n.s.	n.s.	n.s.	
Age at which they started to learn English			n.s.	n.s.
Ever visited an English-speaking country			Yes > no	n.s.
Linguistic model	Catalan > Spanish/Both	Spanish > Catalan/Both	n.s.	
Size of hometown	n.s.	+ 100,000 > − 100,000	n.s.	
Predominant language in hometown	Catalan > Spanish	Spanish > Catalan	n.s.	

Data derived from statistical contrast between the predominant language in the city and attitudes towards the three languages should be interpreted in the same way: while people living in basically Catalan-speaking cities have better attitudes toward Catalan than people living in Spanish-speaking cities [F 1, 294 = 54.760 ($p < 0.001$)], the opposite happens in Spanish-speaking cities, as attitudes are more favourable towards Spanish than towards Catalan [F 1, 294 = 40.623 ($p < 0.001$)].

A significant correlation between the self-perception of competence in the three languages and the attitudes shown towards them has been observed: $R^2 = 0.220$ ($p < 0.001$) in the case of Catalan, $R^2 = 0.291$ ($p < 0.001$) in the case of Spanish and $R^2 = 0.404$ ($p < 0.001$) in the case of English. These results also help to confirm the strong relationships between linguistic attitudes and competence in a given language (Baker, 1992).

Discussion

The objective of this chapter was to analyse the linguistic use and attitudes of university students following formal and nonformal education in Catalonia. The first really relevant finding is the high level of competence in Catalan and Spanish among the sample members (99% have a good or a very good level of both languages). These results coincide with previous research studies revealing that population of this age reaches a peak regarding knowledge of Catalan language. This is to a large extent due to the process of recovery of the language through school (Institut d'Estadística de Catalunya, 1998).

But this high level of competence in the knowledge of official languages is notably reduced when we refer to the English language; only one third of the students state they have a similar level of competence in this language or in a second foreign language.

We found it striking that the success of bilingual education in Catalonia does not extend to the learning of foreign languages. If, on the one hand, there is a well known relationship between attitudes towards a language and academic success (Baker, 1992; Gardner, 1985; Lasagabaster, 2003; Muñoz, 2000), on the other hand we need to point out that initial attitudes towards a language are as important as keeping these attitudes through the whole process of teaching and learning. The dynamics at the Nursery School usually entail approaching the foreign language through playing with a global scope, but from a certain age onwards (8–9 years) this circumstance is modified remarkably into not strictly communicative approaches, but the repetition of formal structures (syntaxes, vocabulary, morphology, etc). Thus, the aim is not that pupils do things in this language any more, but the fact that they dominate some aspects of the language in an isolated way. This approach has effects not only upon the teaching and learning activities *per se*, but upon the pupils' attitudes towards the language being studied (Vila, 1993).

Consequently, if the didactic bases of bilingual education have proved that the best way to learn a language is to do things in this language by giving priority to a communicative approach, it seems clear that this conceptualisation should be valid for both, present languages and foreign languages (Muñoz, 2000). In other words, going beyond the debate about early introduction of a foreign language in education, the key question would be how to make such an approach prevail beyond Primary and Secondary Education to ensure that, regardless of the moment when a pupil comes into contact with the foreign language, an instrumental perspective of the language is guaranteed.

Another interesting question that can emerge from our research study refers to the use of the Catalan language and the importance attributed to it in daily activities. As we have seen, in spite of being the most used in family relationships (70% of cases), its usage is remarkably reduced as we move away from the individual's family nucleus and Spanish takes its place. This aspect is confirmed by the existing balance between language and communication media, which indicates the importance of Spanish as a language of social use in Catalonia and, even more, its significance for living normally in our community (see Table 1.4).

But in spite of the imbalance in favour of Spanish in many social activities, attitudes towards Catalan are more positive in percentage than towards Spanish or English. While 80% present favourable attitudes towards Catalan, neutral attitudes are more important towards the other languages, and moreover there are no negative attitudes towards the Catalan language.

Finally, we will refer to the relationship between the main controlled variables and the attitudes towards the three languages. Contrary to the results from other reviews (Huguet & Llurda, 2001; Lasagabaster, 2003), the gender variable is not significant in any case. This fact can be due to the mainly feminine component of the sample linked to teacher training and the selection of male members that decide to study this subject. We need, nevertheless, to be cautious about this statement as we believe further research needs to be done in this regard.

On the contrary, according to previous reviews (Huguet & Llurda, 2001), L1 was significant for attitudes towards Catalan and Spanish: the nearer the family to a given language, the more positive the attitudes towards it. It may be that the sense of threat from the other language against the status of our own language makes us give predominance to our own language to the detriment of the other one.

The families' socioprofessional level did not prove significant. This variable does not seem to be connected with the attitudes towards Catalan or Spanish; the described parameters are kept regardless of the social groups. The same happens with regard to the English language and its role as an international lingua franca: it seems to be above the families' socioprofessional level.

We need to add, with regard to English, that the age of learning does not influence the attitudes towards this language. This would confirm the previous appreciation about the importance of keeping positive attitudes throughout school life rather than focusing the debate on whether an early learning is convenient or not. In this sense, having visited an English-speaking country has proved significant, so it could be inferred that a better knowledge of the Anglophone society and culture is a positive influence in determining the attitudes towards the language of these societies.

Finally, we need to point out that, even if attitudes towards English do not seem to be influenced by the linguistic model followed at school or by the size and the dominant language of the place of residence, these variables do have some influence on the attitudes towards Catalan and Spanish. The linguistic model and the language of the place of residence act in a similar way as they do for L1, so the bigger presence of one or the other results in more favourable attitudes towards that given language. Also, living in bigger cities (over 100,000 inhabitants) brings more positive attitudes towards Spanish. This probably has to do with the migration movements in Spain during the 1960s and the 70s that brought many workers from Spanish-speaking communities to the most important cities in Catalonia.

The relationship between success in a given language and the attitudes shown towards it needs to be pointed out (Baker, 1992). Our data confirm this relationship in the three languages analysed, but as this is a correlational study, the debate is still alive: which is the cause and which is the effect?

Acknowledgements

This study was possible thanks to a research project funded by the *Dirección General de Investigación* of the Ministry of Education and Science (SEJ2005-08944-C02-02/EDUC).

Notes

1. A thorough revision of the Catalan linguistic community can be seen in Pradilla (2001).
2. The rate of understanding of Catalan is over 98% in all groups of age 5–24 years old. In the same way, the rate of people who can speak Catalan is at its maximum between 10 and 24 years of age (over 90%, with peaks of about

95% between 10 and 19 years of age). Similar behaviour can be observed in reading and writing abilities, according also to the population's literacy levels. Thus, reading comprehension levels are at their maximum (90%) between the ages of 10 and 24, and the maximum skills in writing are obtained at ages between 10 and 19 (87%) and between 20 and 24 (81%).

3. The Centre's Linguistic Project (PLC) integrated within the Educational Project is the instrument used by schools to decide the language policy in a particular school. For this purpose, a period of reflection is necessary in order to adapt the current regulations to the school's particular needs, objectives and characteristics. Thus, for a PLC to be viable, it necessarily needs to part from the school's present reality and from its real means and possibilities. In the beginning, the school will need to assess the students, teaching staff and parents' language levels of knowledge and use, and also the language presence in the school's social environment. It will also be necessary to assess the basic indicators that allow a diagnosis of the state of the question, both at the teaching and organisational levels (number of tuition hours, areas in which each language is used for teaching, the use of the school's linguistic resources, to what extent are teachers organised to coordinate methodological questions, etc). This analysis of the school's current situation is the departing point for the school to decide upon each of the issues mentioned, so that achievable goals are set for the short, medium and long terms, both at the teaching and organisational level, and so that an order of priorities is established.

4. The percentages in this review would have been different had the sample been taken in Barcelona, where the percentage of population with Spanish as L1 is bigger than in the rest of the Catalan provinces.

References

Areny, M. and Van der Shaaf, A. (2000) *Catalan: The Catalan Language in Education in Catalonia, Spain.* Leeuwarden: Mercator Education.

Arnau, J. and Artigal, J.M. (1995) El programa d'immersió a Catalunya. In J.M. Artigal (coord.) *Els programes d'immersió als territoris de llengua catalana* (pp. 21–47). Barcelona: Fundació Jaume Bofill.

Arnau, J., Bel, A., Serra, J.M. and Vila, I. (1994) A comparative study of the knowledge of Catalan and Spanish among 8th-grade EGB schoolchildren in Catalonia. In Ch. Laurén (ed.) *Evaluating European Immersion Programs. From Catalonia to Finland* (pp. 107–127). Vaasa: Universidad de Vaasa.

Baker, C. (1992) *Attitudes and Language.* Clevedon: Multilingual Matters.

Bel, A. (1991) *Deu anys de normalització lingüística a l'ensenyament 1978–1988.* Barcelona: Departament d'Ensenyament de la Generalitat de Catalunya.

Bel, A., Serra, J.M. and Vila, I. (1993) Estudio comparativo del conocimiento de catalán y del castellano al final del ciclo superior de EGB. In M. Siguan (ed.) *Enseñanza en dos lenguas* (pp. 97–110). Barcelona: ICE-Horsori.

Bel, A., Serra, J.M. and Vila, I. (1994) Estudio comparativo del conocimiento de catalán en sexto, séptimo y octavo de EGB en 1990. In M. Siguan (ed.) *Las lenguas en la escuela* (pp. 229–252). Barcelona: ICE-Horsori.

Comet, M.C. (1992) Adaptación y adecuación de la didáctica de la lengua catalana al programa de inmersión lingüística. In J. Arnau, C. Comet, J.M. Serra and I. Vila (eds) *La educación bilingüe* (pp. 153–213). Barcelona: ICE-Horsori.

Consell Superior d'Avaluació del Sistema Educatiu (2003) *La situació de la llengua anglesa a l'Ensenyament no universitari de Catalunya*. Barcelona: Generalitat de Catalunya – Departament d'Ensenyament.

Consell Superior d'Avaluació del Sistema Educatiu (2004) *Estudi PISA 2003*. Barcelona: Generalitat de Catalunya – Departament d'Educació.

Consell Superior d'Avaluació del Sistema Educatiu (2005) *La llengua anglesa al batxillerat. Avançament de resultats*. Barcelona: Generalitat de Catalunya – Departament d'Educació.

Farràs, J., Torres, J. and Vila, F.X. (2001) El coneixement del català 1996. Mapa sociolingüístic de Catalunya: Anàlisi sociolingüística de l'Enquesta Oficial de Població de 1996. Barcelona: Institut de Sociolingüística Catalana.

Gardner, R.C. (1985) *Social Psychology and Second Language Learning: The Role of Attitude and Motivation*. London: Edward Arnold.

Huguet, Á. (2004) La educación bilingüe en el Estado español: situación actual y perspectivas. *Cultura & Educación* 16 (4), 399–418.

Huguet, Á. and Llurda, E. (2001) Language attitudes of school children in two Catalan/Spanish bilingual communities. *International Journal of Bilingual Education and Bilingualism* 4 (4), 267–282.

Huguet, Á. and Suïls, J. (1998) *Contacte entre llengües I actituds lingüístiques. El cas de la frontera catalana-aragonesa*. Barcelona: Horsori.

Institut d'Estadística de Catalunya (1998) *El coneixement del català l'any 1996*. Barcelona: Generalitat de Catalunya.

Instituto Nacional de Calidad y Evaluación (1998) *Elementos para un diagnóstico del Sistema Educativo español. Informe global*. Madrid. Ministerio de Educación y Cultura.

Lambert, W.E. (1974) A Canadian experiment in the development of bilingual competence. *Canadian Modern Language Review* 31 (2), 108–116.

Lasagabaster, D. (2003) *Trilingüismo en la enseñanza. Actitudes hacia la lengua minoritaria, la mayoritaria y la extranjera*. Lleida: Editorial Milenio.

Mateu, R.M. and Vila, F.X. (1994) *Com parlem a la UPC: Enquesta sociolingüística de la UPC 1991–1992*. Barcelona: Universitat Politècnica de Catalunya.

Muñoz, C. (2000) *Segundas lenguas: adquisición en el aula*. Barcelona: Ariel.

Muñoz, C. and Tragant, E. (2001) Motivation and attitudes towards L2: Some effects of age and instruction. *EUROSLA Yearbook* 1, 211–224.

Ouellet, M. (1990) *Synthèse historique de l'immersion française au Canada*. Quebec: CIRB.

Pradilla, M.A. (2001) The Catalan-speaking communities. In M.T. Turell (ed.) *Multilingualism in Spain* (pp. 58–91). Clevedon: Multilingual Matters.

Sanuy, J., Huguet, Á., Pifarré, M. and Vendrell, C. (2002) Relaciones entre conocimiento del catalán, el castellano y el rendimiento matemático. Un estudio empírico. *Revista de Educación* 328, 383–394.

Serra, J.M. (1997) *Inmersió lingüística, rendiment acadèmic i classe social*. Barcelona: ICE-Horsori.

Serra, J.M. and Vila, I. (1996) Coneixement lingüístic i matemàtic d'escolars de nivell sociocultural baix en programes d'immersió. *Articles de Didàctica de la Llengua i la Literatura* 8, 15–23.

Servei d'Ensenyament del Català (1994) *Dades sobre l'ús de la Llengua en la docència a l'Ensenyament Primari de Catalunya el curs 1992–1993*. Barcelona: Departament d'Ensenyament de la Generalitat de Catalunya.

Servei d'Ensenyament del Català (2001) *Estadístiques generals de parvulari, ensenyament primari i ensenyament secundari*. Barcelona: SEDEC. On WWW at http://www.xtec.es/sedec/. Accessed 23.2.04.

Siguan, M. (1992) *España plurilingüe*. Madrid: Alianza Editorial.
Siguan, M. (1994) *Conocimiento y uso de las lenguas en España*. Madrid: Centro de Investigaciones Sociológicas.
Tragant, E. and Muñoz, C. (2000) La motivación y su relación con la edad en un contexto escolar de aprendizaje de una lengua extranjera. In C. Muñoz (ed.) *Segundas lenguas: adquisición en el aula* (pp. 81–105). Barcelona: Ariel.
Vicerectorat de Relacions Institucionals i Política Lingüística (1998) *Enquesta sobre les actituds lingüístiques de l'alumnat de la UB*. Barcelona: Universitat de Barcelona.
Vila, I. (1992) La educación bilingüe en el Estado Español. In J. Arnau, C. Comet, J.M. Serra and I. Vila (ed.) *La educación bilingüe* (pp. 53–103). Barcelona: ICE-Horsori.
Vila, I. (1993) Psicología y enseñanza de la lengua. *Infancia y Aprendizaje 62/63*, 219–229.
Vila, I. (1995) *El català i el castellà en el Sistema Educatiu de Catalunya*. Barcelona: Horsori.
Vila, I. (1998) *Bilingüisme i educació*. Barcelona: Proa.
Woolard, K.A. and Gahng, T.J. (1990) Changing language policies and attitudes in autonomous Catalonia. *Language in Society* 19, 311–330.

Chapter 2

Language Use and Language Attitudes in Galicia

XAQUÍN LOREDO GUTIÉRREZ, ANTONIO FERNÁNDEZ SALGADO,
ISABEL SUÁREZ FERNÁNDEZ and HÅKAN CASARES BERG

Introduction

Galicia is one of the 17 autonomous communities that make up the Kingdom of Spain and it is situated in the North-West of the Iberian Peninsula. It borders the Bay of Biscay in the north, the Atlantic Ocean in the west, the Principality of Asturias and the Autonomous Community of Castile-León in the east, and Portugal in the south (see Figure 2.1).

Galicia became an autonomous community in 1981 incorporating the provinces of A Coruña, Lugo, Ourense and Pontevedra. It was in this year that the Statute of Autonomy for Galicia was established after the restitution of the democratic system in Spain. This Statute granted the Galician language the status of 'Galicia's own language' and established Galician alongside Spanish as the official language of the Community.

The Galician-speaking territory covers the present administrative Galicia and the adjoining regions of Terra Eo-Navia in Asturias, Os Ancares Orientais and O Bierzo Occidental in the province of León, and As Portelas in the province of Zamora. Other variants that have to be included in this group are those spoken in the province of Cáceres (Extremadura) and the areas that were repopulated by Galicians during

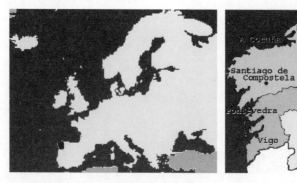

Figure 2.1 Position of Galicia in Europe

Table 2.1 Inhabitants per area

Percentage		Inhabitants
35.4	50,000 or more inhabitants	955,569
30.6	From 10,000 to 50,000 inhabitants	826,438
34	Less than 10,000	913,873
100	Total	2,695,880

Source: Revision of the Municipal Register of Inhabitants (2001)

the reconquest of the Middle Ages, i.e. the spoken dialects of San Martín de Trevejo, Eljas and Valverde del Fresno (see Figure 2.2).

In 2001 the population of Galicia was 2,695,880, 35.4% of which lived in towns with a population of 50,000 or more inhabitants, 30.6% lived in towns of between 50,000 and 10,000 inhabitants and 34% in villages and small towns of less than 10,000 inhabitants (see Table 2.1).

According to the data of the Sociolinguistic Map of Galicia (Socio-linguistics Seminar 1994, 1995, 1996), almost everyone understands the Galician language (97% of the population), but their command of reading and writing is far less than their competence in oral skills. The most recent data (IGE, 2004) show a vast improvement in writing skills. In the younger generations we have noticed a very important recovery of these abilities – it is a similar effect that takes place in those at secondary education and undergraduate level – a phenomenon that is in some way predictable because of the recent incorporation of Galician in the education system. In addition, according to the calculations of the Government of Galicia, 1,400,000 Galicians are estimated to be living outside Galicia, and this figure does not take into account the number of second-generation immigrants.

At the beginning of the 20th century more than 90% of the population spoke only Galician. However, according to the most recent sources (IGE, 2004), the percentage of Galicians who usually speak Galician or more Galician than Spanish is 61% (see Table 2.2). The number of Galician speakers has thus fallen despite the current favourable social circum-stances, but it has regained some social prestige.

The linguistic attitudes towards Galician appear to be clearly positive. Seventy-two percent of the population have a favourable attitude, 68.7% think that Galician is the same as, or more useful than Spanish, and 66% think that Galician should be the language used in schools (Socio-linguistics Seminar, 1995).

In the group of European Union languages, Galician is considered a minority language that is well established, in a similar way to Catalan or

Figure 2.2 Galician-speaking territory

Basque. Taking into account the data supplied by *Euromosaic. Producción e reproducción dos grupos lingüísticos minoritarios da Unión Europea* (1996) and *Mercator Guide to Organizations: Providing Information on Lesser Used Languages* (1998), Galician has a privileged position among the 48 minority languages of the European Union.

Galician is a Romance language (the same as French, Spanish, Catalan, Portuguese and Italian). It evolved from Latin, the language spoken by the Romans who settled in the North-West of the Iberian Peninsula, in

Table 2.2 Language use in Galicia

	Percentage
Only Galician	42.62
More Galician than Spanish	18.38
More Spanish than Galician	18.78
Only Spanish	19.75
Other language/s	0.53

Source: IGE (2004)

the Roman province of Gallaecia. The evolution of this Latin towards the Romance language took place gradually. Towards the 12th century it was a Romance language that was clearly different from Latin. As well as the oldest troubadour compositions, the first legal documents written in Galician–Portuguese date from this century. Between the 12th and 14th centuries this language became the language of poetry in the Iberian Peninsula. The poetry is usually labelled as Galician–Portuguese poetry, because until the middle of the 14th century Galician and Portuguese were part of the same branch.

After the golden age of the Galician language during the Middle Ages, the arrival of the reign of the Catholic Sovereigns and the foreign nobility that supported the new dynasty caused the Galician language to be absent in written form in an era when the other Romance languages became established. This period, which spans from the 16th century to the 18th century, constitutes the Dark Ages.

With the Enlightenment began the vindication of the use of Galician in all domains of public life. In the 19th century and with the Literary Resurgence, Galicia continued its literary, cultural, political and historical recovery.

The arrival of the 20th century marked the advancement of this early regionalism towards the birth of a nationalism that would demand a more important role for the language. The birth of the *Irmandades da Fala* (Galician Language Brotherhoods) and the publication of the journal *Nós*[1] date from this period. And it was the name of this journal which identified a generation that would be in charge of putting the Galician culture and the Galician language in touch with contemporary European aesthetic ideals. Due to the start of the Civil War (1936–1939), the Statute of Autonomy that was approved in 1936 was not applied. During these years, Galician culture, language and identity protected itself in exile and within the country thanks to the initiatives organised by groups of intellectuals and cultural associations.

With the end of Franco's dictatorship and the arrival of democracy Galicia became an autonomous community by means of the enactment of the Statute of Autonomy for Galicia (1981). The statute recognised Galician as the accepted language of Galicia. This acknowledgement means that Galician is the historic language that marks out Galicia from a linguistic point of view and constitutes one of its fundamental elements of difference. That is that Galician must be the language used by the majority of the Galician population, regardless of the official standing of Spanish or Galician, that Galician must be the language of all the institutions of Galicia and the language of preference used by the Administration of the Spanish State in Galicia, by other institutions and by the firms and establishments that offer public services in general. It also maintains that Galician and Spanish are both the official languages of the Community.

In 1983 the Parliament of Galicia passed the Law of Linguistic Standardisation so that it could finally restore the Galician language in a progressive way in all the domains from which it was excluded, e.g. civil service, schools, the media, etc. This law is a legal tool that is indispensable in exercising the linguistic rights in the framework of the statutory sanction of both languages. Its aim is to respect the individual linguistic rights in order to be able to surpass the relationship of inequality between the two official languages of our Community, Galician and Spanish.

Nevertheless, despite the equality of duties and rights of Galician and Spanish in Galicia, there is an inequality that derives from the standing that the Spanish Constitution gives to the Spanish language. While Spanish is a language that all citizens must know, there is no reciprocal acknowledgement stating that it is compulsory to know the other co-official languages of the State.

At the present moment, when the transmission of Galician to the next generation is falling (Sociolinguistics Seminar, 1994; IGE, 2004), schools have to attain a higher importance as an environment in which to learn Galician. Schools, together with the media, are one of the fundamental areas within which a language policy favouring Galician has been implemented. The Royal Decree 1981/1979, known as the 'Bilingualism Decree', sets out that learning the Galician language is compulsory. However, its use as the official language in education was not legislated until four years later, the subjects and areas of education to be taught in Galician being established for the first time in 1988.

According to what is decreed in the statutes of the three Galician universities, Galician is the official language both in university lecturing and in all the internal and external acts. The three universities (University of Santiago de Compostela, University of A Coruña and University of Vigo) have linguistic standardisation services that advise the departments and devise specific vocabulary to facilitate the use of Galician in the different teaching areas.

The recognition of Galicians as a very different people in the Spanish State is rooted in the perception that the Community obtains through its language and culture. The promotion of the normal use of the Galician language in social domains, especially in education, should contribute in a fundamental way to the standardisation and expansion of the use of the language throughout Galician society. The Parliament of Galicia finally passed the *General Plan for the Normalization of the Galician Language* in September 2004 and it made a decisive contribution to the way that Galician should face the new challenges of Galician society in the 21st century.

The Galician Educational System

The model of bilingual education designed by the government of Galicia has been gradually introduced over the last two decades. For many centuries the paradox was that a society that was almost universally monolingual in Galician was schooled in Spanish, and consequently Galicians could not write the language they spoke.

This situation did not prove decisive in the loss of speakers, as the access to education was restricted to a minority until well after the 20th century and besides, primary education socialisation was only in Galician. However, this marginalisation was crucial in the confirmation of a bilingual mentality and hierarchical relations between the two languages in the population (Silva, 2002).

It was only when the Statute for Galicia was approved in 1981 that Galician, together with Spanish, was recognised as an official language. With its approval, the situation of the Galician language in different fields, especially education, became regulated. The following aspects of this Statute appear in Law 3/1983:

- Galician as the official language in all levels of education;
- the right of children to receive their first teachings in their mother tongue;
- the pupils will not be separated in different centres because of their language;
- Galician will be a compulsory subject in all levels of education prior to going to university;
- all things considered, when completing their statutory education, pupils must know how to speak and write to the same level in Galician as in Spanish.

The linguistic model that is specified in the Statute for Galicia and in the subsequent Decree of 1995 is portrayed by two characteristics:

(1) The schooling in nursery and primary school of Galician children in their L1.
(2) The curricular distribution between the two official languages, and the establishment of a minimum number of areas that are to be taught in Galician in the rest of their statutory education.

The schooling of children in their L1, during their first years of education, derives from the implementation of the section of the Law of Standardisation about the right of children to receive their first schooling in their mother tongue. This aspect, accompanied by the impossibility of separating the pupils in centres or different classrooms because of their language, except in exceptional circumstances, prevents the application of *linguistic immersion programmes*, or the possibility of choosing from a variety of different linguistic models. Another factor that arises from the implementation of this model, which seeks to avoid segregation of linguistic groups, is that in Galicia there are no unified language situations, which is why we find children in one class who speak one language and others who speak another. If we choose the language of the majority, the minority who speak the other language would be discriminated against.

At preuniversity level there is a curricular distribution between the two official languages and an establishment of the minimum of areas that must be taught in Galician. It stemmed from a criterion according to which the centre was responsible for the assignation of the same number of hours for Galician as for Spanish until the Decree of 1995, where the minimum number of subjects in Galician was set out. As regards the rest of the curriculum, it would be up to the centre to plan how to act linguistically.

The introduction of Galician in education had an important repercussion in the awareness of the written competences. When we compare the data from the Sociolinguistic Map of Galicia collected in 1991 (Sociolinguistics Seminar, 1994) with the data from the Galician Institute of Statistics collected in 2003 (IGE, 2004), we come across some clearly significant differences. For example, only 45.9% of those surveyed in 1991 said they had a good or very good competence in reading, whilst in 2003 the figure had risen to 85.6%. A similar increase was also recorded in the competence for writing, as it rose from 27.1% in 1991 to 49.8% in 2003.

The data indicate that in about 40% of classrooms in nursery education, where the presence of Galician is marginal, the learning of reading and writing is mainly carried out in Spanish (50% in Spanish and 30% in Galician; Department of Education, 1999). However, most Galician students have Galician as their background and familiar language.

These findings were confirmed in another study carried out in 2001, where it was observed that Galician was rarely used in urban centres (Monteagudo & Bouzada, 2002). The fulfilment of regulations in statutory secondary education is more encouraging. The centres declared that they were going to adhere to compulsory teaching in Galician.

The main aim of language policy in Galicia is to achieve equal linguistic competence in Galician and Spanish. However, there is no research that evaluates its implementation. Hypotheses that are based on observation studies of students maintain that the oral competence in the two languages is very different depending on the main language of the users. Thus, it has been noted that while predominantly Spanish-speaking youngsters have difficulties speaking Galician fluently and correctly, Galician speakers show no difficulties expressing themselves in Spanish (Silva, 2002).

A series of changes with regards to the learning of foreign languages in the Galician education system are about to take place. Due to social demands, the University Department of Education and Regulation is undertaking a series of steps to improve the learning of other European languages. Research carried out in our community (Vez & Martínez, 2002) shows deficiencies in the development of communication capabilities in English and French when finishing their statutory education (16 years old). These results confirmed the social expectancy on the effective learning of foreign languages in teaching.

The promotion of foreign languages among Galician students was set out in the Experimental Plan for the Promotion of Foreign Languages. This programme began in the academic year 1999/2000 and considers the teaching of a foreign language during the last two years of nursery education (5–6 years old) and during the first two years of primary education (7–8 years old). There is also the project titled *The European Section*, which consists of the teaching of one or several bilingual subjects, be it Galician or Spanish, and another foreign language spoken in the European Union in the second cycle of statutory secondary education (15 and 16 years old).

The results of the dominance of English over other foreign languages are clear. The general data of preuniversity teaching show that 87.6% of the pupils study English as opposed to 19.4% who study French, 0.2% German and 0.2% other languages. The results in educational stages can be seen in Table 2.3.

The results by educational stages (nursery education, primary education, secondary education and postsecondary education) indicate the predominance of English at all these stages. The data for nursery and primary are clear, as opposed to 45.5% and 92.5% respectively who studied English, and only 0.3% and 1.3% studied French. The situation is slightly different in secondary education where the percentage for French increases to 50.2% as opposed to 99.1% in English. The comparison of the Galician situation with the Spanish one indicates a lesser diversity of foreign languages in the Galician school population.

Table 2.3 Foreign languages learnt by preuniversity students (2001–02 academic year)

Galicia	English	French	German	Others
Nursery education in Galician	45.5	0.3	0.0	0.5
Nursery education in Spanish	39	0.8	0.2	0.2
Primary education in Galician	92.5	1.3	0	0.2
Primary education in Spanish	85.2	2.6	0.2	0.2
Secondary education in Galician	99.1	50.2	0.5	0
Secondary education in Spanish	98.8	40.5	2	0.1
Postsecondary education in Galician	93.9	19.8	0.4	0
Postsecondary education in Spanish	96.2	28	1.1	0.3

Source: Office of Statistics of the MEC (Spanish Ministry of Education)
The figures that add up to percentages higher than 100% are due to the existence of students who study more than one foreign language

Already in the dawn of the democratic transition, the Galician university positioned itself at the forefront of the defence of the Galician language. Teachers and students demanded a wider use of Galician in this environment, a matter that appears in the first statute of the University of Santiago de Compostela, which was approved in 1985. The new universities created between 1989 and 1990 (University of A Coruña[2] and University of Vigo) are also committed to this, and sign up to sociolinguistic studies in order to study their position (Lorenzo et al., 1997; Rodríguez et al., 1998).

The research studies undertaken show that nearly all the university students understand Galician without any difficulty: 98.2% at the University of Vigo and 97.3% at the University of Santiago, 91.6% and 83.2% respectively are able to speak it, 96.4% and 94.4% can read it and 86.6% and 86.4% are able to write it. Yet, there are important differences regarding its use: Galician is the everyday language used by 30.8% of the students at the University of Santiago and by 10% of the students at the University of Vigo. The linguistic attitudes of the students are very positive regarding Galician and, in fact, we find a high proportion of students who are demanding much greater usage of their native language in the academic environment (44.3% in the University of Vigo and 47.3% in the University of Santiago).

Studies on Language Attitudes Carried Out in Galicia

In Galicia linguistic attitudes have been researched for three decades. The first empirical studies on the topic identified the attitudes towards

Galician as the main problem for the future of this language (Ayestarán & De la Cueva, 1974; De Miguel, 1970). As opposed to the high frequency of use of the Galician language by the population, the data that referred to the attitudes pointed out the danger of linguistic substitution, especially in the urban environment (Castillo & Pérez Vilariño, 1977; Del Campo & Tezanos, 1977). After the recognition of the bilingual status of Galician by the Spanish Constitution in 1978, the attitudes towards Galician began to shift with great speed. In a study about primary education in 1979 the results showed for the first time more favourable attitudes to the minority language (Rojo, 1979). Subsequent studies continued showing positive attitudes towards Galician, but pointed to a decline in its use. The majority of them were focused on the educational system (Monteagudo *et al.*, 1986; Rodríguez *et al.* 1988; Rubal & Rodríguez, 1987; Rubal *et al.*, 1992), but there are also studies dealing with different environments such as the church (López Muñoz, 1989) or the socioeconomic sphere (Bouzada, 1993). In all cases the data were gathered through questionnaires.

The first study where the linguistic attitudes of the Galician population as a whole were analysed was published in 1996 (Sociolinguistics Seminar, 1996). This survey, known as the Sociolinguistic Map of Galicia (SMG), puts forward the results referring to attitudes. It was carried out on a sample of 38,897 individuals aged 15 and over. The instrument used was a questionnaire made up of Likert scales, consisting of 53 items. The main conclusion of this research was a wide acceptance of Galician. The average score was 3.60, on a scale of 1 to 5, and the lowest did not fall below the centre point. This favourable attitude was mainly observed in the younger generation (the average of the group aged between 16 and 25 was 3.75, whilst in those who were over 65, it was 3.44), with Galician speakers (the average of the monolinguals in Galician was 3.79, as opposed to 3.06 of the monolinguals in Spanish) and in the most rural habitat (3.68 in the rural-II[3] as opposed to 3.49 in the urban habitat). The study also highlighted the importance of Galician as a feature of identity, as 90.9% considered that all the people who reside in Galicia should know Galician. But the answers by the people who took part in the questionnaire mostly identified a general belief rather than an intention related to real behaviour. In fact, whilst 85.8% pointed out that if Galician were not spoken a great part of the Galician culture would be lost, 58.1% considered that Galicians should speak 'both languages'. Only 16.3% thought that the use of Galician determined the Galician identity of the speakers. Regarding its usefulness, 57.3% stated that it served 'the same purpose' as Spanish, but the study was set up to measure the degree of acceptance of a prejudice, rather than a personal attitude.

Most of the research studies undertaken to evaluate the linguistic attitudes since the publication of the SMG used a similar method to the one utilised by the SMG, ending up with similar results (Lorenzo *et al.*, 1997; Rodríguez *et al.*, 1998; Vaamonde, 2003).

Recent research studies with different questionnaire methods show the strength of prejudices towards the prosodic and phonetic features of Galician among the younger population (Sociolinguistics Seminar, 2004). In research based on the 'matched-guise' technique, which was carried out on a representative sample made up of 400 adolescents, it was found that the speakers who express themselves in linguistic varieties where Galician phonetics is pervasive, independently of the language being used, were categorised as approachable people but not well equipped for social success. They were associated with low social status professions and physical stereotypes that are not very appealing. On the other hand, the speakers who did not show the phonetics that are typical of the Galician language, whether they spoke Galician or Spanish, were considered less accessible and belonging to a group with social success.

Studies that are based on the use of qualitative methods showed the coexistence of general beliefs that favour Galician but point negatively towards determining its usefulness amongst the youth and the population (Fernández Salgado, 2002; Iglesias, 2003; Sociolinguistics Seminar, 2003). Two differing content titles were found to socially categorise the Galician speakers. On the one hand, we would have the stereotype known as 'coarse', that is associated with the rural speakers who express themselves using the correct Galician phonetics. And on the other hand, we would have the 'nationalist', who is associated with the 'new speakers of Galician' who have no Galician accent and live in the cities. Regarding Spanish speakers, however, no stereotype images were found (Sociolinguistics Seminar, 2003). From these studies it emerges that the use of Galician among the youth was motivated by symbolic and group reasoning, rather than being of a pragmatic kind. Galician would not be able to carry out the instrumental needs of the younger population. This is an aspect that would at least partially explain the continuous decline in the use of Galician among young people.

In the study of linguistic attitudes in Galicia important gaps can still be found. We still do not have data that compares bilingual competence with attitude factors. The study of linguistic attitudes was centred almost exclusively on the attitudes towards the minority language, as there is hardly any data on the attitudes towards Spanish or foreign languages such as English. Moreover, most of the instruments used for the measurement of the linguistic attitudes do not fulfil the requisites of reliability and validity. Nowadays, the second part of the SMG (in progress) intends to surpass these weaknesses.

The Galician Study

The sample

A sample of 207 university students who were in their first year of Teacher Training or Pedagogy was drawn. Forty-three percent were training to be nursery school teachers, 12.1% were training to be primary school teachers, 28% were training to be music teachers and 16.9% were studying Pedagogy. The data were gathered in three different Galician cities: Lugo (30%), Santiago de Compostela (58.5%) and A Coruña (11.5%). The average age of the participants was 20 years and 4 months, the youngest was 18 years old and the oldest 35 years and 9 months old (91.9% of the sample were within the age range of 18–24 years old). As expected, given the predominance of the female gender in this kind of university study, 78.3% of the sample were women and only 21.7% were men. The distribution of the sample according to their mother tongue can be seen in Figure 2.3.

The majority of the future teachers' mother tongue was Galician (37.7%), as opposed to 26.5% whose mother tongue was Spanish. The high percentage (33.8%) of bilingualism (Galician–Spanish) of the participants in the study is prominent. Also important is that 2% of the people had a different language to Galician or Spanish as their first language. Regarding socioprofessional status, 17% (35) belonged to the upper class, 31.1% (64) were middle class and 51.9% (107) were working class.

23.8% of the sample lived in cities with more than 100,000 inhabitants, whilst the majority (76.2%) lived in rural nuclei or towns, and 62.4% of the students lived in areas where Galician is predominantly spoken (62.4%), as opposed to the 37.6% living in areas where more Spanish is spoken.

As for foreign languages, 27.5% started studying English before they were 8 years old, 37.3% started when they were 8 and 38.2% after they were 8 years old. As for their contact with the English language outside of formal settings, 21.7% had been to an English-speaking country, but 89.3% never (60.4%) or hardly ever (29.4%) watched TV in English, whereas only 5.8% watched it once or twice a week, 1.9% watched it more than three times a week and just 5 individuals (2.4%) watched TV on a daily basis.

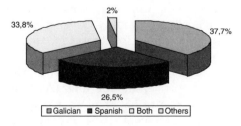

Figure 2.3 The students' L1

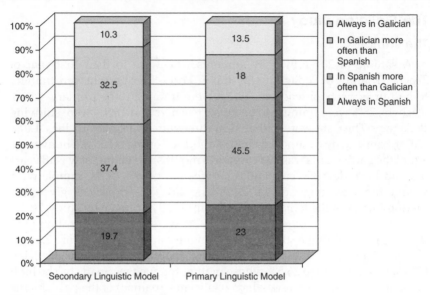

Figure 2.4 Linguistic model

As can be seen in Figure 2.4, the majority had lessons mainly in Spanish at primary school (68.5%) and at secondary school (57.1%), despite their first language being mainly Galician.

The instrument and the procedure

The instrument and the procedure of this study are the same as those used by the rest of the participants in this volume. As explained in the introductory chapter, the only important factor is that the students were given the possibility of completing the questionnaire in either Galician or Spanish. The data were compiled during the first two months of the academic year, between September and October 2004.

Results

Analysing the general competence perceived in the three languages that belong to the school curriculum of the Autonomous Community of Galicia, we find that the individuals who were part of the sample show a much higher competence in Spanish, followed by Galician and finally English (see Figure 2.5). Analysing the results for competence in English, we find that only 2% (5 people) from the sample think that their competence in English is very good and 70% of the participants had a low level of English. These results agree with those of Vez and Martínez (2002), who concluded that the students of the last year of ESO had an average competence in understanding of English and a low competence in communication. On the other hand, 93.1% of the participants chose the option good or very good

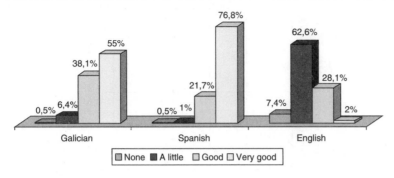

Figure 2.5 Level of competence in the three languages

when asked about Galician, and only 6.9% chose the option little or none. With regard to the issue of Spanish, 98.5% of those surveyed expressed having a good or very good competence in this language. Only 1 person stated that he/she could not speak Galician properly. When asked about a second foreign language only 18.7% expressed a knowledge of one. Of those 18.7%, 45.1% answered that they have some knowledge, 39.2% that their knowledge is good and 9.8% that it is very good.

The data of linguistic uses in the heart of the family (see Table 2.4) show a larger presence of Spanish in communication with parents (46.4% always or more often speak with their father in Spanish and 50.2% with their mother) as opposed to Galician (41.3% always or more often speak in Galician with their father and 39.3% with their mother). Another interesting point from communication with their parents is the existing difference between communication with the father as opposed to communication with the mother: the students spoke to their mother more in Spanish than to their father. We also verified that there is a generational difference between communication with their parents and communication with their brothers. Gradually, there is a tendency to a more 'Spanishised' communication together with a fall in bilingual uses.

In the education context Spanish is used more widely, as 49.5% of the students always or more often spoke to their teachers in Spanish and 51.2% spoke to their classmates in Spanish. This percentage drops to 43.7% when the students speak to their neighbours.

The use of media communications in Galician only is anecdotal (see Table 2.5). In fact, just 2% state that they watch television in Galician only and 1% declare reading the press in Galician only. These results are understandable, as there is only one channel (TVG) and one newspaper (*Galicia Hoxe*) exclusively in Galician. However, 31% declare watching television equally in Galician as in Spanish. Due to the inequality amongst the channels in Spanish and Galician the data are understandable. The data on the reading of the press are similar to that of

Table 2.4 Language used when talking to the following people

	Always in Galician (%)	In Galician more often than Spanish (%)	In Galician and Spanish about equally (%)	In Spanish more often than Galician (%)	Always in Spanish (%)
Father	37.2	4.1	12.2	11.2	35.2
Mother	33.8	5.5	10.4	13.9	36.3
Brothers and sisters	35.5	2.7	9.3	11.5	41
School friends	22.4	7.3	19	21	30.2
Other friends	23.4	7.3	16.6	19.5	33.2
Teachers	22.8	11.7	16	20.4	29.1
Neighbours	31.4	11.3	13.7	16.7	27

Table 2.5 Importance attached to the Galician language to do the following activities

	Always in Galician (%)	In Galician more often than Spanish (%)	In Galician and Spanish about equally (%)	In Spanish more often than Galician (%)	Always in Spanish (%)
Watching TV	2	2	31	47.8	17.2
Reading newspapers	1	6.4	31.9	36.8	24
Listening to music	0	2.5	19.1	36.7	41.7
Listening to the radio	1	4.5	26.6	40.2	27.6

television: 31.9% declare reading equally in Galician and in Spanish. It should be pointed out that the availability of Galician press is greater, as the majority of the newspapers have a percentage of their contents in Galician. The percentage falls when we refer to listening to the radio, as only 26.6% say that they listen to it equally in Galician and Spanish.

However, if we combine all the categories of answers except 'always in Spanish', the percentages for the use of Galician are not low: 82.8% of the participants who took part in the study generally watched television in Galician, 76.1% read newspapers and 72.3% listened to the radio in Galician and 58.3% listened to music in Galician. If we analyse the data in this sense looking at the various media available in one or other language, the use of the media in Galician is quite high.

With reference to the importance that is given to the Galician language (see Table 2.6), it is not considered important for people to be liked (83%), to go shopping (81.6%), to make telephone calls (76.6%), to be accepted by the community (74%) and to watch television (60.3%). The people of the study did not consider it discriminatory in order to establish new relationships, nor its use in their daily activities.

On the other hand, in terms of reading and writing, it was considered an important language by 81.2% and 80.4% respectively. Only 20.1% considered that it was not important when bringing up a child and 34.6% that it was not important for getting a job. Finally, only 16.7% consider the Galician language not to be important for living in Galicia.

When we analyse the attitudes towards the three languages that are now present in schools in Galicia, it is found that the most favourable attitude of the participants tends to be towards Galician (see Figure 2.6), whilst the least favourable is towards English, with Spanish in the middle: 73.43% of the sample showed positive attitudes towards Galician, 56.04% towards Spanish and only 30.92% towards English. It is noticeable that only 1.45% of the sample shows negative attitudes towards Galician and Spanish. These negative attitudes are slightly higher when referring to the foreign language.

To continue, we shall analyse those independent variables that significantly influence the dependent variables. These are defined as attitudes towards Galician, Spanish and English. The first analysis points towards the influence that gender has on linguistic attitudes. The results indicate gender does not significantly influence attitudes towards Spanish or English. However, it does influence attitudes towards Galician [$F = 2.443$ ($p = 0.015$)]. Thus, the data show women have more positive attitudes towards Galician than men. These results are consistent with the other results of other surveys, which show women have a more positive attitude towards different languages, especially minority languages (Lasagabaster, 2003).

Table 2.6 Importance attached to the Galician language to do the following activities

For people to:	Important (%)	A little important (%)	A little unimportant (%)	Unimportant (%)
Make friends	20.2	14.8	23.2	41.9
Read	41.7	38.7	10.8	8.8
Write	43.3	37.9	11.8	6.9
Watch TV	15.2	24.5	40.7	19.6
Get a job	33.7	31.7	22.8	11.9
Be liked	10	7	35	48
Live in Galicia	60.8	22.5	9.8	6.9
Bring up children	45.6	34.3	12.3	7.8
Go shopping	8.4	9.9	36.6	45
Make phone calls	15.7	11.3	38.2	38.4
Pass exams	28.4	17.2	28.9	25.5
Be accepted in the community	11.3	14.7	35.3	38.7
Talk to friends at university	14.2	20.6	35.3	29.9
Talk to teachers at university	21.1	19.6	33.3	26
Talk to people out of university	16.7	16.7	37.3	29.4

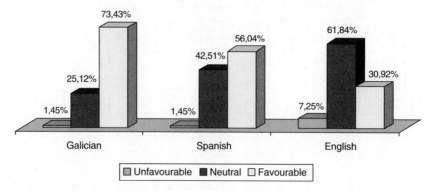

Figure 2.6 Attitudes towards the three languages

The first language has a clear influence on the analysed dependent variables. Those students who spoke Galician as their first language [$F2 = 17$ ($p < 0.001$)] or both [$F2 = 12.77$ ($p < 0.001$)] have better attitudes towards this language than those who speak Spanish as their first language. On the other hand, the opposite occurs with the attitudes towards Spanish. Those people whose first language is Spanish [$F2 = 10.588$ ($p < 0.001$)] or both [$F2 = 13.05$ ($p < 0.001$)] show better attitudes towards Spanish than those who speak Galician as their first language. However, when analysing the influence of L1, the attitudes towards English did not show significant differences.

When considering socioprofessional status, we came across some interesting results. When we analysed their attitudes towards Spanish we did not come across any marked differences. However, there are differences when we analyse English and Galician. The upper social classes show more favourable attitudes towards English than the lower social classes [$F2 = 9.65$ ($p < 0.008$)]. The upper social classes also manifest more negative attitudes towards Galician than the lower social classes [$F2 = 7.37$ ($p < 0.036$)].

For the next analysis we categorise the variable when they started to learn English, Galician and Spanish, 'before the age of 8' and 'after the age of 8'. The analyses do not show significant differences in the average of attitudes. On the other hand, there are significant differences in the attitudes towards this language between the people who have visited an English-speaking country and those who have not [$F = 4.356$ ($p < 0.001$)]. The people who have visited an English-speaking country have more positive attitudes than those who have not. The knowledge of a second foreign language, regardless of the level of that knowledge, does not have a significant influence on the attitudes towards the other languages.

The linguistic model in Galicia in each centre has its own peculiarities. It is more diversified in primary education and more homogenous in

Table 2.7 Summary of the most influential variables on language attitudes

Independent variable	Attitudes towards Galician	Attitudes towards Spanish	Attitudes towards English	Competence in English
Gender	Women > men	n.s.	n.s.	
L1	Galician > Spanish/both	Spanish > Galician/both	n.s.	
Socioprofessional status	Low > high/middle	n.s.	n.s.	
Age at which they started to learn English			High > Middle/low	n.s.
Ever visited an English-speaking country			Yes > no	n.s.
Knowledge of other foreign languages			n.s.	
Primary linguistic model	Always Spanish < Spanish more often/Galician more often/always Galician	n.s.	n.s.	
Secondary linguistic model	Always Spanish < Spanish more often/Galician more often/always Galician	Always Galician < Galician more often/Spanish more often/always Spanish		
Size of hometown	− 100,000 > + 100,000	+ 100,000 > − 100,000	n.s.	
Predominant language in hometown	Galician > Spanish	Spanish > Galician	n.s.	

secondary education. This variable has a significant influence on the attitudes towards Galician and Spanish. In primary education those who had an almost monolingual education in Spanish, except for Galician language lessons, show more negative attitudes towards Galician than those whose education was mainly in Spanish [$F2 = 7.31$ ($p = 0.042$)], those whose education was mainly in Galician [$F2 = 13.74$ ($p < 0.001$)] and those whose education was almost monolingual in Galician [$F2 = 11.65$ ($p = 0.009$)].

A similar trend is identified in secondary education, where there are some more negative attitudes towards Galician in the monolingual education model in Spanish compared to the rest of the options, i.e. mainly in Spanish [$F2 = 9.31$ ($p = 0.008$)], mainly in Galician [$F2 = 14.7$ ($p < 0.001$)] and only in Galician [$F2 = 16.78$ ($p < 0.001$)]. There are no significant differences in the attitudes towards Spanish.

When analysing the size of habitat and the predominance of one or other language in its place of residence, significant differences can be found in the measurement of attitudes. In this case, the people who inhabit a locale of under 100,000 inhabitants have more positive attitudes towards the minority language [$F = 3.32$ ($p = 0.001$)], whilst in the nuclei of more than 100,000 inhabitants have more positive attitudes towards the majority language [$F = 2.51$ ($p = 0.013$)]. In the same way, those individuals who reside in places where Galician is mainly spoken show better attitudes towards Galician [$F2 = 4.02$ ($p < 0.001$)], whilst those who live in areas where Spanish is predominantly spoken exhibit better attitudes towards Spanish.

Finally, the analysis of the relationship between attitudes and perceived competences shows some significant correlations between the attitudes towards one language and the self-perceived competence in that language, as is the case in Galician [$R^2 = 0.429$ ($p < 0.01$)], Spanish [$R^2 = 0.113$ ($p < 0.01$)] and English [$R^2 = 0.298$ ($p < 0.01$)].

Conclusion

This research, carried out with new university entrants who are studying to become teachers, tried to analyse the uses and linguistic attitudes not only towards the two official languages in Galicia, but also towards a foreign language with as much scope as English. This combination of variables has never been researched before in this community.

The first results extracted from this research are those that refer to competence. A piece of information that caught our attention was the perception that competence in Galician is inferior to competence in Spanish when the majority of the participants had Galician as the first language. In fact, whilst 76.8% declared that their competence in Spanish was good, that percentage fell to 55% in their competence in Galician.

The fact that these students had more contact with Spanish during their education could explain this result. This asymmetry in the perception of these competences might be a problem when implementing objectives that attempt to guarantee that the students acquire comparable attitudes in the two official Galician languages at the end of their statutory education.

With reference to the English language, the means for perceived competence are very low. Seventy percent of those polled revealed that they had little or no competence in English, whilst 6.9% judged their competence to be very good. These statistics are particularly worrying if we remember that 64.8% had been studying English since before they were nine years old. The lack of competence in foreign languages is not a new revelation. Galician statistical research carried out by Vez and Martínez (2002) already informed us of student deficiencies, especially in their oral communicative competences at the end of their statutory education. In fact, one of the recommendations made by these authors relates to the training of nursery and primary school teachers in foreign languages and proposes the alteration of areas and methods of teaching of the languages. The Galician Government is taking into account the results of the performance in foreign languages and is starting to adopt the first measures to resolve the problem. These measures consist of introducing these languages at an earlier age, in multilingual pilot teaching programmes in secondary education and in facilitating the training of teachers.

When talking about a second foreign language the results are still more frustrating: 81.3% revealed that they do not have any competence in another language. It is even worse when we analyse the 18.7% of the remainder and nearly half reveal having little knowledge. In the section where we analysed the education system the data provided by the Ministry of Science and Education on foreign languages already informed us of the little weight that other foreign languages have, apart from English, in the school curriculum.

The results confirm the intergenerational downward trend of the use of Galician (Sociolinguistics Seminar, 1995). The high level of usage of Spanish in all fields of interaction of those polled was prominent. Except when speaking to their neighbours, in all situations the future teachers used Spanish more than Galician, but above all when communicating with people of their own generation. So whilst 41.3% choose Galician to speak to their father, those who speak to their brothers total 38.2%. It was also very interesting to find that Galician is spoken more in the family environment than in the educational one, and that in this environment more Galician is spoken with the teachers (34.5%) than with their classmates (29.7% in class). As happened with the competence, we came across an inconsistency in the data of the first language with the data of linguistic uses. The surveyed students learnt to speak mainly in Galician, but speak more Spanish than Galician in nearly all situations.

With reference to the linguistic uses related to the media, it should be pointed out that these are influenced by the language on offer. In all the Galician media there is a larger presence of Spanish than Galician, which limits the choice of language in this environment.

In this study the hypothesis shown by previous qualitative studies of the existence of negative attitudes towards the use of Galician is confirmed (Iglesias, 2004; Sociolinguistics Seminar, 2004). Whilst 65.1% of the participants considered that Galician is important to live in Galicia, only 33.7% confirmed that it is necessary when looking for a job, 45.6% considered that it is important when having a child, and the most surprising data, when referring to the integrating dimension of the language, is that 65.1% of the future teachers consider Galician not to be at all important when making friends. Along this same lines, only 11.3% point out that it is important in order to be accepted by the community. It is also not considered important when communicating with classmates in the education environment. Galician is only considered important for reading and writing activities that are limited to the world of education. These data are very worrying for the future teaching of the Galician language by teachers, as the general belief of the importance of Galician for life in Galicia does not correspond with motives of an instrumental or integrational kind that will benefit its use. The fact that these students had a strong Spanish-language influence in their educational experience very probably favours this perception.

The results of the analyses of the linguistic attitudes towards Galician, Spanish and English point out that the future teachers have more positive attitudes towards Galician than Spanish and thirdly English. After having analysed the effect of different independent variables in language attitudes, we find that the women, who learnt to speak Galician or both languages, who come from the lower social classes, who had more Galician presence in their education, who reside in areas where there are less than 100,000 inhabitants and who live in mainly Galician-speaking areas, are those that show the most favourable attitudes towards Galician. Perceived competence also has a significant relationship with the attitude towards Galician, in the sense that those who point out a major competence also show better attitudes. With regard to Spanish, those who spoke this language as their L1, whose model of education was mainly in Spanish, who reside in areas of over 100,000 inhabitants or where Spanish is the predominant language, and who have better competence in that language, are those that have better attitudes.

Finally, attitudes towards English are more positive in the upper social classes, amongst those who have travelled to an English-speaking country and amongst those who have a high competence in this language. Different studies undertaken in Galicia (Lorenzo *et al.*, 1997; Rodríguez Neira *et al.*, 1998) have found that the attitudes of the university students towards the minority language are generally positive. However, this study has found the existence of negative appraisals towards Galician in the motivational, instrumental and integrational dimensions by using a questionnaire as an instrument of direct study for the first time. These conclusions are more worrying owing to the profile of the participants in the study, as those who participated will in the near future be nursery or primary school teachers. Taking the function of the teaching profession as a model and communicator of beliefs, attitudes and values, especially in these ideals, we believe in the necessity of training future schoolteachers in the importance of language attitudes.

Notes

1. *Nós* was the flagship journal of the Nós Generation. It was a key piece in the construction of the Galician national identity and activism around the Galician language. It included articles on anthropology, ethnography, folklore and literature from contributors such as Vicente Risco, Alfonso R. Castelao, Otero Pedrayo and Florentino Cuevillas, among other intellectuals.
2. No records have been published yet about the sociolinguistic situation of the University of A Coruña.
3. The habitat classified as rural-II included areas of less than 2000 inhabitants within a dispersed settlement.

References

Ayestarán Aranaz, M. and De la Cueva, J. (1974) *Las familias de la provincia de Pontevedra en 1974: Galleguidad y conflicto lingüístico gallego*. Sevilla: Instituto de Ciencias de la Familia.

Bouzada, X. (1993) A lingua galega no sector dos servicios ou as racionalidades, dilemas e paradoxos presentes en usos cotiáns da lingua galega. *Cadernos de lingua* 8, 5–18.

Castillo Castillo, J. and Pérez Vilariño, J. (1977) *La Reforma educativa y el cambio social en Galicia*. Santiago de Compostela: ICE.

Comisión Europea (1996) *Euromosaic. Producción e reproducción dos grupos lingüísticos minoritarios da Unión Europea*. Santiago de Compostela: Centro de Investigacións Lingüísticas e Literarias Ramón Piñeiro-Xunta de Galicia.

Consellería de Educación e Ordenación Universitaria (1999) Estudio sobre o uso do idioma galego. Unpublished manuscript, Xunta de Galicia.

Consello da Cultura Galega (1990) *Informe sobre a situación da lingua*. Santiago de Compostela: Consello da Cultura Galega.

Del Campo, S. and Tezanos, J.F. (1977) Galicia. In S. Del Campo Urbano, M. Navarro López and J. F. Tezanos (eds) *La cuestión regional española* (pp. 226–237). Madrid: Edicusa.

De Miguel, A. (ed.) (1970) *Informe sociológico de la situación social de España: 1970*. Madrid: Fundación Foessa, Euramérica.

Fernández Salgado, B. (2002) As linguas dos estudantes de Publicidade e Relacións Públicas: usos e actitudes. In G. Constenla (ed.) *Linguas non normalizadas*. Vigo: Universidade de Vigo – ASPG.

Iglesias Álvarez, A. (2003) *Falar galego: no veo por qué*. Vigo: Xerais.
Instituto Galego de Estatística (IGE) (2003) *Coñecemento e uso do Galego*. Santiago de Compostela: Xunta de Galicia.
Lasagabaster, D. (2003) *Trilingüismo en la enseñanza. Actitudes hacia la lengua minoritaria, la mayoritaria y la extranjera*. Lleida: Editorial Milenio.
López Muñoz, D. (1989) *O idioma da igrexa en Galicia*. Santiago de Compostela: Consello da Cultura Galega.
Lorenzo Suárez, A., Luaces Pazos, R., Pin Millares, X., Sánchez Bello, P., Vaamonde Liste, A. and Varela Caruncho, L. (1997) *Estudio sociolingüístico da Universidade de Vigo: Profesores, P.A.S. e Estudiantes*. Vigo: Servicio de publicacións da Universidade de Vigo.
Monteagudo Romero, H., Novo Folgueira, P., Costas González, X.H. and Rodríguez, E. (1986) *Aspectos sociolingüísticos do bilingüismo en Galicia segundo os alumnos da 2ª etapa de E.X.B.* Santiago de Compostela: Xunta de Galicia.
Monteagudo, H. and Bouzada, M.X. (eds) (2002) *O proceso de normalización do idioma galego, Vol. II Educación*. Consello da Cultura Galega: Santiago de Compostela.
Rodríguez Neira, M.A. and López Martínez, M.ªS. (1988) *O galego na Universidade*. Santiago de Compostela: Consello da Cultura Galega.
Rodríguez Neira, M. and Rubal Rodríguez, X. (1987) *O galego no ensino público non universitario*. Consello da Cultura Galega: Santiago de Compostela.
Rodríguez Neira, M.A., García Ares, M.C., Núñez Singala, M.C. and Varela Vázquez, B. (1998) *O idioma na Universidade*. Santiago de Compostela: Consello da Cultura Galega.
Rojo, G. (1979) *Aproximación a las actitudes lingüísticas del profesorado de E.G.B en Galicia*. Santiago de Compostela: ICE-Universidad.
Rubal Rodríguez, X.R. and Rodríguez Neira, M.A. (1987) *O galego no ensino público non universitario*. Santiago de Compostela: Consello da Cultura Galega.
Seminario de Sociolingüística (1994) *Lingua inicial e competencia lingüística en Galicia*. A Coruña: Real Academia Galega.
Seminario de Sociolingüística (1995) *Usos lingüísticos en Galicia*. A Coruña: Real Academia Galega.
Seminario de Sociolingüística (1996) *Actitudes lingüísticas en Galicia*. A Coruña: Real Academia Galega.
Seminario de Sociolingüística (2003) *O galego segundo a mocidade*. A Coruña: Real Academia Galega.
Seminario de Sociolingüística (in progress) *Avaliación das competencias bilingües ao final do ensino obrigatorio*. A Coruña: Real Academia Galega.
Seminario de Sociolingüística (in progress) *Revisión do Mapa Sociolingüístico de Galicia*. A Coruña: Real Academia Galega.
Silva, B. (2002) A lingua galega no sistema educativo de Galicia. Unpublished manuscript, Universidade de Santiago de Compostela.
Tjeerdsma, R.S. (ed.) (1998) *Mercator Guide to Organizations: Providing Information on Lesser Used Languages*. Ljouwert/Leeuwarden: Fryske Akademy/Mercator-Education.
Vaamonde Liste, A. (ed.) (2003) *Estudio sociolingüístico sobre a situación da lingua galega no Concello de Vigo*. Vigo: Concello de Vigo.
Vez, J.M. and Martínez Piñeiro, E. (eds) (2002) *Competencia comunicativa oral en lenguas extranjeras: Investigación sobre los logros del alumnado gallego de inglés y francés al finalizar la ESO*. Santiago de Compostela: Universidade de Santiago de Compostela, Servicio de Publicacións e Intercambio Científico.

Chapter 3
Language Use and Language Attitudes in the Basque Country

DAVID LASAGABASTER

Introduction

The Basque Country is a small Basque-speaking area with about 2,800,000 inhabitants. It covers an area bordering the Pyrenees and the Bay of Biscay, that in the north of the Pyrenees being part of France and that in the south belonging to Spain. The Basque Country refers therefore to the area occupied by the *Euskera* (Basque) speech community. The *Euskaldun* (Basque speaker) community is split up into three political units: the Basque Autonomous Community (BAC henceforward) and Navarre in Spain, and the Atlantic Pyrenees Department in France (see Figure 3.1), also known as continental Basque Country (*Iparraldea* in Basque). This chapter deals with the BAC, which is one of the 17 autonomous communities of Spain.

The BAC, established by the Statute of Autonomy of 1979, encompasses three provinces: Araba, Bizkaia and Gipuzkoa. Since 1982, and as a result of the Basic Law on the Standardisation of Basque, this has become a bilingual community where both Basque (the minority language) and Spanish (the majority language) are official languages. The Basque community speaks what is considered to be the oldest Western European

Figure 3.1 The Basque Country

language, a language spoken by just some 700,000 speakers in the three political entities into which the Basque-speaking community is divided.

The Basque language can be seen as one of the main symbols representing the identity of our community. It was the only pre-Indo-European language in the Spanish State that managed to resist the pressure exerted by Latin. Most European languages stem from two language families: the Indo-European and the Uralic families. However, the origin of the Basque language is an unresolved question, as it has no known linguistic relatives. Whereas most Western European languages stem from Indo-European, this is not the case with Basque.

The Basque language has undergone a remarkable development in the last 25 years. This change has been brought about by the evolution of the political situation since Franco's demise in 1975 and the transition from a dictatorship to democracy. As a result of this political process, certain minority languages that coexisted in Spain – Basque, Catalan and Galician – have recovered their presence in society in general and in education in particular, whereas others did not (Aragonese or Asturian, for example).

The most recent attempt by the Basque speech community to reverse the decline of its mother tongue can be divided into two phases (Gardner, 2000). The first phase spans the period from the 1950s to the end of the 1970s, and the second one from then to now. The key for this division is the period from 1975 to 1980, that is to say, the transition from a dictatorship to a constitutional monarchy. The first phase was characterised by very harsh conditions for all those involved in the defence and survival of the Basque language, as they lacked official support, minimum resources or any legal framework. Thus, the situation was extremely precarious due to the lack of trained Basque-speaking teachers, shortage of teaching materials and extremely limited economic resources. Zuazo (1995) also points out that there are three main factors that have determined and still determine the evolution of the Basque language nowadays; the small number of Basque speakers, its limited territory, and the administrative division that it has suffered.

The second phase started when Basque acquired co-official status with Spanish in 1978, which facilitated funding and the setting up of a campaign for literacy. The situation that the Basque language underwent for more than five centuries was also the cause for the rather late evolution of literature in Basque: 'From 1545, when the first book was published, Bernard Etxepare's *Linguae Vasconium Primitiae*, to 1879, only some 100 books were published in Basque' (Olaziregi, 2004: 14). Most Basques, being basically illiterate, had little contact with the written version of the language. Basque was not used in the administration and its sociolinguistic situation was a very good example of diglossia.

However, the aforementioned evolution can be observed in the fact that nowadays more than 1500 books are published in Basque every year.

Since Basque acquired co-official status with Spanish in 1978, efforts to revive the language have been made on the part of both public and private institutions. Research carried out in the BAC by the Basque Statistics Institute (*Eustat*) divides language speakers according to three categories:

- Basque speakers: this group is made up of fluent Basque speakers.
- Quasi-Basque speakers: those who can speak Basque with difficulty and who can understand it well or reasonably well.
- Spanish speakers: those people who can neither speak nor understand Basque.

The last large sociolinguistic survey undertaken by the Basque Government reveals that the numbers of speakers in each of these three groups in 2001 are as follows: 29.4% of its population can speak Basque fluently, while a further 11.4% speak it with difficulty and understand it well or reasonably well. However, 59.2% are monolingual Spanish speakers, people who can neither speak nor understand Basque (Table 3.1). In 1991, 24.1% were bilingual, whereas nowadays 29.4% are Basque–Spanish bilingual speakers. In the same period, the percentage of bilingual subjects in the age range 16–24 has risen from 25% to 48% (the figures have almost doubled), which clearly demonstrates the impact of the educational system on the increase in the number of bilingual youngsters.

This effect can also be observed in the most recent large-scale study carried out by the Basque Government. In 2004 the so-called *Observatory of the Youth*, under the auspices of the Department of Culture of the Basque Government, analysed (among other issues) the language use of 1500 subjects in the age range 15–29. The results showed that 63% of them usually speak Spanish at home, 27% Basque and the remaining 10% both Basque and Spanish. Nevertheless, when it comes to the language used with their friends, those who preferably speak Spanish amount to 51%, which means that almost half of them speak either Basque or both Basque and Spanish with their peers: 27% preferably spoke in Basque

Table 3.1 Number of Basque, quasi-Basque and Spanish speakers in the BAC

BAC	*2001*
Basque speakers	29.4%
Quasi-Basque speakers	11.4%
Spanish speakers	59.2%

Source: Basque Government (2003)

and 22% in both languages. Thus, it can be concluded that there is an increase in the use of Basque amongst youngsters in their everyday life, especially in their relationships with friends.

Nevertheless, while the last two decades have seen a small but steady increase in the number of people who can and do speak Basque in their everyday life – especially among children and young people due to the ever more popular immersion programmes – Basque is still clearly a minority language. It is also worth noting that nearly half of the Basque speakers are found in the province of Gipuzkoa. In the BAC the percentages according to mother tongue are the following: Basque (18.8%), Spanish (76.1%) and both Basque and Spanish (5.1%).

Hence, it can be stated that the sociolinguistic situation of Basque is better than ever before: it has a legal status, the number of speakers is steadily increasing, it has widespread social support, more printed books are published than in the previous four centuries combined, and it is being used in new areas (university, technology, etc). It seems that its survival is ensured, but Basque institutions should proceed with utmost caution. It needs to be remembered that among those who can speak Basque, some rarely do or their command is considerably weak. Furthermore, the role played by international languages cannot be ignored, particularly that of English, regarded by many people as essential for work. And we must also consider the arrival of immigrants who speak an additional language (L4) and who represent a linguistic challenge for the future (Lasagabaster & Sierra, 2005; Siguan, 1992).

Therefore, and despite the reverse language shift efforts, the Basque language still faces many challenges, the most important being that of securing intergenerational transmission and public use (Fishman, 1991). It is a fact that the educational system has given the Basque language a timely boost, as is shown in the number of young people who can speak it. The role of the school is vital, but the production of competent second-language speakers is not enough to ensure the survival of Basque; it cannot improve the situation on its own. Institutional action alone, without the support of social movements, is incapable of carrying out this task successfully. In this respect it has to be emphasised that the Basque Government has taken a first step aimed at stimulating the social use of Basque with the publication in 1999 of its comprehensive strategy designed to promote the use of Basque.

The Basque Educational System

Since the passing in 1983 of the law establishing the use of the Basque language at preuniversity levels in the BAC, and due to the existence of different social attitudes towards bilingualism, there are three linguistic models in which children can complete their studies:

- *Model A.* This is a programme in which Spanish is the vehicle language and Basque is taught only as a subject (4–5 h per week). The L1 of the students is Spanish. Although it was originally designed to include some subjects in Basque in the last years of compulsory education, which would make it comparable with the Canadian late partial immersion, this original resolution has been discarded.
- *Model B.* This is an early partial immersion programme in which both Basque and Spanish are used as means of instruction. These students' L1 is usually Spanish, although there may be some rare exceptions with Basque as their L1. In this model the first three schooling years (kindergarten) are generally taught through Basque. At the age of six, that is to say, the first year of primary education, they start to learn the reading–writing process and mathematics in Spanish. Many schools have evolved towards a more *intensive* model B, in which the reading–writing process and part or the whole subject of maths is implemented in Basque. Without any doubt this is the most heterogeneous model, and depending on different factors such as the sociolinguistic setting in which the school is located or the availability of Basque teaching staff, the time allotted to each of the languages varies considerably.
- *Model D.* A total immersion programme for those students whose L1 is Spanish and a maintenance programme for those with Basque as L1 (unlike Finland or Canada, where total immersion programmes are only used with students who have no knowledge of the vehicle language). Basque is the language of instruction and Spanish is only taught as a subject (4–5 h per week).

The evolution of these linguistic models is shown in Table 3.2. There has been a change from a monolingual educational system to a bilingual one, in which Model X (this was the only model available during the dictatorship, in which Basque was not taught at all) has practically disappeared. Enrolment figures in Model A go steadily down, whereas Models B and D go steadily up (207,408 students were enrolled in immersion programmes at preuniversity levels in the 2002–03 school

Table 3.2 Evolution of the three linguistic models at preuniversity level

	1983–84	*1990–91*	*1996–97*	*2002–03*
Model A (%)	72.8	50.6	31.5	30.6
Model B (%)	10.5	24.9	27.7	22.5
Model D (%)	16.5	24.4	40.7	46.4

year). Nonetheless, this shift is far more gradual in secondary education, something that could be attributed to the factors below:

(1) Model B is less widespread at this level, particularly in technical colleges.
(2) Some students who started their schooling process in Model B move into Model A in secondary education, because they are afraid of dealing with a greater cognitive effort in Basque; they consider their command of the minority language to be insufficient to succeed academically at a higher level.

The enrolment figures for 3 year olds in the 2003–04 school year in the BAC merit consideration, as they indicate the way trends are moving. These figures were the following: Model A, 8.4%; Model B, 30.1%; and Model D, 61.4%. Even in Araba, the province where there is a lower percentage of Basque speakers, Models B and D are much more popular than Model A at kindergarten. That this new generation of parents is in favour of the immersion programmes is thus beyond any doubt. As for academic results, research studies demonstrate that Model D students are the only ones who are close to balanced bilingualism and clearly outperform Models B and A in Basque, whereas Model B obtains better results in the minority language than Model A (whose students' command of Basque is really poor). In the rest of the academic subjects and Spanish, no differences have been observed, except in English, where Model D students also seem to take advantage of their higher degree of bilingualism (Cenoz, 1991; Lasagabaster, 2000).

The age at which students start learning English (the predominant first foreign language in the Basque educational system) has been gradually lowered, and since the 2000–01 school year it has been taught to children as young as four. This is an attempt on the part of the Basque Government to respond to social pressure in this direction, as Basque society supports and demands constant improvement in the teaching of this international language, and this early teaching is widely believed to be the correct way forward, despite the lack of research that clearly bears out this belief in formal contexts (Lasagabaster & Doiz, 2004). Therefore, all pupils have contact with three languages from a very early age, irrespective of their linguistic background. The Basque educational system attaches growing importance to trilingualism and multilingual education. The Department of Education has put its faith in trilingual education, as proved by the implementation of trilingual experimental programmes in secondary education. In fact, during the 2003–04 academic year 12 state schools taught their subjects in Basque, Spanish and English, following the lead of certain private schools, whose academic results are not generally made public.

Table 3.3 Foreign languages learnt by preuniversity students (2000–01 academic year)

BAC	English	French	German	Others
Nursery education (%)	50.9	0.6	0.4	0
Primary education (%)	97.8	1.1	0.6	0
Secondary education (%)	100	20.7	2.2	0.7
Postsecondary education (%)	98.6	6	0.1	0.03

Source: Basque Institute of Statistics (Eustat)

The hegemony of English as the main foreign language can be clearly seen in Table 3.3 The data are overwhelming. The presence of English in Primary (from 6 to 12 years of age), Secondary (13–16) and Postsecondary (17–18) education is superior to that of any other foreign language, at all levels above 97% and reaching 100% in Secondary education. This is due to the fact that even those few students who are enrolled in German or French schools have English as their second foreign language. Most conspicuous are the low percentages of German and French in Nursery and Postsecondary education. This monochromatic tendency is only broken in Secondary education, where one out of five students (20.7%) studies French, but this percentage plummets in Postsecondary education, where only 6% learn French. And this despite the proximity of French-speaking areas and the obvious cultural bonds with the continental Basque Country or *Iparralde*.

As far as tertiary education is concerned, the University of the Basque Country obviously has a role of paramount importance in sustaining and reinforcing Basque's everyday use, facing up to the challenge of the *Basquisation* of its degree courses with a view to providing society with Basque-speaking graduates ready to use the language in all social spheres. As is usually the case, the main stumbling block is an economic one. Currently, out of 87 university degrees available at this university, more than 30 (34%) can be completed in Basque. Ten years ago 17% of the students were studying in Basque, whereas nowadays this percentage has risen to 41%. As for the teaching staff, it consists of 3591 lecturers and professors, of whom 29% (1066) are bilingual speakers.

To summarise, teacher training and the creation of materials in Basque are the two crucial difficulties the University of the Basque Country has to cope with. According to its linguistic planning, it is expected that 50% of tertiary education students will complete their degrees in Basque in the academic year 2005–06. Nonetheless, and despite the positive increase in the number of Basque-speaking lecturers, much has yet to be done to reach a balanced presence of the two official languages.

Studies on Language Attitudes Carried Out in the BAC

The attitudes of the Basque population towards their languages have raised the interest of researchers in the BAC, as a result of which several studies have been undertaken. These studies can be divided into three main categories (Perales, 2001): (1) studies completed by institutions; (2) studies whose sample is made up of adults learning the Basque language – these are the people who did not have the chance to learn the language at school; and (3) studies carried out among students enrolled in primary, secondary or tertiary education.

As far as the first group is concerned, the samples are usually very large, which is why the questionnaire has become the most habitual instrument used in gathering data. Due to space constraints (for a detailed review see Lasagabaster, 2003), reference will only be made to one study (Basque Government, 2003), in which 3600 over-15s participated. The most relevant data taken from this study – dealing with the percentage of population who can speak Basque and/or Spanish – has already been provided in the first section of this chapter. However, it is worth pointing out that there are important differences between the three provinces that make up the BAC. Thus, and although there was widespread agreement in support of the measures taken to foster the use of Basque in society, support varied according to province: the measures were greeted most favourably in Gipuzkoa, where 72% approved, dropping to 69% in Bizkaia and 64% in Araba. Similarly, the percentage of those who can speak only Spanish is higher in Araba (75.5%) than in Bizkaia (64.9%) or Gipuzkoa (42.6%).

Studies whose samples consist of adults learning Basque indicate that the students' attitudes towards the minority language seem favourable. Amonarriz (1996) examined the attitudes of more than 2800 students in the age range 20–39, 76% of whom harboured positive or very positive attitudes, 23% neutral and only 1% negative attitudes. It has to be borne in mind that, although some of these students are basically instrumentally orientated (getting a job, generally in the public service sector), integrative orientation is most conspicuous. Arratibel (1999) studied the effect of both types of orientation, and factor analyses demonstrated that integrative orientation explained 30.4% of the variance, a percentage which almost doubled that of instrumental orientation (15.5%). The integrative factor included issues such as the desire to better understand the Basque people and their way of life, the desire to take part in cultural events and to get to know the Basque culture in more depth, or the wish to be able to communicate in Basque and feel more at ease among Basque speakers. This author concludes that the integrative orientation fosters the use of Basque to a greater extent, while helping the subject to really assimilate and absorb the Basque language. Likewise, in this type of study (Perales, 2000) the effect positive attitudes have on achievement in the L2 – Basque in this case – has also been corroborated.

Regarding the third category, studies completed among students during the 1990s and the first years of the new millennium (Etxebarria, 1995; García, 2001; Larrañaga, 1995; Lasagabaster, 2004; Madariaga, 1994) in the BAC have demonstrated that attitudes towards Basque and Spanish are sharply influenced by several factors, irrespective of the age of the students (these results have been confirmed with primary, secondary and tertiary education students): (1) Those whose L1 is Basque usually harbour more positive attitudes towards the minority language than those with Spanish as their L1. (2) The same applies to those who can speak Basque when compared with those who cannot speak it. (3) Those who have studied in Basque are more positive towards this language than those who have attended programmes in which Spanish is the vehicle language. (4) The clear effect of the sociolinguistic context: the higher the percentage of Basque speakers, the more positive people's attitudes are. These results led Madariaga (1994) to conclude that the sociolinguistic context is the variable that has a greater impact on achievement in Basque and, consequently, if a bilingual society is to be achieved, this task cannot be simply delegated to the school. Encouraging and endorsing the use of Basque in the social environment requires the participation of all social institutions and not just the school system. As with the second grouping, the research studies comprised in this third category have also confirmed the clear-cut effect attitude plays on the degree of competence achieved in Basque.

However, it has to be said that the vast majority of the studies completed so far in the BAC have been focused on both the majority and the minority language, but not on the foreign language, which overwhelmingly corresponds to English in the Basque educational system.

The Basque Study

The sample

The participants in the study were 222 university students studying for their Teacher Training Degree, which enables them to teach in Primary Education (6–12 year olds). Although all the subjects were completing the first year of their different degrees in Vitoria-Gasteiz, the political capital of the BAC, they came from the three provinces that make up the BAC. The mean age of the subjects was 20 years and 4 months, the youngest being 17 and the oldest 46 (93.2% of the sample was in the age range 17–24). Regarding their specialisation, 31.1% were studying Nursery Education, 28.4% Primary Education and 40.5% Physical Education. As is usually the case among would-be teachers,

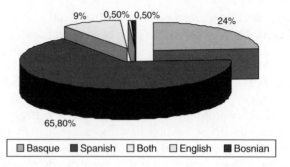

Figure 3.2 The students' L1

the vast majority of students were female (68.5%). The distribution of the participants depending on their mother tongue can be seen in Figure 3.2.

Although almost a quarter of the future teachers' mother tongue was Basque, plus 9% who had both Spanish and Basque as L1, the majority of them had Spanish as L1 (65.8%). Two students were English and Bosnian respectively. Regarding their parents' socioeconomic status, 19.8% (44 subjects) had high status, 38.3% (85) were middle-class and 41.9% (93) lower-class. 56.4% lived in towns with more than 100,000 inhabitants versus 43.6% who lived in smaller towns or villages, whereas 75.9% of them lived in predominantly Spanish-speaking areas.

In the case of the foreign language, 48.2% had started to learn English before the age of 8 and the remaining 51.8% at the age of 8 or later. As for their contact with the English language out of formal settings, 40.5% (90 subjects) had been to an English-speaking country, but 92.3% never (66.2%) or hardly ever (25.8%) watched TV in English, whereas only 4.5% watched it once or twice a week, 0.9% more than three times a week and just 5 subjects (2.3%) on a daily basis. It has to be remembered that Spain is one of the few European countries where all foreign films, documentaries, etc. are still dubbed, which explains the lack of contact with the English language – generally only accessible via pay-channels – through this nowadays ubiquitous and influential means of communication.

Last but not least, it has to be said that 32% of the students had been enrolled in Model A at preuniversity levels, 13.1% in Model B and more than half of the sample (55%) completed their studies in the more popular Model D.

The instrument and the procedure

The instrument and the procedure used in this study were the same as those followed by all the contributors to this volume, as explained in the introductory chapter. Students were given the possibility of filling out the questionnaire in either Basque or Spanish. The data were gathered in September 2004, the very beginning of the academic year.

Results

As for the degree of perceived competence attained by the participants in the three compulsory languages in the Basque school curriculum (see Figure 3.3), the highest competence is found in Spanish, followed by Basque and finally English. It is worth highlighting the fact that only 2% (5 subjects) of the students considered their command of English to be very good, whereas nearly 60% considered their level of proficiency in the foreign language to be very low. The students' own perceptions appear to corroborate those of Cenoz (1991) and Lasagabaster (1998), whose studies point to the generally poor command of English that Basque students have at preuniversity level. Contrastingly, 81% of the students regarded their command of Basque as good or very good, which clearly demonstrates that the objectives aimed at through the *Basquisation* process are on the right track, as this percentage is higher than that of the population in general, among whom 60% have little or no knowledge of Basque. The role of Spanish as the majority language is demonstrated by the fact that a meagre percentage of 1.4% (just three subjects) stated they could not speak Spanish well. The knowledge of other languages (French or German) apart from the three compulsory ones is not widespread at all. As a matter of fact, and as far as their general competence in a second language is concerned, 88.7% have no knowledge, 7.2% (16 students) a little and just 4.1% (9) have a good general command. The percentage is even lower amongst those who can speak it well: 2.3%, that is to say, just five individuals. Furthermore, out of more than 220 students, none of them has a *very good* command of a second foreign language. This situation clearly depicts the previously mentioned lack of tradition in

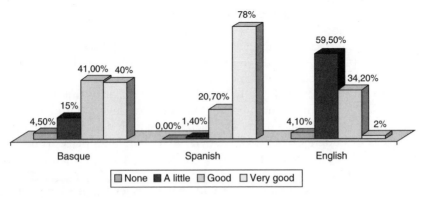

Figure 3.3 Level of competence in the three languages

foreign-language learning, as well as the preponderant position of English as the *only* foreign language really worth learning.

The language used with the family verifies that there is a generational difference (see Table 3.4). On the one hand, more than 75% of the students speak only or mostly Spanish to their fathers, and a similar percentage do so when addressing their mother. On the other hand, this percentage drops to 50% when it comes to their siblings, which demonstrates that amongst the younger members the presence of Basque is becoming more evident, as can be observed in the 'In Basque and Spanish about equally' column (Table 3.4). However, Spanish is still the most widely used language. This trend is maintained when they are asked about their friends in and outside the classroom.

Basque is most widely spoken to teachers (55.4% of the students talk to them always or more often in Basque), whereas the percentage of use of Basque diminishes when conversing with neighbours, where only 17.2% always or more often speak in Basque. These percentages are a reflection of the comments made in the introduction with regards to the use of the Basque language in everyday life, as there is a dire need to cultivate its use in many social spheres. It is a fact that the number of students who do speak Basque at the different educational levels is on the increase, but it is also true that the use of the minority language decreases enormously once they leave their respective educational settings and are immersed in their social sphere.

The use of Basque only as an input medium for the mass media (see Table 3.5) is minimal amongst the future teachers and the Spanish language seems to be predominant. As a matter of fact, only 0.5% watch TV only in Basque, whereas the percentage rises slightly as regards the press (1.8%). Nevertheless, it is worth pointing out that of the 10 or so daily newspapers on sale, only one (*Berria*) is completely in Basque, and there is just one TV channel (*ETB-1*) that broadcasts exclusively in Basque. Yet, 53.6% watch TV in Basque and Spanish equally, a high percentage if it is considered that in the BAC there are five open channels – plus some local ones – in Spanish. The highest use of Basque as the sole media interface is radio; 12.6% of the students listen to the radio only in Basque, plus 18% who listen to it more often in Basque than Spanish, despite the remarkable imbalance between the presence of Spanish and Basque (always overwhelmingly in favour of the majority language) also in this case. It is worth remembering that there are several radio stations that broadcast in Basque, many of which have a high music content, thus of appeal to students; and it is an activity that often takes place when the listener is alone, much more so than TV, which is often a group activity. It is also less intrusive.

However, if we except the 'Always in Spanish' category, the percentages for use of Basque as the medium may be seen as encouraging, even if it

Table 3.4 Language used when talking to the following people

	Always in Basque (%)	In Basque more often than Spanish (%)	In Basque and Spanish about equally (%)	In Spanish more often than Basque (%)	Always in Spanish (%)
Father	14.4	2.3	5.9	6.8	68.5
Mother	15.3	5.4	2.3	11.7	64.9
Brothers and sisters	17.6	4.5	15.3	18	32
Friends in the classroom	11.7	20.7	22.1	11.3	33.8
Friends outside school	8.6	10.8	25.2	20.3	35.1
Teachers	44.1	11.3	3.6	6.3	34.7
Neighbours	10.4	6.8	17.1	18	47.3

Table 3.5 The media and language medium

	Always in Basque (%)	In Basque more often than Spanish (%)	In Basque and Spanish about equally (%)	In Spanish more often than Basque (%)	Always in Spanish (%)
Watching TV	0.5	5.9	53.6	27	13.1
The press	1.8	5	33.8	29.3	30.2
Music	0.5	15.8	50	21.2	12.6
Listening to the radio	12.6	18	30.6	19.8	18.9

has to be accepted that there are *different degrees of utilisation*. To a greater or lesser degree, almost 87% watch TV in Basque, nearly 70% read journals and newspapers in Basque, more than 87% listen to music and 81% to the radio in the minority language. This leads us to conclude that use is not so low, especially if we take into account how Spanish language media massively outweighs that available in Basque. In any case, it is obvious that the percentage of use of the two languages varies considerably from subject to subject.

As far as importance attached to the Basque language is concerned (see Table 3.6), 81.1% do not consider it important when going shopping, more than 75% of the sample believe that Basque is not important in order to be liked, 68.5% to be accepted in the community, 65.3% to make phone calls and 59% to talk to people outside the university setting. Therefore, the main conclusion to be drawn is that university students do not regard Basque as a discriminatory language that hinders new relationships from being established or may become a hurdle in carrying out the regular activities of everyday life.

However, there are activities in which Basque is observed as important, such as for getting a job (only 7.7% think it is not important in this respect), for living in the Basque Country (just 10% consider it of little consequence) and when it comes to bringing up children (the percentage of those who do not see the Basque language as significant in this respect amounts to just 14.4%). Thus, the ability to communicate in Basque is clearly recognised as being important in order to live in the Basque Country and to bring up children here. The significance of the instrumental orientation is also well worth emphasising.

When analysing the attitudes towards the three languages in contact at school, the first thing that draws our attention is that attitudes towards Basque are the most positive (see Figure 3.4), whereas the attitudes harboured regarding the foreign language are the least, with the majority language being placed in between: 71% of the sample showed positive attitudes towards Basque, 41.9% towards Spanish and only 24% towards English. It is worth pointing out that unfavourable attitudes towards the three languages are very rare (8 subjects in the case of Basque, 12 in that of Spanish and 8 for English).

In the following text the independent variables that exerted a greater influence on the dependent variables (attitudes towards Basque, Spanish and English) in the Basque context will be dealt with. The first striking result is that although previous studies completed in the BAC, such as Aiestaran and Baker's (2004) and Lasagabaster's (2003), found significant differences when considering gender, in our sample this did not wield a statistically significant influence on the students' language attitudes, which may be due to their choice of specialisation. Habitually, women hold more positive attitudes towards the different languages, especially

Table 3.6 Importance attached to the Basque language to do the following activities

For people to:	Important (%)	A little important (%)	A little unimportant (%)	Unimportant (%)
Make friends	22.1	30.2	28.4	18.9
Read	39.6	32.9	22.5	5
Write	41.9	29.3	22.5	5.9
Watch TV	20.3	36	38.3	5.4
Get a job	76.1	15.8	7.2	0.9
Be liked	8.6	16.2	40.5	34.7
Live in the Basque Country	61.3	28.8	8.6	1.4
Bring up children	62.6	22.1	7.7	7.7
Go shopping	2.3	16.7	51.8	29.3
Make phone calls	10.8	23.9	43.2	22.1
Pass exams	55	21.2	14.4	9
Be accepted in the community	9.5	22.1	41.9	26.6
Talk to friends at university	31.1	27	26.1	15.8
Talk to teachers at university	46.8	19.8	20.3	13.1
Talk to people out of university	16.7	24.3	38.3	20.7

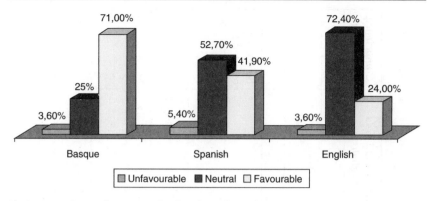

Figure 3.4 Attitudes towards the three languages

the minority language, but in this case the choice of a career over-whelmingly dominated by women might have an impact on their male counterparts' language attitudes. In any case, this is a question that requires further investigation.

Conversely, the students' L1 did have a clear-cut influence on their attitudes. Thus, those students who had Basque as L1 were more favourable towards the minority language than those whose L1 was Spanish [$F2, 196 = 9.584$ ($p < 0.001$)] or both languages [$F2, 71 = 2.710$ ($p = 0.008$)], whereas the L1 = both group was also more favourable than the Spanish = L1 group [$F2, 163 = 4.191$ ($p < 0.001$)]. In the case of Spanish the results were just the opposite, as those who had Spanish as L1 were more positive towards the majority language than those who had Basque [$F2, 197 = 8.963$ ($p < 0.001$)] or both languages as L1 [$F2, 164 = 3.274$ ($p = 0.001$)], whereas the 'both' group was also more favourable than the Basque group [$F2, 71 = 2.794$ ($p = 0.007$)]. As far as the foreign language was concerned, those with Spanish as L1 were more positive towards English than those who had Basque [$F2, 197 = 3.605$ ($p < 0.001$)].

When the students' socioprofessional status was considered, the only significant difference was observed in the case of attitudes towards Spanish, where those from a low socioprofessional background hap-pened to be significantly more favourable than their high [$F2, 135 = 2.588$ ($p = 0.005$)] and middle-class [$F2, 176 = 2.436$ ($p = 0.016$)] counterparts.

The age at which the students started to learn English did not have an effect on their attitudes towards the foreign language, although it did with regards to their self-perceived level of competence. Thus, those who had started to learn before the age of 8 considered that their competence was better than those who learnt it for the first time at the age of 8 or later [$F1, 220 = 4.439$ ($p < 0.001$)]. Whether they had ever visited an English-speaking country did not affect their self-perceived competence,

Table 3.7 Summary of the most influential variables on language attitudes

Independent variable	Attitudes towards Basque	Attitudes towards Spanish	Attitudes towards English	Competence in English
Gender	n.s.	n.s.	n.s.	
L1	Basque > Spanish/both Both > Spanish	Spanish > Basque/both Both > Basque	Spanish > Basque	
Socioprofessional status	n.s.	Low > high/middle	n.s.	
Age at which they started to learn English			n.s.	Before 8 > at or after 8
Ever visited an English-speaking country			Yes > no	n.s.
Knowledge of other foreign languages			Yes > no	
Linguistic model	Model D > Model A/B Model B > Model A	Model A > Model B/D Model B > Model D	Model A > Model B/D Model B > Model D	
Size of hometown	− 100,000 > + 100,000	+ 100,000 > − 100,000	n.s.	
Predominant language in hometown	Basque > Spanish	Spanish > Basque	n.s.	

although it did have an impact on their attitudes, as those who had ever been to an English-speaking country were more favourable towards the foreign language than those who had not [$F1$, $219 = 2.620$ ($p = 0.009$)]. Similarly, their knowledge of a second foreign language brought about more positive attitudes towards English, as those who knew a fourth language (irrespective of their degree of competence) held more positive attitudes towards the foreign language [$F1$, $221 = 2.111$ ($p = 0.030$)] than those who could not speak any.

The linguistic model also turned out to exert a great influence on their language attitudes. Those who had completed their preuniversity studies in Model D were more favourable towards Basque than those enrolled in Models A [$F2$, $190 = 10.545$ ($p < 0.001$)] and B [$F2$, $148 = 3.769$ ($p < 0.001$)], as were Model B students when compared to those from Model A [$F2$, $98 = 6.180$ ($p < 0.001$)]. In the case of attitudes towards Spanish, the results were just the opposite. Model A students were significantly more positive than their Model B [$F2$, $98 = 5.091$ ($p < 0.001$)] and D [$F2$, $191 = 11.164$ ($p < 0.001$)] counterparts, whereas those who had been enrolled in Model B were also more favourable than those who completed their studies in Model D [$F2$, $191 = 11.164$ ($p < 0.001$)]. The same pattern is maintained with regards to English, as Model A students were more positive than Model B [$F2$, $98 = 2.069$ ($p = 0.041$)] and D [$F2$, $190 = 6.005$ ($p < 0.001$)] students, and the latter also held more favourable attitudes towards the foreign language than Model D students [$F2$, $148 = 2.112$ ($p = 0.036$)].

Both the size and the predominance of the majority/minority language in their hometown also revealed significant differences: those living in locations with less than 100,000 inhabitants were more positive towards the minority language [$F1$, $217 = 4.999$ ($p < 0.001$)], whereas those living in places with more than 100,000 inhabitants held more positive attitudes towards the majority language [$F1$, $218 = 4.602$ ($p < 0.001$)]. Similarly, those residing in a predominantly Basque-speaking area were more favourable towards this language [$F1$, $216 = 5.744$ ($p < 0.001$)], while those living in predominantly Spanish-speaking areas supported more earnestly the majority language [$F1$, $217 = 4.201$ ($p < 0.001$)].

Finally, it is worth pointing out that in all three cases, Basque [$R^2 = 0.699$ ($p < 0.001$)], Spanish [$R^2 = 0.383$ ($p < 0.001$)] and English [$R^2 = 0.311$ ($p < 0.001$)], there is a significant correlation between the students' self-perceived language competence and their attitudes towards each of the three languages, which would bear out the results of all those studies that claim a direct relationship between language attitudes and language achievement (see Section 3). As this study did not aim to delve into the cause and effect question (it is cross-sectional), it can only be confirmed that there is a significant relationship between language competence and attitudes.

Discussion

The main objective of this chapter is to examine the language use and language attitudes of university students who will become teachers in the BAC in the near future, as their teaching will undoubtedly wield great influence on their future pupils. The first piece of data that drew our attention was the high command of Basque of 81% of the sample, well above the mean of Basque society in general, but perhaps still not sufficient for the demands of a Basque educational system where there is a clear trend among parents to choose bilingual programmes for their children. If this trend continues, it seems obvious that *all* those who want to become teachers will need to be highly proficient in the minority language to cater for the linguistic needs of near-future students. Moreover, if the objective is to achieve a bilingual society, all teachers need to be bilingual. As for Spanish, only three subjects acknowledged their less than fluent command, which clearly reflects its role as the majority language. We see a different picture regarding the English language, as only 2% of the future teachers had a very good command of a language that has become the main lingua franca all over the world, but what is more preoccupying, 60% consider their command of the foreign language to be very low. This paper does not aspire to explain this issue, but the reason for this could be found in the lack of a foreign-language learning tradition in the BAC in particular and Spain in general. In fact, this is a shortcoming that the Basque educational authorities are endeavouring to correct in order to foster linguistic diversity and multilingualism (see pp. 68ff.).

The fact that Spain is one of the few European countries that still dubs cinema films and TV is worth considering in this respect. In a study carried out in Finland, Lasagabaster (2001) observed that Finnish teachers of English (Finland is one of those European countries where there is no dubbing) coincided in stating that Finnish students' command of the English language at the end of compulsory education was very good, one of the main reasons being the lack of a dubbing industry. As a matter of fact, the vast majority of teachers interviewed pointed out that the amount of passive vocabulary the students possess before starting English at school is flabbergasting (Dewaele, 2002, also makes reference to this question in Belgium), a clear effect of the positive influence of screening TV and films in their original language. This is a question to be borne in mind by the Basque Government (and, by extension, by the Spanish Government).

To make foreign-language matters worse, nearly 89% of the participants had no knowledge of a second foreign language at all and only 4.1% considered that they had a good command, whereas none of them regarded themselves as being proficient; this despite the European Union's efforts to boost second foreign language learning and the ever increasing presence of immigrant students in the Basque educational system. It can therefore be concluded that if Europe's historical linguistic and cultural diversity is to be maintained, there is a dire need to boost foreign-language learning amongst Basque students in general and future teachers in particular, as otherwise we run the risk of English becoming not just the main but the *only* lingua franca. Much is said about our Europe without frontiers, but is it perhaps time to have at least some native teachers of foreign languages working in the state system?

Another interesting issue is related to the use of Basque with different members of the family and friends. Whereas it is used with parents only by 25% of the participants, when it comes to brothers, sisters and friends, the percentage is doubled (50%). Thus, it seems obvious that Basque is used more widely amongst the younger generation, which sheds some positive light on the future of the minority language. Moreover, the item 'If I have children, I would like them to be Basque speakers regardless of other languages they may know' displays the second highest mean score, a key issue if the language reversal shift efforts carried out so far are to be secured via intergenerational transmission. However, and as regards public use, Basque is only used by 17.2% in the neighbourhood and not seen as important in everyday life, which reveals the need to implement language policies to foster the social use of the minority language.

The analysis of the use of Basque with respect to the media indicates a similar trend. Basque is more widely used when listening to the radio (30% listen only or more often in Basque), but the presence of Spanish is much more habitual and this has a diaphanous impact on its use. To give an example that clearly demonstrates that Basque is still a minority language, on 1 January 2005 the successful film *Harry Potter and the Sorcerer's Stone* was broadcast on Basque television. It was the first time that a film was broadcast in both Spanish and Basque at the same time; however, the Basque version was followed by 1.8% of the audience, while the Spanish version reached 37% of the viewers. Being a film that appeals primarily to youngsters – of whom the vast majority can speak Basque – it could be said that there is an obvious mismatch between the knowledge and the use of the minority language. If the gap between school and everyday use is to be bridged, the use of the minority language in the media needs to be encouraged and increased.

As for the importance attached to the Basque language, this is highly regarded when it comes to living and raising children in the BAC, but not to carry out everyday activities such as going shopping or making phone calls. More importantly, the results clearly manifest that there is no discrimination on linguistic grounds, as the minority language is not seen as being consequential in order to be liked or accepted in the community. There is an open instrumental orientation to Basque (important to gain employment), and these future teachers are well aware of how important, even fundamental, being able to speak Basque has become, as the vast majority of teaching positions in the BAC require a linguistic profile, meaning the ability to communicate well or very well in Basque. In fact, this was the item whose importance was more widely supported by the trainee teachers.

One of the most prominent elements to emerge from this study has to do with the fact that Basque is the language towards which more positive attitudes were harboured, even though students pointed out that it is a difficult language to learn and that there are more useful languages than Basque. This positive attitudinal stance, an important question if social use is to increase, will probably be reflected in their future pupils. It is important to remember that research (Aiestaran & Baker, 2004) carried out in the BAC has shown that the effect of favourable attitudes to the minority language on Basque language and Basque cultural identity, actual use of Basque outside the family and potential use of Basque is positive and strong. On the other hand, in our survey the attitudes towards Spanish and, above all, English are not so positive (students also agreed on finding English a difficult language to learn). Therefore, it seems obvious that there is a need to work on language attitudes at preuniversity level to try to change this trend.

When analysing the effect of the different independent variables, it was observed that those living in predominantly Basque-speaking small towns or villages had more favourable attitudes towards the minority language, whereas those living in predominantly Spanish-speaking and bigger towns went more clearly for the Spanish language. Yet there are two variables whose effect on the three languages was definitive: the students' L1 and the linguistic model. It has to be considered that these two variables are closely linked, as those whose L1 is Basque are enrolled in Model D, and the percentage of students enrolled in this model is much higher in predominantly Basque-speaking small towns than in the predominantly Spanish-speaking big towns. Thus, those students who completed their studies in Model D were the ones who more positively backed the Basque language, followed by Model B and finally Model A students. In the case of the two international languages (Spanish and English), the effect of this variable was just the opposite, those in Model A being most favourable. As Model D is nowadays the most popular linguistic model, it seem obvious that there is a need to pay attention to language attitudes, which are usually part of what has been termed the *hidden curriculum*, as they are theoretically regarded as very important at preuniversity level, but the reality is that not much consideration is given to them in the classroom (Lasagabaster, 2003). In the case of English, those who had at some time visited an English-speaking country were more positive towards the foreign language, which would lead us to affirm that the student exchange programmes already existing in some Basque schools have to be made as widely available as possible, as contact with the target society and culture also improves students' language attitudes. Although those students who set out to learn English before the age of 8 did not hold more positive attitudes, it has to be remembered that its teaching from the age of 4 onwards has almost become universal at Basque schools during the last few years, which, according to our results, should have a positive impact on students' competence.

Hence, it can be concluded that there is a need to work on language attitudes at teacher training courses, bearing in mind that there are significant differences between individuals and between different languages. I have emphasised elsewhere (Lasagabaster, 2005) that explicit language awareness activities could be included in the curriculum, discussing the different languages in contact at school, which would mitigate feelings of inferiority amongst those who speak the minority language. It would also improve the attitudes towards Basque of those who do not exhibit a favourable stance. It is important to foster better feelings regarding the different languages by arousing students' awareness of the characteristics of the different languages and their place in the world. Linguistic tolerance does not come naturally; it has to be learned and to be worked at if we are to avoid a society marked by a high degree of linguistic parochialism. In a previous study (Lasagabaster, 2003), whose sample was made up of 1087 university students taking 17 different degrees, the knowledge of languages other than Basque, Spanish and English had a significantly positive effect on the students' attitudes regarding English. This is also the case in the present sample and, consequently, it can also be affirmed that the learning of second foreign languages should also be fostered at preuniversity and university levels, as this may help to improve attitudes towards foreign languages and help to maintain Europe's linguistic and cultural diversity.

Acknowledgements

This chapter was made possible thanks to the financial patronage awarded by the Spanish Ministry of Education and Science (SEJ2004-06723-C02-02/EDUC) and the Basque Government (PI98/96).

References

Aiestaran, J. and Baker, C. (2004) Bilingual education in the Basque Country: A model of its influence. *Cylchgrawn Addysg Cymru/The Welsh Journal of Education* 13, 8–29.

Amonarriz, K. (1996) Helduen euskalduntzea: eskaintza eta eskariaren egoera eta etorkizunerako aurrikuspenak. *Bat Soziolinguistika Aldizkaria* 19, 63–78.

Arratibel, N. (1999) *Helduen euskalduntzean eragiten duten prozesu psikosozialak: motibazioaren errola*. Bilbao-Bilbo: Universidad del País Vasco – Euskal Herriko Unibertsitatea.

Basque Government (2003) *Euskararen jarraipena III: Euskal Herriko soziolinguistikazko inkesta 2001*. Vitoria-Gasteiz: Gobierno Vasco – Eusko Jaurlaritza.

Cenoz, J. (1991) Enseñanza-aprendizaje del inglés como L2 o L3. San Sebastián-Donostia: Universidad del País Vasco – Euskal Herriko Unibertsitatea.

Dewaele, J.-M. (2002) Psychological and sociodemographic correlates of communicative anxiety in L2 and L3 production. *The International Journal of Bilingualism* 6, 23–38.

Etxebarria, M. (1995) Competencia y actitudes lingüísticas en la Comunidad Autónoma Vasca. In *Actas del simposi de demolingüística/III trobada de sociolingüistes* (pp. 119–125). Barcelona: Generalitat de Catalunya.

Fishman, J. (1991) *Reversing Language Shift: Theoretical and Empirical Foundations of Assistance to Threatened Languages*. Clevedon: Multilingual Matters.

García, I. (2001) *Euskararen erabileran eragiten duten prozesu psikosozialak: identitate etnolinguistikaren garrantzia*. San Sebastián-Donostia: Universidad del País Vasco – Euskal Herriko Unibertsitatea.

Gardner, N. (2000) *Basque in Education in the Basque Autonomous Community*. Bilbao-Bilbo: Departamento de Educación, Universidad e Investigación del Gobierno Vasco.

Larrañaga, N. (1995) *Euskararekiko jarrerak eta jokabideak*. Bilbao-Bilbo: Universidad de Deusto.

Lasagabaster, D. (1998) *Creatividad y conciencia metalingüística: incidencia en el aprendizaje del inglés como L3*. Bilbao-Bilbo: Universidad del País Vasco – Euskal Herriko Unibertsitatea.

Lasagabaster, D. (2000) Three languages and three linguistic models in the Basque educational system. In J. Cenoz and U. Jessner (eds) *English in Europe: The Acquisition of a Third Language* (pp. 179–197). Clevedon: Multilingual Matters.

Lasagabaster, D. (2001) The learning of English in Finland. *Interface, Journal of Applied Linguistics* 16, 27–44.

Lasagabaster, D. (2003) *Trilingüismo en la enseñanza. Actitudes hacia la lengua minoritaria, la mayoritaria y la extrajera*. Lleida: Editorial Milenio.

Lasagabaster, D. (2004) Attitudes towards English in the Basque Autonomous Community. *World Englishes* 23, 211–224.

Lasagabaster, D. (2005) Attitudes towards Basque, Spanish and English: An analysis of the most influential variables. *Journal of Multilingual and Multicultural Development* 26, 1–21.

Lasagabaster, D. and Doiz, A. (2004) The effect of the early teaching of English on writing proficiency. *International Journal of Bilingualism* 8, 527–542.

Lasagabaster, D. and Sierra, J.M. (eds) (2005) *Multilingüismo y multiculturalismo en la escuela*. ICE/Horsori.

Madariaga, J.M. (1994) Jarreren eragina hezkuntza elebidunean: A eta D hizkuntza-ereduen artean egindako konparaketa-azterlana. In I. Idiazabal and A. Kaifer (eds) *Hezkuntzaren eraginkortasuna eta irakaskuntza elebiduna*

Euskal Herrian (pp. 111– 128). Oñati: Herri Arduralaritzaren Euskal Erakundea (IVAP).

Olaziregi, M.J. (2004) *An Anthology of Basque Short Stories*. Reno, NV: University of Nevada, Reno.

Perales, J. (2000) *Euskara-ikasle helduen ikas-prozesua: ikaslearen baitako zenbait aldagairen eta arrakastaren arteko erlazioa*. San Sebastián-Donostia: Universidad del País Vasco – Euskal Herriko Unibertsitatea.

Perales, J. (2001) Gainbegirada bat hizkuntz jarrerei Euskal Herrian. *Bat Soziolinguistika Aldizkaria* 40, 89– 110.

Siguan, M. (1992) *España plurilingüe*. Madrid: Alianza Editorial.

Zuazo, K. (1995) The Basque Country and the Basque language: An overview of the external history of the Basque language. In J.I. Hualde, J.A. Lakarra and R.L. Trask (eds) *Towards a History of the Basque Language* (pp. 5– 30). Amsterdam/Philadelphia: John Benjamins.

Chapter 4

Language Use and Language Attitudes in the Valencian Community

MARIA PILAR SAFONT JORDÀ

Sociolinguistic Context

At present, more than seven million people around the world speak Catalan as their mother tongue. We find Catalan speakers in Catalonia, Andorra, the 'Franja' in Aragon, the French Rousillon, l'Alguer in Sardinia, the Balearic Islands and the Valencian Community. In Spain there are three main areas quoted above where Catalan is spoken, namely those of the Balearic Islands, Catalonia and the Valencian community, which is the focus of our study (Figure 4.1).The Catalan language developed in the later period of the Roman Empire from a variety of Latin spoken in the northern and eastern parts of the Pyrenees. As a romance language, it shares many similarities with the Spanish language that is spoken in all the Spanish territory. The constant contact with Spanish is particularly manifested in those regions where both languages, Catalan and Spanish, are used. However, the Catalan language history and its evolution in these areas (Catalonia, the Balearic Islands and the Valencian Community) are different, as shown by the existing dialectal varieties.

The origin of the Catalan language in territories now known as the Valencian Community dates back to the 13th century when King James I settled in this area. At this time, Valencian society used the language for administrative, political, cultural, economic and social purposes. The Catalan language was then a common instrument that connected the Valencian region to Catalonia and the Balearic Islands. This privileged status of the language continued until the 16th century, when castilianisation of the territory gradually increased. Upper social classes started adopting Spanish as a sign of prestige linked to the Castilian Crown. In the 17th century, with the triumph of Philip V, the use of the Spanish language was expanded to all territories belonging to his empire, which included the Valencian region. The superiority of Spanish over Catalan would continue during the 18th and 19th centuries. However, Catalan was still used by people in towns, rural areas and in informal everyday conversations. In the 19th century there were two contradictory

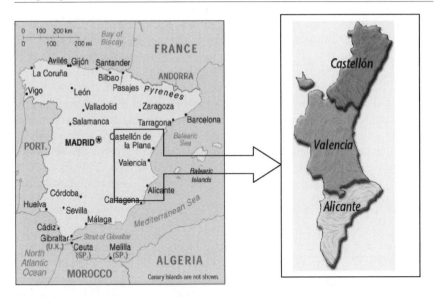

Figure 4.1 Spain and the Valencian Community

occurrences, namely the literary recovery of Catalan and the social prestige attributed to the Spanish language.

The literary movement in Valencia quoted above, known as the *Reinaixença*, gave rise to fundamental changes for the Catalan language in the 20th century. In fact, standardisation and orthographical normalisation of Catalan took place in that period. At the beginning of the 20th century, that is, during the First Republic, an organised Valencianist political movement developed parallel to the increased literary production in Catalan, and led to the creation of the *Societat Castellonenca de Cultura* (Castelló Cultural Society) in 1919. The fact that the use of the Catalan language had been long reduced to oral encounters had promoted high dialectal variability that required urgent grammatical normalisation. Bearing this purpose in mind, intellectuals concerned about the language met in 1932 in Castelló and produced a document known as '*Les Normes de Castelló*', which involved certain orthographical and grammatical codes. These norms were influenced by certain spelling rules previously approved by *Institut d'Estudis Catalans* (Catalan Studies Institute) in 1913 and by a former Catalan grammar, namely that of Pompeu Fabra's *Gramàtica Normativa de la Llengua Catalana* (Normative Grammar of the Catalan language), both of them developed in Catalonia.

As might be shown by certain historical facts mentioned above, in the Valencian territory the Catalan language has often been considered as inferior to Spanish. Unlike the social status of the language in Catalonia at the end of the 19th and beginning of the 20th centuries, Catalan was mainly spoken in towns and rural areas, whereas Spanish was seen as a prestigious language. However, possibilities for using the language after its total normalisation and standardisation would soon diminish in both communities. The dictatorship period in Spain that lasted for 40 years, from 1936 to 1976, also involved the nonofficial and unadvised use of Valencians' and Catalans' mother tongue. During this time, Spanish was the only official language of the Spanish State and Catalan, as well as other languages like Basque and Galician, was totally forbidden and only used in very reduced settings (i.e. family, rural areas). This fact was a determinant factor for the supremacy of Spanish over Catalan in the Valencian community.

From the birth of the Spanish Constitution in 1978, where all languages spoken in Spanish regions were recognised as official within their own respective communities, there has been an increasing tendency to maintain Catalan and to spread its use both in informal and formal settings. In 1982, the *Estatut d'Autonomia* in the Valencian Community proclaimed the existence of Catalan and Spanish as official languages in this community, and the right of every inhabitant to use and learn them. As a consequence, it was the responsibility of the Autonomous Government to guarantee the learning and use of both languages. The *Estatut d'Autonomia* gave rise to the regulation and use of the Catalan language by the *Llei d'ús i ensenyament del Valencià* in 1983, where incorporation of the Catalan language in education is made compulsory. This law addresses the issue of the obligatory knowledge of Catalan for both teachers and students regarding oral as well as written production. Yet the law does not address one issue that has recently raised some controversy, that of the name of the language.

For the purposes of the present chapter we will be referring to the language as Catalan in line with the document (i.e. *les Normes de Castelló*, 1932), which includes all normative criteria responsible for the standardisation process related to written language use in all territories employing the Catalan language. Nevertheless, the term Valencian may also be employed in cases where reference is made to the use of the language in Valencian territories exclusively, and specially in those laws and norms that regulate its employment within the Valencian Community. In fact, politicians refer to the Catalan language employed in the Valencian Community as Valencian (see rules and norms related to language use and mentioned in this section of the chapter), instead of referring to it as Catalan used in the Valencian Community. Some would argue that it is a solution to the identity problems that the name Catalan may involve, as it is also employed to refer to people living in Catalonia. Yet the name Valencian is also subject to criticisms. On the one hand, the term Valencian also refers to those living in Valencia, hence, excluding those living in Castelló or Alacant, on the other; it is one dialectal variety of the Catalan language, and the actual academic and agreed name of the language is Catalan as stated in *Les Normes de Castelló* mentioned before. Besides, the use of the dialectal term to refer to the language in general has promoted the idea that it might be a different language from that of Catalan, although this is only an opinion not grounded in any philological criteria, and it is promoted by specific political parties. Actually, those using Catalan and those having Catalan as their mother tongue have no problems in referring to their language as either Valencian or Catalan. They worry about its teaching and its use rather than about its name.

Various laws and rules have attempted to regularise the inclusion of the Catalan language in the Valencian community educational system by means of various bilingual educational programmes. These programmes affect mainly primary as well as compulsory secondary school curricula.

The Valencian Educational System

In 1990 a global modification of the Spanish educational system took place that also affected autonomous communities. This modification is commonly known as LOGSE (*Llei d'Ordenació General del Sistema Educatiu* – Law for the General Regularisation of the Educational System). Within this law certain issues affecting bilingual education in the Valencian Community have been tackled in subsequent years, as curricula for primary and secondary education have been redefined from 1992 to 1997. The main goal for all bilingual education models is to guarantee that students obtain a good command of Spanish and Catalan at the end of their compulsory educational period, which includes primary as well as part of secondary education. In the first stages of the implementation of these curricula modifications, a bilingual model was applied in schools, namely that of the Progressive Incorporation Programme or PIP (*Programa d'Incorporació Progressiva*). According to this programme, some school subjects would be taught in Catalan and others in Spanish. However, the programme received criticism from certain regions in the Valencian Community whose first language is Spanish. Additionally, Catalan speakers were a bit reluctant about the inclusion of their language in their children's school curricula. Indeed, that inclusion took place at a time when Catalan-speaking parents spoke Spanish with their sons and daughters with the idea that it would be much more useful for them to know the majority (Spanish) than the minority (Catalan) language, which they considered useless, and even, to a certain extent, equivalent to informal language use. Hence, they complained against the PIP incorporation. A similar reaction was that of Castilian speakers who felt threatened by a language they had no command of and that they hardly ever used. These facts showed a need for shifting people's beliefs and attitudes about their own language (in the case of Catalan speakers), and the language of the territory in which they were living (in the case of Castilian speakers).

For this reason, and after examining results of the PIP incorporation, two other programmes were developed in order to embrace the socio-linguistic and psycholinguistic reality of all inhabitants in the Valencian Community. These programmes are known as the PEV (*Programa d'Ensenyament en Valencià* or Valencian Teaching Programme) and the PIL (*Programa d'Immersió Lingüística* or Linguistic Immersion Pro-gramme).

The very first programme mentioned before, PIP, addresses now non-Valencian-speaking areas in the community, most of them located in areas fairly closed to Spanish-speaking communities. The PIP pro-gramme is assumed to be a transitional step towards bilingualism. In the early stages of education adopting the PIP programme, learners receive instruction in Spanish and only one subject is taught in Catalan. In the following years the number of subjects that are taught in Catalan progressively increases, until for most school subjects Catalan is a vehicle of instruction, except for Spanish language and literature. In this way, bilingualism is then ensured, and thus, the main goal of the new educational system is reached.

Besides, a second programme has also been developed for Catalan-speaking regions, which is the case of most areas in the community. This model is best known as the PEV (*Programa d'Ensenyament en Valencià* or 'Valencian' Teaching Programme), and it includes the use of Valencian as a vehicle for instruction from the early stages of primary education. The Spanish language is only employed in the instruction referred to this language, its literature or history. Therefore, we may say that this model involves 90% of instruction in Catalan, whereas only 10% includes Spanish, which may correspond to the learners' second language. Yet in these regions we also find Spanish speakers, and the PIL programme (*Programa d'Immersió Lingüística* or Linguistic Immersion Programme) was also adopted in some school centres in order to address the characteristics of these inhabitants. This programme includes Catalan as a means for instruction, hence coinciding with PEV characteristics. However, unlike the PEV programme, it addresses Spanish-speaking students whose parents have chosen a Catalan-based educational programme in order to guarantee the integration of their sons and daughters in the target language community.

The above description of the PIP, PIL and PEV models is based on the guidelines provided by the autonomous government in terms of their recommended application. According to the *Conselleria d'Educació i Ciència* – the division of the Autonomous Government that deals with education and linguistic policy affairs – and the Valencian Institute of Statistics, a number of schools include one or two of these programmes in their curricula, as illustrated in Table 4.1. We have subdivided existing centres on the basis of the three main geographical areas that make up the Valencian Community.

As shown in Table 4.1, Castelló is the province where most schools have adopted bilingual programmes, both in primary (aged between 6 and 11 years) and secondary (aged between 12 and 16 years) education. Concerning primary education centres, about 60% of schools (62.9%) seem to have applied bilingual programmes in Castelló, whereas approximately 60% of primary schools in Valencia (58%) and 75% in Alacant (75.1%) have not incorporated any of these programmes. A similar pattern is followed by secondary education centres, as 70% in Castelló include bilingual programmes, whereas approximately 30% of these centres in Valencia (31.65%) and Alacant (25.6%) have chosen to follow such models. A whole array of factors might have caused these differences between the three territories. One of these factors may refer to the sociolinguistic situation of each province. Concerning the language that is mainly used in their capital cities, we may state that most people employ Catalan both in formal and informal encounters in Castelló city, whereas in Valencia and Alacant the number of Catalan speakers is fairly reduced. In fact, according to the Valencian Institute of Statistics (IVE), Castelló is the province where Catalan is mostly spoken, involving more than 50% of its total inhabitants, followed by Valencia, where approximately 40% of its total population speak the language. Finally, we may say that Alacant is the region where Catalan is least used, as the number of Catalan speakers accounts for less than one third of the total number of its inhabitants.

Added to the inclusion of Catalan and Spanish in educational programmes, there has always been an interest in including English as a foreign language. In 1998 the Valencian Autonomous Government implemented an educational multilingual programme, namely that of

Table 4.1 Number of schools officially applying the PIP, PEV or PIL programmes

	Primary schools	*Percentage of total*	*Second. schools*	*Percentage of total*
Castelló	144	62.9	37	72.5
Valencia	355	42.0	112	31.65
Alacant	145	24.9	48	25.60

Source: IVE (*Institut Valencià d'Estadística* – Valencian Statistics Institute)

Enriched Bilingualism (*Bilingüisme Enriquit*, rule published in *DOGV n. 3285. 3-7-1998*). It consisted in the introduction of a foreign language in the three existing bilingual programmes described above. The basic amount of foreign language tuition required in all bilingual programmes (PIP, PIL and PEV) was set to be identical, and in all cases it was to gradually increase. According to the planning provided by educational authorities, there would be at least one and a half hours of tuition during the first cycle of primary education. In the second cycle, foreign language instruction should amount to two hours and a half per week, while three hours and a half minimum tuition would be provided in the third cycle of primary education. The hours of foreign language instruction could be increased in each cycle depending on the specific circumstances and requirements in each school.

At present the IVAQE (*Institut Valencià d'Avaluació i Qualitat Educativa* or Valencian Institute for Quality in Education) is conducting a series of studies to evaluate the implementation of the above quoted programmes (PEV/PIL and PIP) and, thus, may modify their implementation on the basis of the results obtained. One aspect that may be worth mentioning is the fact that educational authorities in the Valencian Community advised the implementation of the PIP programme (instruction is mainly conducted in Spanish) in those schools that did not follow any of the above-quoted programmes. In so doing, the perceived differences between the three provinces in incorporating the educational programmes mentioned above, which aimed at promoting bilingualism, may diminish, and the presence of monolingual programmes (i.e. only Spanish is considered as means of instruction) may then disappear. It seems, though, that some schools following the PIL programme, on the one hand, and those centres which have recently opted for implementing the PIP programme on the basis of educational authorities' recommendation seem to follow a Spanish-based model of instruction. This may be so to the extent that people refer to those programmes as '*línea en valencià*' (i.e. Catalan-based) or '*línea en castellà*' (i.e. Spanish-based). In fact, we believe that such an idea may explain one aspect of the results derived from the study presented in this chapter, as far as former PIL students are concerned. However, we need data and further studies that corroborate the above-quoted claim.

Previous Studies on Language Attitudes Carried Out in the Valencian Community

The situation of the Valencian Community in studies dealing with multilingualism phenomena is scarcely present (Hoffmann, 1991). In fact in recent volumes dealing with multilingualism in Spain (Siguan, 1992; Turell, 2001) the Valencian Community and its sociolinguistic reality is almost omitted. The issue of language attitudes is not an exception. We find many studies dealing with attitudes towards the Catalan language (Bernaus *et al.*, 2004; Huguet & Llurda, 2001), but they have focused on Catalonia and other Catalan-speaking areas, like the Franja in Aragó (Huguet & Llurda, 2001). Hence, we may state that in accounting for the sociolinguistic reality underlying language instruction and factors influencing attitudes towards languages, the Valencian Community should also be taken into account.

In this area many studies have addressed the acquisition of English from a second/foreign language perspective (Alcón, 2004; Alcón & Codina, 1996; Alcon & Guzmán, 1995). However, very few have considered bilingualism or multilingualism as a point of departure in examining and identifying factors influencing English acquisition and use (Safont, 2005). In cases where a multilingual perspective has been adopted, the focus has not been that of attitudes, but the development of English learners' interactional competence.

As far as we are concerned, very few descriptive studies have accounted for attitudes and education in the Valencian Community. One of these studies was conducted by the Valencian Institute of Educational Quality (IVAQE) (Seoane *et al.*, 2004). Nevertheless, the purpose is to show the extent to which the existing educational laws are accepted by parents, teachers and students, as well as aspects that could be improved. Yet, language attitudes are not taken into account.

As reported by Lasabagaster (2003), two more studies have tackled attitudes in the Valencian Community. More specifically, Blas Arroyo (1995) dealt with attitudes towards two Spanish dialects, the Northern dialect and that employed in the Canary Islands, and towards two Catalan dialects, the one used in Barcelona (i.e. Eastern variety) and the one used in Valencia (i.e. Western variety). Participants consisted of bilingual (Catalan–Spanish) and monolingual (Spanish) speakers studying the course previous to university studies (i.e. *COU*) in Valencia, and who were aged 17 or 18 years. Results showed that monolingual subjects' attitudes towards Catalan were rather unfavourable, whereas their attitudes towards Spanish were favourable. Bilingual subjects' attitudes towards their mother tongue, that is, Catalan, were even more negative than attitudes from Spanish monolingual subjects. A higher status was related to the Catalan variety used in Barcelona than to the one employed in Valencia. According to Blas Arroyo (1995), the results may be connected to political issues and ideologies. In our view, a very different picture would have been obtained if data had been collected in Castelló, as sociolinguistic, ethnolinguistic and pscyholinguistic characteristics may differ.

Blas Arroyo (1995) made use of the matched guise technique in reporting language attitudes in Valencia. A similar version of the instrument was used by Casesnoves (2001), which is the second study on attitudes in the Valencian Community reported by Lasagabaster (2003). Participants in Casesnoves' study (2001) did not relate a higher status to the Catalan used in Catalonia than to the Catalan used in Valencia, as had been the case in Blas Arroyo's results (1996). Therefore, we may state that further research on language attitudes in the Valencian Community involving participants from other areas may help us understand the apparent divergence in results reported. Furthermore, none of these studies included attitudes towards a foreign language, which is the case for our analysis.

Hence, this chapter may contribute to widen our knowledge of multilingual communities in Spain, and it may provide more data on attitudes towards minority, majority and foreign languages.

The Valencian study

The sample

The sample for the present study consisted of 200 university students who were engaged in two different degree courses, those of Teacher Training and Psychology, the latter involving a specialisation in Education, thus preparing students to assist learners in schools and high schools. Our subjects were completing their first and, in a few cases (only 10% in our sample), their second year at university Jaume I in Castelló. Their mean age was 20 years and 2.7 months, the youngest being 19 and the oldest 33. Most participants were female (81.5%) and only some of them were male (18.5%). The distribution of our subjects in terms of their L1 is illustrated in Figure 4.2.

As may be observed, about half of our participants stated that Spanish was their mother tongue (52%) whereas the other half (46%) considered Catalan or both (Catalan and Spanish) as their first language. A very low percentage (2%) were subjects with Romanian as their mother tongue. Regarding their parental occupation, which reflects their

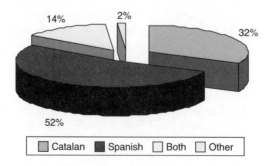

Figure 4.2 The students' L1

socioprofessional status, most cases indicated low (50%) and middle-class (27.5%) status and only 18.5% were participants with a high status. Most participants (73.5%) were living in towns with less than 100,000 inhabitants, whereas 36.5% lived in bigger towns and cities. The language employed in these towns according to our subjects' perception was Catalan in 56.6% and Spanish in 43.5%. Although they all lived in Catalan-speaking and Catalan–Spanish-speaking towns, their reports about the language employed in their hometowns may be related to the educational model in which they were engaged during primary and secondary education. In fact, 67% of the students had completed their studies in the PIL model (where Catalan and Spanish are both used as means of instruction), 31% of participants had been engaged in the PEV model and only 2% (4 students) in the PIP model.

In addition to that, we should also consider the sociolinguistic reality of the Valencian Community stated in the previous section of this chapter. We particularly refer to the fact that in capital cities of the Valencian community, namely those of Castelló, Valencia and Alacant, Spanish is widely employed. On the contrary, there exists a prevalence of Catalan over Spanish use in towns and small villages.

Regarding the knowledge of the foreign language, we may state that our subjects started learning English at the age of 8 or later in 69% of cases, and 31% of students engaged in English courses before the age of 8 for the first time. Related to their contact with the English language, 73% of participants had never been to an English-speaking country, while 27% had visited a foreign country at least once. Apart from these visits, their exposure to the foreign language in their hometown relates to the input from audiovisual material like TV. Participants claimed that they never (60.3%) or hardly ever (26.1%) watched TV in English; only 15 students (7.5%) watched TV in English once or twice per week, while 3% (6 students) were exposed to English on TV more than three times a week or on a daily basis.

The instrument and the procedure

The instrument and the procedure used in this study were the same as those followed by all the contributors to this volume. Students filled out the questionnaire in Catalan. The reason why Spanish was not used was related to the fact that Catalan is the only official language in Jaume I University, so learners are used to being distributed important information in that language. In fact, when asked to evaluate their teachers and professors, or when they apply for their degree courses, all documents and information about these aspects are provided in Catalan. The data were gathered at the very beginning of the academic year, that is to say, in October 2004.

Results

In reporting our results we will focus on three main aspects: (1) the students' proficiency level in Catalan, Spanish and English, (2) their global attitude towards these three languages, and (3) those variables that influenced their reported attitudes most. Regarding our participants' perceived level of competence in the minority, majority and foreign language (see Figure 4.3), we may state that students reported to have better competence in Spanish than in any other language, as 79% of them claimed to have a very good command of that language. Yet we should also state that their perceived knowledge of Catalan is also very high, as 34% and 41% reported a very good and a good command of the language respectively. In cases where they claimed to have just a little knowledge, 15% of subjects referred to Catalan and just a single student referred to Spanish. Furthermore, 6% of students claimed to have no competence at all in Catalan, whereas only one student reported to have no competence in Spanish.

Regarding learners' knowledge of a foreign language other than English, percentages are very low. Almost 80% stated they have no competence in any foreign language other than English, and in cases where some knowledge was pointed out (28%), they all referred to French, with one exception who referred to Romanian knowledge, but in this case it was the subject's mother tongue, not a foreign language. Among those who stated to have some knowledge of French, they evaluated their competence as good in 32.1% of cases, and 46.4% of students reported to have some idea of the language. Only 8.9% claimed to have very good knowledge of French and 12.5% stated to have no idea about the language.

As regards their competence in English as a foreign language, only 2% reported to have a very good command. In fact, most students (51%)

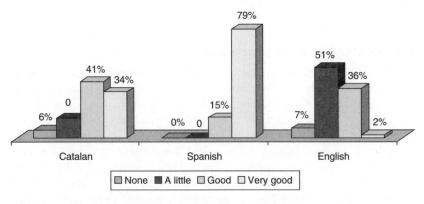

Figure 4.3 Level of competence in the three languages

stated to have a little knowledge in English, and 36% reported a good command in the language. A similar number of students (6% and 7%) reported no command in both Catalan and English. Nevertheless, the reasons for the above-quoted reports in these two languages may be quite distinct. Students stating no competence in Catalan had been engaged in the PIL and PIP programme during primary and secondary education, thus, their contact with Catalan language might have been minor (see Section 2 of this chapter for a description of each model). We should also point out that although our students start learning English at school, and they may be in contact with that language in formal contexts for over ten years, they still show difficulties in using the language for communicative purposes. This last aspect is not exclusive to the Valencian Community, but common to most areas in Spain given the shared policy of autonomous governments in terms of exposure to a foreign language. Unlike in other European countries, films are dubbed into Spanish or Catalan. Consequently, this fact reduces people's chances of being exposed to oral input in English. On the contrary, opportunities for listening and using the majority and the minority language are very high, as these languages share a co-official status in this community.

Regarding this last point, participants were asked about their use of Catalan and Spanish in different contexts, their presence in the media, and the importance participants attached to each language. Participants' regular use of the minority and majority language is best described in Table 4.2.

Percentages related to their use of Spanish seem to be higher than those related to Catalan use, especially as far as language use outside their homes is concerned. Thirty-six percent of students employed Spanish when talking with their friends in the classroom, and a similar number used that language when speaking to friends outside the school context. However, only 6% employed Catalan with friends in the classroom, and a slightly higher percentage (15%) used that language outside the university context.

At home participants used Catalan or Spanish with their parents (38.5% always in Catalan and 46% always in Spanish), and brothers and sisters (31.5% in Catalan and 41.5% in Spanish). Percentages of the use of both languages at home are rather low, as shown in Table 4.2 (2.5% 'In Catalan and Spanish about equally'), yet they increase a little when referring to the use of 'Spanish more often than Catalan' with brothers and sisters (10.5%). We should point out the fact that at home students either use Catalan or Spanish, as illustrated by the percentages stated before. However, there are no cases in which both the majority and minority language are employed with similar frequency. In fact, there is a clear tendency to make regular use of one or the other. The language employed to speak to their teachers and neighbours varied (12% 'in

Table 4.2 Language used when talking to the following people

	Always in Catalan (%)	In Catalan more often than Spanish (%)	In Catalan and Spanish about equally (%)	In Spanish more often than Catalan (%)	Always in Spanish (%)
Father	37	4.5	2.5	4	49.5
Mother	38.5	2.5	4	6	46
Brothers and sisters	31.5	2	6.5	10.5	41.5
Friends in the classroom	6	14.5	21	21.5	36
Friends outside school	15	11.5	16	17	40.5
Teachers	4.5	14	26.5	12.5	41.5
Neighbours	17	12	18.5	17.5	35

Catalan more often than in Spanish' and 17.5% 'in Spanish more often than in Catalan'), with a prevalence of Spanish over Catalan (41.5% 'always in Spanish').

On the whole, we may state that about half of our participants always use Spanish, whereas the other half either use Catalan or both Catalan and Spanish. That prevalence of the use of the majority language is also connected to the presence of that language in the media, as illustrated in Table 4.3.

Percentages related to participants' preference for the Catalan language in watching TV, reading the press, listening to music or to the radio are very low, ranging from 0.5% to 2%. On the contrary, about half of them always use Spanish in their contact with the media, with the exception of TV, as illustrated in the last three columns of Table 4.3. More students watch TV in both Catalan and Spanish (30.5% and 36.5%) than in Spanish (26%) exclusively. The presence of the minority language on TV shows its role in society, and the fact that it is not only employed in informal situations or rural areas, but also as a means of communication. In an attempt to further examine the role of Catalan in the Valencian Community, participants were asked to evaluate the importance of knowing the minority language for some activities, as shown in Table 4.4.

The highest percentages related to the importance attached to Catalan are found in literacy issues, like reading (31.5%) or writing (33.5%), getting a job (38%) or living in the Valencian Community (35.5%), while it appears to be less important in maintaining relationships, like talking to friends (8.5%), or teachers (11.5%) at the university, being accepted in the community (6.5%), going shopping (6%) and being liked (5.5%). There seems to be different views about the importance attached to Catalan in passing exams, 21% consider it important and 31% unimportant, or bringing up children, 27% consider Catalan use important while 19.5% find it unimportant.

According to data in Table 4.4, we may state that Catalan does play a role in society, as its use and knowledge is considered important for the development of some activities connected to life in the Valencian Community. The importance attributed to a language by members of a given speech community might reflect their attitude towards that language. We will next describe participants' attitudes towards the three languages that are in contact at school.

Figure 4.4 shows participants' attitudes towards Catalan, Spanish and English. We may state that the most favourable attitudes are toward the majority language (67.5%), followed by the minority one (49%). In the case of the foreign language the highest percentage refers to neutral attitudes (63%), unlike in the two previous cases. Regarding negative attitudes, percentages were very low, 11% being the highest and attributed to Catalan. Only 1% of students presented negative attitudes

Table 4.3 Means of communication and language used

	Always in Catalan (%)	In Catalan more often than Spanish (%)	In Catalan and Spanish about equally (%)	In Spanish more often than Catalan (%)	Always in Spanish (%)
Watching TV	2	5	30.5	36.5	26
The press	0.5	3	18.5	32	45.5
Music	1	2	16	24.5	56
Listening to the radio	2	5.5	24	26	42.5

Table 4.4 Importance attached to the Catalan language to do the following activities

For people to:	Important (%)	A little important (%)	A little unimportant (%)	Unimportant (%)
Make friends	10	14	25.5	47.5
Read	31.5	35	17	16.5
Write	33.5	35	14	17
Watch TV	13	24.5	39	23
Get a job	38	31	19	11.5
Be liked	5.5	11	23	59.5
Live in the Valencian Community	35.5	33	19	12
Bring up children	27	32	20.5	19.5
Go shopping	6	6.5	37.5	49
Make phone calls	6.5	15	34.5	42.5
Pass exams	21	20	25.5	31
Be accepted in the community	6.5	10	26.5	53
Talk to friends at university	8.5	17.5	33.5	37.5
Talk to teachers at university	11.5	26	32	30
Talk to people out of university	12.5	15.5	28.5	39.5

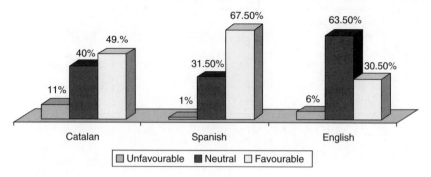

Figure 4.4 Attitudes towards the three languages

towards Spanish, and 6% towards English. It may be worth pointing out that the difference between neutral and favourable attitudes towards Catalan are not very high, as 40% of students present neutral attitudes whereas 49% show favourable attitudes. In the case of Spanish, the difference between neutral (31.5%) and favourable (67.5%) attitudes are higher, thus highlighting the role of Spanish as the majority language in the community.

The attitudes towards the three languages were not affected by participants' socioprofessional background, which, as has been described before, points to low (50%) and middle-class (27.5%) status in most cases, and only 18.5% had a high status. Unlike in other studies (Dewaele, 2005), another variable that does not show a significant influence on students' attitudes is their gender. As reported before, our sample included more female (81.5%) than male participants. Nevertheless, their attitudes were significantly influenced by specific variables, which we will now point out. The students' mother tongue influenced their attitudes towards the minority and majority languages, as shown by the ANOVA results described below. On the one hand, participants whose mother tongue was Catalan or both Catalan and Spanish presented favourable attitudes towards Catalan, whereas those with Spanish as L1 showed neutral attitudes towards the minority language. Differences in attitudes were statistically significant [F, 191 = 43.642 ($p = 0.000$)]. On the other hand, attitudes towards Spanish were neutral on the part of students with Catalan as L1, and they were favourable on the part of participants with Spanish or Spanish and Catalan as mother tongue [F, 191 = 27.622 ($p = 0.000$)]. The students' mother tongue did not affect either competence or attitudes towards English.

The predominant language in their hometown also affected students' attitudes towards Catalan [F, 198 = 45.884 ($p = 0.000$)] and Spanish [F, 197 = 23.119 ($p = 0.000$)]. On the one hand, inhabitants from Spanish-speaking towns had neutral attitudes towards Catalan and favourable attitudes towards Spanish. On the other, those living in Catalan-speaking areas showed favourable attitudes towards Catalan and Spanish. Correlation indexes were significant regarding attitudes towards Catalan and hometown language (0.434 sig. = 0.000), and attitudes towards Spanish and hometown language ($-$0.324 sig. = 0.01).

A third influencing factor was the linguistic model in which participants were engaged at school. It affected their attitudes towards the minority and the majority language, although no effects can be reported regarding its effect on attitudes towards the foreign language. Attitudes towards Catalan varied significantly as reported by statistical analysis of our data [F, 199 = 29.917 (p = 0.000)]. Those participants from the PEV model showed more favourable attitudes towards Catalan, while the attitudes of students from PIP and PIL model were neutral. Regarding attitudes towards Spanish, we find a similar pattern in the sense that those having studied within the PEV framework presented neutral attitudes towards Spanish, and PIL and PIP students' attitudes towards this majority language were favourable. As reported by ANOVA (*post hoc* Scheffé) results, the differences were statistically significant [F, 198 = 15.724 (p = 0.000)].

Another aspect of our subjects' hometown that significantly affected their attitudes towards Catalan [F, 199 = 7.976 (p = 0.005)], Spanish [F, 198 = 4.175 (p = 0.042)] and English [F, 197 = 4.332 (p = 0.039)] was its size. Participants living in towns with more than 100,000 habitants showed neutral attitudes towards Catalan and favourable attitudes towards Spanish and English. Those students from towns with less than 100,000 had favourable attitudes towards Catalan, and neutral attitudes towards the majority and the foreign language.

The next variable related to their educational background refers to their specialisation in their actual degree courses, that is, whether they were studying psychology (specifically related to education) or teacher training. Unlike previous variables, subject's specialisation affected attitudes towards the minority language, but no effects can be reported about attitudes to the other two languages or to their perceived competence in English. Given the distribution of our data (Kolgomorov–Smirnov index = 0.75), we decided to make use of a *t*-test in ascertaining whether differences in attitudes towards Catalan were statistically significant (p < 0.01). Results showed that attitudes of psychology students were neutral, while teacher training students' attitudes were favourable, the difference being statistically significant (sig. < 0.01).

Connected to participants' previous language-learning experience may be their visit to an English-speaking country. This fact affected their attitudes towards English significantly [F, 198 = 2.242 (p = 0.000)], as well as their perceived competence in that language [F, 191 = 15.944 (p = 0.000)]. Those participants who had visited an English-speaking country had positive attitudes towards English and they scored their competence as good. Students who had never been to an English-speaking country had neutral attitudes towards English and they evaluated their competence in English as 'a little'.

As has been raised in this section, while the socioprofessional status and gender of the participants had no effect either on attitudes towards Catalan, Spanish or English, or on their perceived competence in these languages, the variables that significantly influenced our subjects' attitudes may be subdivided into two main groups: those related to the participants' sociolinguistic situation and those connected to their educational background. Regarding factors connected to the participants' sociolinguistic situation, results pointed out the powerful role of the students' mother tongue, and the language and size of their hometown. Related to their educational background, the variables that influenced learners' language attitudes and competence in English were the linguistic model within which they received instruction during primary and secondary education, the age at which they started learning English, whether they had visited an English-speaking country, their perceived competence in their Catalan and Spanish, and the degree course they were studying at university. In fact, results from a Pearson analysis show significant correlation indexes between (1) attitudes towards Catalan and level of competence in that language [$R^2 = 0.568$ ($p = 0.000$)] and in Spanish [$R^2 = -0.158$ ($p = 0.03$)], (2) attitudes towards Spanish and level of competence in Spanish [$R^2 = 0.164$ ($p = 0.024$)] and Catalan [$R^2 = -0.445$ ($p = 0.000$)], and finally, (3) attitudes towards English and level of competence in English [$R^2 = 0.340$ ($p = 0.000$)].

A summary of our main results is presented in Table 4.5.

Discussion

The purpose of this paper was to analyse language attitudes and language use of university students in the Valencian Community. We have particularly focused on teacher training and psychology students at University Jaume I in Castelló. In reporting our results, we have first considered our participants' perceived level of competence in Catalan, Spanish and English. The superiority of Spanish over the other two languages seems clear, as indicated by participants' perceived competence in that language. In fact, 79% of students judged their competence as 'very good'. Similarly, their competence in Catalan is quite highly evaluated (e.g. 'good' for 41% and 'very good' for 34% of subjects), thus illustrating the role of the Catalan language in Valencian society nowadays. Only 6% of students indicate no knowledge at all, and they consider that knowing Catalan is important for living in the Valencian Community (see Table 4.2 in Section 5), although it is not so important for

Table 4.5 Summary of the most influential variables on language attitudes

Independent variable	Attitudes towards Catalan	Attitudes towards Spanish	Attitudes towards English	Competence in English
Gender	n.s.	n.s.	n.s.	
L1	Catalan/both > Spanish	Spanish/both > Catalan	n.s.	
Specialisation	Teachers > Psychology Ed.	n.s.	n.s.	n.s.
Socioprofessional status	n.s.	n.s.	n.s.	n.s.
Age at which they started to learn English				n.s.
Ever visited an English-speaking country			Yes > no	Yes > no
Knowledge of other foreign languages			n.s.	
Linguistic model	PEV > PIP > PIL	PIP > PIL > PEV	n.s.	
Size of hometown	− 100,000 > + 100,000	+ 100,000 > − 100,000	+ 100,000 > − 100,000	
Predominant language in hometown	Catalan > Spanish	Spanish > Catalan	n.s.	

establishing and maintaining relationships. This finding shows language contact in this community as we find Catalan as well as Spanish speakers. The later ones relate to migration phenomena from Spanish-speaking areas in Spain (mainly Jaén and some other regions from Andalusia) to Castelló during the 1960s and 70s. The sons and daughters of those immigrants who settled mainly in the capital city (Castelló) continue using Spanish exclusively, although they understand Catalan. We may then state that the Valencian Community is a bilingual area where the two official languages are known by most inhabitants, though in some cases we would find examples of receptive bilingualism.

The presence of a third language in the community is not self-evident, despite its role as a lingua franca both in Europe and in many other parts of the world. As opposed to participants' perceived competence in Spanish and Catalan, only 2% of students judged their command in English as 'very good'. The lack of competence and low proficiency level of students in English is not exclusive to the Valencian Community but common to other areas in Spain. Unlike in Northern European countries, as stated before, input in English outside formal contexts (i.e. school or language centre) is extremely low, not to mention opportunities for using the language. As stated by Pica (2000), there are three main conditions for language acquisition to take place, exposition to input, possibilities for output and feedback. Hence, if we reduce these three conditions to the language classroom, and we still find restrictions for being able to provide learners with them (i.e. large groups, no resources, teacher training, among others), it is not surprising that our students perceive their command as 'low' or 'very low'. This may be so even after having received instruction in English for almost 10 years. In order to provide a solution to this problem, we would need to change methodological practices in the classroom, and political decisions previously informed by research in foreign-language learning if we are to promote multi-lingualism.

Results from our study have focused on competence in Catalan, Spanish and English, which have been discussed above, and attitudes towards these languages. Most positive attitudes are linked to Spanish. As stated before, 52.5% of the participants identify Spanish as their mother tongue. This finding is also in line with their perceived competence in the three languages, which shows Spanish knowledge is ranked higher than the other two languages. Catalan is positively valued, as almost half of the participants demonstrate 'favourable' attitudes, and 40% of students show 'neutral' attitudes. Yet, the percentage for negative attitudes is the highest of all three languages involved (11%). In this respect, it is worth pointing out the fact that, as attitudes are connected to perceived language competence (see Table 4.5 in Section 5 and correlation indexes reported in the previous subsection), they may have been influenced by students' perceived written command of Catalan, which is usually evaluated as low, especially on the part of students from PIP or PIL educational models. This aspect relates to the idea previously mentioned in the first subsections of the chapter related to the actual implementation of PIP and PIL programmes in some schools of the Valencian Community. Although descriptions of these educational programmes state the idea that at the end of instruction students will become bilingual, in the case of the PIP programme, and that students are part of an immersion programme aimed at promoting bilingualism, in the case of PIL model, it seems that sometimes these guidelines are not completely followed. As a consequence, we may find two main 'non-official' models, as suggested before: the Catalan-based and the Spanish-based one. Yet, although this idea might help us explain part of our results, we need more studies analysing what actually takes place in these centres adopting the PIL programme, and empirical data that confirm these ideas. As is suggested, although it cannot be confirmed due to lack of empirical evidence, it seems that instruction may be provided mainly in Spanish with few chances to write or read in Catalan in the PIL classroom. Outside formal instruction, students are frequently exposed to oral input in Catalan, which increases their oral command of the language.

On the contrary, given the lack of opportunities for using the language, oral command in the foreign language is perceived as low. This foreign language has been mainly valued neither negatively nor positively, but attitudes were 'neutral' in most cases (63.5%). Although competence in the language might influence attitudes towards it, as reported above, we also believe that the social importance attributed to it may have affected our students' responses, thus, providing neutral attitudes.

The attitudes illustrated by participants in the study may be best explained by considering other variables that have significantly influenced their reports. Students' competence in English only seemed to be affected by the fact that they had visited an English-speaking country before. Strikingly, and unlike in other studies on language attitudes (Lasagabaster, 2003), gender and socioprofessional status did not have any effect on their attitudes. That was also the case of the variable 'knowledge of other foreign languages', as it did not seem to influence attitudes towards languages. Nevertheless, it is worth mentioning that only a small percentage of our subjects indicated their knowledge of other languages, and in all these cases it was evaluated as 'a little' or 'good'.

Regarding attitudes towards the foreign language, English in our case, we found that the age at which they started learning English did not influence either their attitudes towards the language [$F, 192 = 0.987$

$(p = 0.463)]$ or their perceived competence $[F, 191 = 1.082 \ (p = 0.377)]$. However, results from the ANOVA test show that participants' visit to an English-speaking country affected both their perceived competence in English $[F, 198 = 28.936 \ (p = 0.000)]$ and their attitudes towards that foreign language $[F, 191 = 15.944 \ (p = 0.000)]$.

As regards attitudes towards Catalan and Spanish, we may state that (i) the subjects' mother tongue, (ii) their perceived competence in Catalan, and (iii) the predominant language in their hometown resulted in powerful factors. However, only the size of the hometown seems to have a clear influence on their attitudes towards English, which, as illustrated in Figure 4.2, were mainly 'neutral'. Nevertheless, further research on the relationship between these variables and other psychological and politicultural aspects could provide us with valuable information about their attitudes and perceived competence in the foreign language (Dewaele, 2005) and, thus, help us understand and foster its learning and use in turn.

Additionally, participants' degree course and specialisation in which they were engaged, the linguistic model in which they were educated, and the age at which they started learning English had a powerful influence on their attitudes towards the minority, majority and foreign language, as well as on their perceived competence in English (see Table 4.5 for details). We believe that the results show the importance of sociolinguistic and sociocultural factors in language competence, on the one hand. On the other, they raise the importance of educational frameworks in fostering attitudes which in turn may influence language learning (Dörnyei, 2001). Furthermore, if attitudes may be learnt (Baker, 1992), curriculum planners should take into account findings from studies that show those factors that may influence language attitudes, and they could implement them within current curricula and syllabi. In so doing, results from the present study and the other chapters in this volume may facilitate their task, and promote language learning and multilingualism in turn.

Acknowledgements

Data collection for this study has been funded by a grant from the Spanish Ministerio de Educación y Ciencia (HUM2004-04435/FILO) as part of a research project, co-funded by FEDER, and from Fundació Universitat Jaume I and Caixa Castelló-Bancaixa (P1.1B2004-34).

References

Alcón, E. (2004) Research on language and learning: implications for language teaching. *International Journal of English Studies* 1, 173–196.
Alcón, E. and Codina, V. (1996) The impact of gender on negotiation and vocabulary learning in a situation of interaction. *International Journal of Applied Psycholinguistics* 12, 21–35.

Alcón, E. and Guzmán, J.R. (1995) Interlanguage modifications in NS–NNS oral interactions: A study in an English and Catalan language learning context. Paper presented at the International Conference of Languages in Contact, Valencia (Spain).

Baker, C. (1992) *Attitudes and Language*. Clevedon: Multilingual Matters.

Bernaus, M., Masgoret, A., Gardner, R. and Reyes, E. (2004) Motivation and attitudes towards learning languages in multicultural classrooms. *The International Journal of Multilingualism* 2, 75–89.

Blas Arroyo, J.L. (1995) De nuevo el español y el catalán, juntos y en contraste: estudio de actitudes lingüísticas. *Revista de Lingüística Teórica y Aplicada* 34, 83–99.

Casesnoves, R. (2001) Las actitudes lingüísticas de los jóvenes estudiantes de secundaria en la ciudad de Valencia. In A.I. Moreno and V. Colwell (eds) *Perspectivas Recientes en el Discurso*. León: Universidad de León Servicio de Publicaciones.

Dewaele, J.M. (2005) Sociodemographic, psychological and politicocultural correlates in Flemish students' attitudes towards French and English. *Journal of Multilingual and Multicultural Development* 26, 118–137.

Dörnyei, Z. (2001) *Motivational Strategies in the Language Classroom*. Cambridge: Cambridge University Press.

Hoffmann, C. (1991) *An Introduction to Bilingualism*. London: Longman.

Huguet, A. and Llurda, E. (2001) Language attitudes of school children in two Catalan/Spanish bilingual communities. *International Journal of Bilingual Education and Bilingualism* 4, 267–282.

Lasagabaster, D. (2003) *Trilinguismo en la enseñanza. Actitudes hacia la lengua minoritaria, la mayoritaria y la extranjera*. Lleida: Editorial Milenio.

Pica, T. (2000) Tradition and transition in English language teaching methodology. *System* 28, 1–18.

Safont, P. (2005) *Third Language Learners. Pragmatic Production and Awareness*. Clevedon: Multilingual Matters.

Seoane, J., Garzón, A. and Escamez, J. (2004) Aspectes actitudinals i socials quie incidiesen en el funcionament del sistema educatiu. Estudi de l'Institut Valencià d'Avaluació i Qualitat Educativa.

Siguan, M. (1992) *España Plurilingüe*. Madrid: Alianza Editorial.

Turell, T. (ed.) (2001) *Multilingualism in Spain*. Clevedon: Multilingual Matters.

Part 2
Other European Contexts

Chapter 5

Language Use and Language Attitudes in Brussels

LAURENCE METTEWIE and RUDI JANSSENS

Introduction

Language has always played a central role in Belgian politics (Witte & Van Velthoven, 1998). The confrontation between the French- and the Dutch-speaking communities on language issues has repeatedly dominated Belgian political life just as economic and social problems are often translated into a political–linguistic framework. This tense atmosphere between the linguistic communities must be viewed in the context of the historical heritage of political, economical and cultural dominance of the French-speaking elite in Flanders and Brussels in which every change is considered as a win–lose situation. Subsequent negotiations gave rise to a complex and continuing process of state reform. This evolution is based on the romantic ideal of monolingual areas. The key element of this policy is the principle of territoriality: the official language depends on where one is and not on whom one is speaking it. Belgium recognises three official languages: Dutch, French and German. The official language of a given municipality is clearly defined in the Constitution. The overall majority of the municipalities have only one official language and all relations between its citizens and the government must be administered in this language. Brussels Capital-Region is one of the very few exceptions to this principle. It is the only officially bilingual region, which means that both Dutch and French have the status of official language. Their inhabitants are regarded as members of the Flemish or the Francophone Community while the other citizens are considered as members of the Flemish, Francophone or German-speaking Community depending on the official language of their place of residence.

These three 'communities' live in three 'regions': Flanders, Brussels and Wallonia. Regions and communities only partly overlap (see Figure 5.1). Apart from municipalities with linguistic facilities, only the Flemish Region is monolingual; Wallonia has French- and German-speaking municipalities and the 19 municipalities of Brussels Capital-Region are bilingual. Both regions and communities have their own powers, elections, legislative and executive bodies and their own administration and services. The competencies of the communities include

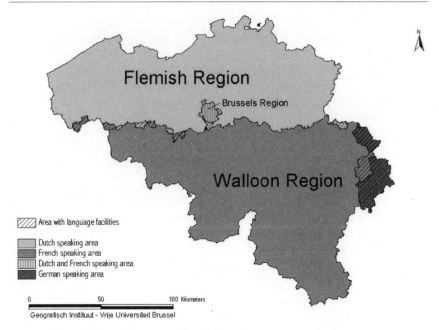

Figure 5.1 Belgium: regions and communities.
Source: VUB – Geographic Institute

culture, education and so-called personalised matters (such as health, welfare, youth protection, minority policies, etc.). The regions are, among other things, responsible for the economy, employment, agriculture, environment, water policy, energy, urbanism, transport, foreign trade and the supervision of provinces, municipalities and interurban companies. The federal government does not bear any responsibility within these domains and cannot overrule a decision of a regional government. Given the specific structure of the country, apart from the Federal Government, the government of Brussels Capital-Region, the Flemish government and the government of the Francophone Community all have their specific say in the different aspects of Brussels' society.

The fact that about 6 million Belgians live in Flanders, 3 million in Wallonia and 1 million in Brussels gives the representatives of the Flemish parties an overall majority in parliament if the 'one man-one vote' principle is applied. However, mechanisms of 'equal representation' and other protective arrangements are built into the Belgian political model so that the Dutch-speaking majority cannot overrule the French-speaking minority. In Brussels, where the majority is French-speaking, other mechanisms, based on a mixture of a guaranteed representation and split responsibilities, are created to protect the Dutch-speaking minority. As a result, the position of the Flemish Community in Brussels and the

Dutch language is not only determined by the number of its native speakers, but also by their position in the country as a whole. Changing the delicate balance on national or regional levels automatically affects the relation between the communities on both levels.

Brussels is the only bilingual region of the country. 'Bilingualism' does not refer to individual bilingualism but to a type of societal bilingualism (Baker, 2001). It is rather a political term covering both a linguistic and an organisational component. Bilingualism refers to the fact that both Dutch and French have the status of official language and to the complex 'bilingual' organisational framework that has been created because of the intricate spread of power over regions and communities. One of the core characteristics of Brussels' political model is the absence of a concept referring to 'subnationality'. There are no official criteria to decide whether a particular citizen can be considered as a member of the Flemish or Francophone Community. At the municipal level, all services are supposed to be bilingual and one always has the free choice to use Dutch or French, although in reality the use of the majority language (French) is often required. The choice in a particular situation does not predetermine the choice in another. For example, one can ask for a passport in Dutch and a driving licence in French. Community issues fall within the competence of the Flemish or Francophone Community and their respective administration. In that case, the citizen has the choice between two separate monolingual alternatives. Here again, a previous choice does not predetermine the next: one can easily decide to send one of his or her children to a French-medium school and the other(s) to a Dutch-medium school, a decision that can be re-evaluated every year. But given the multilingual and multicultural nature of its population, community issues in Brussels often show a different character than in Flanders or in the French-speaking part of Wallonia. Finally the services of the Brussels Capital-Region itself are bilingual, not the civil servant. As a consequence, political bilingualism in the case of Brussels must rather be seen as a kind of dual monolingualism: in his contact with the government every citizen has the choice between both official languages and does not have to master the other.

This dual linguistic landscape does not reflect the actual population. The impact of migration on Brussels is substantial. Half of Brussels' adults have been born outside the capital. Economic motives drove many immigrants to the city. After WWII, the lack of local labour forces called for an influx of poorly schooled foreign workers from South European nations, and later from Morocco and Turkey. These immigrant communities are still present within Brussels. The growing international importance of Brussels as headquarters of both the European Union and the NATO alliance coupled with the inherent economic development of the city has caused a wave of immigration of highly educated West

Europeans. Apart from these trends, Belgium's colonial history in central Africa and the developments in Eastern Europe after the fall of the Berlin Wall have also left their traces in Brussels. As a result, the Brussels population clearly differs from those in the two other regions. Where Brussels accounts for 10% of all inhabitants of the country, almost a third of all non-Belgians lives in the Brussels Capital-Region. Up to 30% of all inhabitants of Brussels do not have Belgian nationality.

This diversity results in a complex linguistic landscape, although till recently no language data for Brussels and Belgian as a whole were available, as the last language census was held in 1947. In those days, the outcome of the census was decisive for the linguistic statute (mono-lingual or a degree of bilingualism) of a municipality. Given the political consequences, no objective results could be guaranteed and tensions between both communities regarding the final outcome resulted in its abolition and the ban on the inclusion of language questions in future censuses. Recent figures based on a representative sample of 2,500 inhabitants of the Brussels Capital-Region, gathered by the Centre for the Interdisciplinary Study of Brussels (see Janssens, 2001), provide an accurate up-to-date view on language use in Brussels. As the base for classification, language use in the family of origin is used (this is the language or languages used in the communication of the respondent with his/her father and mother and the language or languages the parents used among each other). This operationalisation has the advantage that exclusive and exhaustive categories can be built, that people never change category and that more than one language can be considered as the family language. Based on the two official languages, five categories can be discerned: respondents from monolingual Dutch-speaking families (about 10%), respondents from monolingual French-speaking families (about 50%), respondents from families were both Dutch and French were used within the family (about 10%, the so-called 'traditional bilinguals'), respondents who grew up in a family where French was combined with another language other than Dutch (about 10% and labelled 'new bilinguals' in Table 5.1) and finally the respondents who grew up in families where neither Dutch nor French were used (about 20%). Table 5.1 presents an overview for both Belgians and non-Belgians.

The dual community model covers only 60% of the population. In political discussions the others are often forced into a category to reinforce the political power of the original language communities. The new bilinguals are habitually considered as members of the Francophone Community although previous research proves that they seldom identify themselves as such (see Ackaert & Deschouwer, 1999) and in this respect are far more related to the 'other language speakers' who identify themselves with both Brussels' society as a whole and the local immigrant

Table 5.1 Language groups in Brussels

Language groups	Brussels' inhabitants	Belgian nationality	Non-Belgian nationality
Dutch speakers (%)	9.3	10.9	2.9
French speakers (%)	51.5	62.8	9.2
Traditional bilinguals (%)	10.3	12.7	0.4
New bilinguals (%)	9.1	7.4	15.9
Other language speakers (%)	19.8	6.2	71.7

group. The hardest group to classify is the group of traditional bilinguals. Although they are as numerous as the citizens from monolingual Dutch-speaking families, they are seldom mentioned. Whilst in the 1960s and 1970s bilingualism was considered as a transitional stage between monolingual Dutch-speaking families and monolingual French-speakers, it became clear that an important part of this group was bilingual by generation (see Janssens, 2001) or that it was the result of a personal choice.

This context is crucial to understand the attitudes under investigation. Today about 20% of the citizens are raised in a bilingual family, half of them in a family where both Dutch and French is spoken. In the context of this research project, either Dutch or French can be considered as their mother tongue (and as the L1) or both. For the others, their mother tongue might differ from both the L1 and L2 (French or Dutch), just as for the 20% of 'other language speakers'. Not only is the relation towards L1 and L2 dubious but L3 (English) is not a 'neutral' language in Brussels either. English is not only a language taught at school or used on holidays but a lingua franca within the local international community and the economy. Moreover it is a language sometimes in competition with French or used as an alternative language, a neutral code between Dutch speakers and French speakers.

The Educational System in Brussels

The communities are responsible for education. This results in three independent educational systems, one for each language community. Given the fact that up to the second half of the 20th century French was the dominant language among the cultural, political and economic elite, secondary and higher education were almost exclusively in French, as well as in Flanders. The endeavour for education in the local language resulted in a set of language laws based on the principle of territoriality. Today in Flanders, Dutch is the only language of instruction at school

and other languages are taught as separate courses, while in Wallonia –
apart from the German-speaking area and a very few bilingual education
projects – French is the language of instruction. In Belgium there is no
free choice: the language of the school is the language of the region of
residence. Brussels however is the only exception where one has the
choice between Dutch-medium schools (organised by the Flemish
Community and similar to the schools in Flanders) and French-medium
schools (organised by the French Community and similar to the schools
in that part of Wallonia where French is the official language). As already
mentioned, the choice of a particular language does not predetermine the
rest of the curriculum. To complete the picture of the educational system
it is important to mention that within each linguistic pillar one can
discern community schools, a network of free (mainly Catholic)
subsidised schools and schools organised by the local municipality. In
total Brussels has about 200,000 pupils, of which approximately 15%
attend Dutch-medium schools. Whilst 20% of the children attend a
kindergarten where Dutch is the language of instruction, this figure
drops to about 14% in primary and secondary education.

The relation between language and education is an ambiguous one.
Given the position of Brussels in the global economy and the reality of
living in a multilingual city, the daily use of different languages is
inevitable for most inhabitants of the city. Daily experiences emphasise the
importance of language learning. But a multilingual environment gives
rise to linguistic diversity among the pupils in the different classrooms as
well. In this respect, language learning has also become part of the
integration debate of immigrant children. Both aspects will be discussed
briefly.

Strict language laws guarantee children of both official language
communities in Brussels to be taught in their native tongue. It is striking
that for the symbolic value of language, only these laws are applicable to
both communities, whilst all other aspects of the organisation, such as the
pedagogical approach and the content of education, are rigorously kept
apart. First of all, all education is monolingual and other languages are
presented as separate courses. In French-medium schools Dutch is taught
by a Francophone teacher just as a native Dutch speaker is responsible for
the French lessons in Dutch-medium schools. For the Flemish Community, French is considered as the second language and is compulsory from
the 5th year of primary education. In Brussels the Flemish Community
offers the possibility, even in kindergarten and the first years of primary
education, to include French as a course in all classes. For the Francophone Community, Dutch is the second language in Brussels, but in
Wallonia they also offer the opportunity to teach English or German as
second language. This second language is compulsory from the 5th year
on. In Brussels however, Dutch is taught from the third year, comparable

to the timing of second language acquisition in the Dutch-medium schools. In both the French and Flemish educational systems a third language is introduced at secondary level. This third language is always English in Brussels and Flanders. In Wallonia this might be Dutch or German as well, given the different regulations. Depending on the curriculum, a fourth language (German, Spanish or Italian) can also be taught. Table 5.2 presents an overview of the actual situation in both the Flemish and French Communities.

Among the Brussels population a feeling of discontent towards the current language education of their children is noticeable. The majority clearly prefers a kind of bilingual education over the current situation where the second language is offered as a separate course (see Janssens, 2001). Bilingual education, in the sense that both official languages are used as the language of instruction at school, is strictly forbidden by law and only recently some experiments have been allowed. The first attempts to introduce this form of language learning in Belgium were undertaken by the French Community where the so-called 'Onckelinx' decree' has given rise to new possibilities in kindergarten and primary education since 1998. A few Dutch-medium schools in Brussels have recently started experiments as well but in general this type of language education is still a marginal phenomenon. This is due to the historical context in Flanders, where the exclusion of French as a language of instruction was one of the key issues of the linguistic conflict. But because parents in Brussels are free to choose the educational system they send their children to, many Francophone pupils attend the Dutch-medium schools. The growing percentage of these crossovers emphasises the need for bilingualism and the lack of bilingual education in the Belgian capital city. However, the current pedagogical discussion on language learning and language of instruction is deteriorating towards a discussion on the impact of language communities on each other's educational system.

Language issues in education not only refer to language learning but also to the linguistic diversity of the pupils. In Brussels, this diversity goes hand in hand with a social selection. The majority of the richer immigrants working for the European Community and international organisations and companies send their children to European or international schools or to schools organised by their country of origin. Children of the poorer immigrants are found in the Dutch- and French-medium schools, together with the Belgian children. For most of them the school language (Dutch or French) is not their mother tongue. Given the historical background, Flemish education is very sensitive to these linguistic issues while the Francophones tend to treat this problem as an ethnic or social one. Because of this, data about the home language of pupils attending French-medium schools are not available. The only recent public figures available are those collected by the Flemish

Table 5.2 Languages of instruction and foreign languages taught at school

	Flemish Community		*French Community*	
	Flanders	*Brussels*	*Brussels*	*Wallonia*
Language of instruction L1[a]	Dutch	Dutch	French	French
First foreign language L2[a]	French	French	Dutch	Dutch or English or German
Age started	10	8	8	10
Second foreign language L3[a]	English	English	English	English, Dutch or German
Age started	12	12	12	12
Third foreign language L4[a]	German or Spanish or Italian	German or Spanish or Italian	Spanish or Italian or German	Spanish or Italian or German
Age started	±15	±15	±15	±15

[a]This does not mean these languages are the L1, L2, L3 or L4 of the pupils. It depends on the language background of pupils within each educational system. But in the present chapter we will refer to these languages as L1, L2 and L3

Community Commission. They clearly illustrate the multilingual background of the pupil population in the Dutch-medium educational system (see Table 5.3).

Children of monolingual Dutch-speaking families are a minority within the Flemish educational system in Brussels. In kindergarten, only one out of three families uses Dutch at home and the majority use it in combination with French. This figure rises to 48% in primary education and even 75.3% in secondary education. This evolution can be explained by the fact that the younger the pupils from monolingual French-speaking families are, the more likely they are to attend Dutch-speaking schools because the parents want their children to become bilingual so that they have better job opportunities later on. The presence of bilingual pupils next to Francophone crossovers and pupils from other linguistic backgrounds testifies to the multilingual composition of the population in Brussels.

Whereas in general knowing a second language is an asset, here the 'other' language is often considered as a problem, having a negative influence on knowledge transfer in the language of education (Housen *et al.*, 2002; Housen & Pierrard, 2004). Dealing with this situation a political rather than a pedagogical choice. In general, the school policy is to ban the language of origin and replace it as much as possible by the language of instruction. A different approach would be the positive appreciation of the language and culture of the immigrant as the breeding ground for their emancipation. The Foyer model (for a detailed description, see Bryan & Leman, 1990) is an illustration of this approach where starting from their home language (in this case Spanish, Italian and Turkish) Dutch is gradually used as language of instruction. Their results in secondary school are better than those of the immigrants with the same home language who ended up in the Dutch- or French-medium schools. Regarding the current immigration patterns and the enlargement of the European Union, we might expect that the number of

Table 5.3 Home language in Dutch-medium schools in Brussels, September 2002

Home language	Kindergarten	Primary education	Secondary education
Dutch (%)	12.0	19.5	48.7
Dutch/French (%)	21.5	28.4	26.6
French (%)	36.2	29.1	13.5
Other language(s) (%)	29.5	23.0	11.2

Source: VGC

monolingual Dutch- or French-speaking citizens will drop further. Thus, for both educational networks, dealing with linguistic diversity will prove to be the key challenge.

Previous Research on Language Attitudes in Brussels

In a linguistically divided country such as Belgium, where languages have a highly symbolic value because of historical, cultural, political and economic reasons, language attitudes function as a mirror for the status of a language and as a barometer for the relationship between the language communities. Previous research on language attitudes in Brussels and more generally in Belgium have highlighted these functions. Without going into methodological details, attitudes towards the French and Dutch language communities (Mettewie, 2004) and towards language use (Persoons, 1988) reveal – sometimes major – tensions between both linguistic communities. Secondary school pupils have rather negative attitudes towards the 'other' linguistic community or towards its language and express at the same time a strong feeling of in-group favouritism or extremely positive attitudes to their own language.

The only exception to this are bilingual pupils and Francophone pupils attending Dutch-medium schools in Brussels (mentioned above as crossovers). Pupils raised bilingually at home do not show any difference in attitude between both language communities. They nevertheless seem to favour French, the majority language in Brussels, to Dutch. The Francophone crossovers who are in daily contact with the other linguistic community within the school have very positive attitudes towards the Dutch-speaking community. Their attitudes are far more favourable than the usually indifferent attitudes of Francophones in French-medium schools in Brussels and in Wallonia. These results (Mettewie, 2004; Mettewie *et al.*, 2004) seem to indicate that contact between linguistic communities on a daily basis – as is the case for these crossovers – does improve attitudes towards the other language community and hence weaken the tensions perceived in the attitudes of the pupils.

Research on language attitudes confirms these tensions and the rather unfavourable perception pupils have of the language of the 'other' linguistic community. Results from Flanders, Wallonia and Brussels (see Dewaele, 2005; Housen *et al.*, 2000; Lochtman *et al.*, 2004; Mettewie, 1998, 2004) indicate that secondary school pupils have (very) favourable attitudes towards English, whereas their attitudes towards the language of the 'other' linguistic community, respectively French or Dutch, are far less favourable or even unfavourable. Neutral and negative attitudes to Dutch for the French speakers and to French for the Dutch speakers seem to embody the often stereotypical negative views the pupils have about the 'other' linguistic community and its language. This is in sharp contrast with the (extremely) positive attitudes to their own language and to English. English is presumably more popular amongst these youngsters not only because it is a vehicle of youth culture (music, films, show business, Internet, etc.) but also because it is a neutral code, a kind of lingua franca between both linguistic communities. This lingua franca does not carry any social or political connotations or imply any concession or assertion to the other language community as does French or Dutch. English seems to be in Brussels, and in Belgium more generally, a language that is not only an international language, a language of mass media and youth culture, but also a language that overcomes the linguistic tensions that dominate the Belgian society.

The Study in Brussels

The sample

As there is no teacher training at the bachelor level at universities in Belgium, the data ($n = 270$) were gathered in three higher education colleges specialised in teacher training: one was a Dutch-medium college (Europese Hogeschool Brussel, $n = 110$) whereas the two others were French-medium colleges (Haute Ecole Francisco Ferrer and Haute Ecole de Bruxelles – De Fré, $n = 160$). As mentioned earlier, there are two parallel and independent educational systems in Brussels: a Dutch- and a French-medium one. Because these educational systems are so distinctive from one another, it was important for the representativeness of the sample to have data from both systems and to analyse them separately. In the following description of the sample as well as in the presentation and discussion of the results, we will therefore systematically compare both systems in order to obtain a more accurate picture of the attitudes in each educational system and in each language community.

Of the 270 questionnaires that were completed in the three colleges, we only selected those of students who were raised in Belgium. This means that 31 questionnaires, mostly from French-medium colleges, could not be included in the sample as these students mainly came from France, Luxemburg and Morocco. Hence the sample consists of 239 subjects. The students have an average age of 18.9 years in the Dutch-medium college and 19.8 years in the French-medium colleges. There is a significantly higher percentage of girls (75.9% and 78.5% versus 24.1% and 21.5% of boys), which is typical for a highly feminised sector such as education.

When analysing the sample, it is striking to notice that the language background of the students differs greatly according to the school system, except for the small percentage (4.6%) of bilingual students (Dutch/French) both systems host.

Table 5.4 indicates that, contrary to the Dutch-medium college, the population in the French-medium colleges is far more heterogeneous. Next to 67.9% of Francophone students, 22.1% of the students have both French and a migrant language (Arabic, Berber, Turkish, etc.) as mother tongues and a couple of them (2.9%) speak languages other than Dutch and French at home. The population in the Dutch-medium college is highly homogeneous, with 92.6% of the students having Dutch as their mother tongue, next to a couple of Francophone crossovers. This contrast can be explained by the fact that the vast majority of the students attending the Dutch-medium college come from the fairly monolingual Flemish part of the country (95.3% versus 4.7% from Brussels), whereas 70.2% of the students in the French-medium colleges come from the multicultural city of Brussels (next to 22.1% from the Francophone part and 7.7% from the Flemish part of the country).

The regional differences also account for the differences of age at which students started learning the L2, as this depends on the language legislation of each region. The students in the Dutch-medium college mainly attended schools in Flanders, where they started learning French at about 10 years old (5th year of primary school), whereas the students from the French-medium colleges, who mainly attended school in Brussels, started learning Dutch at about 8 years old (3rd year of primary school).

There is no significant difference between both educational systems as to the percentage of students who had been to an English-speaking country (26.9% versus 25.6%). There is however a significant difference between the Dutch-medium college and the French-medium college students in the amount of TV programmes they watch in English: 55.6% of the Dutch-speaking students versus 25.7% of the students in the French-medium schools watch TV programmes at least once a week in English. This difference can easily be explained by the fact that Flemish television very often broadcasts English-speaking programmes, which are subtitled, whereas the English or American series broadcasted by the Francophone channels are systematically dubbed. The English-speaking programmes the Francophone students watch are therefore presumably limited to those from the BBC, which means they have to make a special effort to watch them, contrary to the Flemish students who have them on the Flemish channels.

Last but not least, the description of the sample also reflects the differences in socioeconomic status, as illustrated in Table 5.5. The figures suggest an over-representation of the lower social class in the French-medium colleges (44%) compared to the Dutch-medium college. This difference can be explained by the larger number of students with a migrant background attending the Francophone colleges of the Belgian capital city.

Table 5.4 Language background of the students per educational system ($n = 239$, $\chi^2 = 38.221$, $p = 0.000$)

Language background	Dutch, n (%)	French	Bilingual Du/Fr	French + other	Other
Dutch-medium college ($n = 108$)	100 (92.6)	3 (2.8)	5 (4.6)		
French-medium colleges ($n = 131$)		89 (67.9)	6 (4.6)	29 (22.1)	7 (2.9)

Table 5.5 Socioeconomic status of the students per educational system ($\chi^2 = 23.228$, $p = 0.000$)

Socioeconomic status	High (%)	Medium (%)	Low (%)
Dutch-medium college ($n = 100$)	27	56	17
French-medium colleges ($n = 131$)	28.4	27.3	44
Total	27.8	41.1	31.1

This description of the sample confirms the specificity and complexity of the population in each educational system in Brussels and hence the need to distinguish the situation in the Dutch-medium college from that in the French-medium colleges, by systematically comparing the results in both contexts.

The instruments and procedure

For our research in Brussels, we used a Dutch and French translation of the common questionnaire described in the introductory chapter. For practical reasons however we adapted a few questions concerning the background of the students in relation to the local situation.

The data were collected in the early weeks of the academic year, that is September or October 2004 according to the school system (Dutch- or French-medium education). As a result of the strict language legislation and the language policies of the colleges, we could not give the students the choice between a questionnaire in Dutch or French. Students had to complete the questionnaire in the language of instruction of the school, irrespective of their language background. This means students attending the Dutch-medium college answered the Dutch version of the questionnaire whereas students in the French-medium colleges received the French version.

Results

Language competence

Figure 5.2 and Figure 5.3 illustrate the self-reported general language competence of the students for their L1, L2 (French or Dutch according to the educational system) and for English. These figures show that the students think they have a good to very high competence in the L1. For the L2 the results indicate that even after 6–10 years of L2 instruction at primary and secondary school, 51% of the Dutch-speaking students and only 28% of the French-speaking ones estimate they have a good or fluent command of their L2. Although the students only started learning English from secondary school onwards, the figures for the self-reported

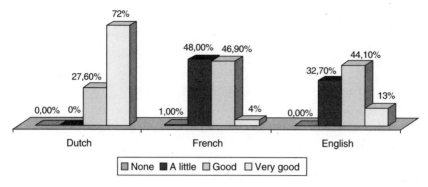

Figure 5.2 Self-reported language competence of students from Dutch-medium colleges (L1 = Dutch, L2 = French, L3 = English)

competence in English (L3) are more positive than those for the L2, as 57% of the Dutch-speaking students and 44% of the Francophones evaluated their proficiency in English as good or fluent. Perhaps this difference in contact with English media can partially account for the higher self-perceived language competence in English of the Dutch-speaking pupils. Although we have to remain careful whilst interpreting results based on self-reported competence, they highlight two important facts: (1) the students in the Dutch-medium college seem to have a better command of both their L2 (French) and L3 compared with the students in French-medium colleges, confirming the general opinion that Dutch-medium education has an efficient language education policy; (2) in both systems, there is a significant difference between the fluent and/or good command of the L2 versus the L3. The self-reported competence for English is always higher than that for the L2, confirming previous

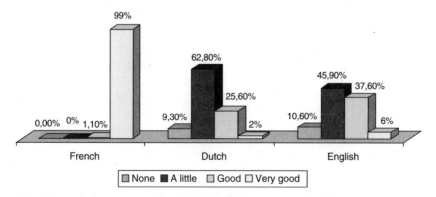

Figure 5.3 Self-reported language competence of students from French-medium colleges (L1 = French, L2 = Dutch, L3 = English)

findings (Dewaele, 2005; Housen *et al.*, 2000) and emphasising the fact that the language of the 'other' community (L2) is not very successful amongst youths, contrary to English.

Language use and language importance

The analyses of the items in the questionnaire concerning language use (see Table 5.6 and Table 5.7) confirm the trends described in the introduction contrasting the societal bilingualism of Brussels with the individuals' monolingualism. Except for the small number of bilinguals in our sample, the students do not resort to a diglossic system in their daily language use. The result shows that more than 90% of them always and/ or mainly use their L1 (either French or Dutch, depending on the educational system they are involved in). In a few cases, some of them use the L2 with neighbours or watch certain TV programmes in the L2. These results are very comparable in both the Dutch- and the French-medium colleges. This suggests, as previously mentioned, firstly that Francophones in Brussels are mainly monolingual in their language use and have hardly any contact with Dutch, and secondly that, as most students in the Dutch-medium college in Brussels come from Flanders, they use Dutch in most situations and have very little contact with French, their L2, and the majority language of the city where they study.

Table 5.8 gives an overview of the situations in daily life in Brussels where the two major groups of students consider the L2 to be important or not.

The analyses of the items on the importance of the L2 in daily situations (see Table 5.8) partly confirm the results for language use, indicating that in most situations the L2 is considered to be unimportant. Students are nevertheless aware of the importance of the 'other' language in some particular domains described hereafter. Contrary to language use, there are some major differences in the evaluation of the importance of the L2 according to the home language of the students. We will therefore compare the results for the three main language groups: Dutch speakers, French speakers and students who speak both French and a migrant language at home. The group of bilinguals and of students who only speak a language other than French and Dutch are too small to be taken into account.

These figures clearly show that the L2 is mainly important for the Dutch speakers in Brussels, where French as the majority language is used as the lingua franca and Dutch an official language but spoken by a minority of the inhabitants. The importance of French for the Dutch speakers is nevertheless restricted to situations of contact outside their in-group (shopping, living in the city versus family, friends, college, media). The L2 however is very important for all linguistic groups when

Table 5.6 Language used by students from Dutch- (D) and French-medium schools (F) when talking to the following people

	Always in Dutch (%)		In Dutch more often than French (%)		In Dutch and French about equally (%)		In French more often than Dutch (%)		Always in French (%)	
	D	F	D	F	D	F	D	F	D	F
Father	94.3	0.0	1.9	0.0	0.0	0.9	0.0	2.7	3.8	96.4
Mother	93.4	0.0	0.9	0.0	1.9	0.9	0.9	4.3	2.8	94.9
Brothers and sisters	94.2	0.0	1.0	0.8	0.0	0.8	1.9	4.2	2.9	94.1
Friends in classroom	94.3	0.0	3.8	0.0	1.9	0.8	0.0	1.6	0.0	97.7
Friends outside school	74.8	0.0	16.5	1.6	4.9	2.3	2.9	10.9	1.0	85.3
Teachers	100	0.8	0.0	0.0	0.0	0.0	0.0	0.0	0.0	99.2
Neighbours	76.6	2.3	10.3	0.0	3.7	1.5	0.9	8.4	8.4	87.8

Table 5.7 Means of communication and language used by students from Dutch- (D) and French-medium schools (F)

	Always in Dutch (%)		In Dutch more often than French (%)		In Dutch and French about equally (%)		In French more often than Dutch (%)		Always in French (%)	
	D	F	D	F	D	F	D	F	D	F
Watching TV	65.4	1.5	26.2	3.8	6.5	28.0	1.9	0.8	0.0	65.9
The press	77.8	0.0	16.7	0.0	4.6	3.8	0.9	20.5	0.0	75.8
Music	41.2	0.0	43.1	0.0	10.8	2.4	3.9	10.2	1.0	87.4
Listening to the radio	65.4	0.8	23.4	0.8	8.4	6.1	0.9	13.7	1.9	78.6

Table 5.8 Importance attached to the L2 to do the following activities (D if L1 = Dutch, F if L1 = French)

For people to:	Important (%)		A little important (%)		A little unimportant (%)		Unimportant (%)	
	D	F	D	F	D	F	D	F
Make friends	10.2	8.0	22.4	11.5	57.1	47.1	10.2	33.3
Read	19.4	11.5	39.8	35.6	33.7	28.7	7.1	24.1
Write	13.3	11.6	26.5	30.2	50.0	33.7	10.2	24.4
Watch TV	7.4	0.0	10.5	17.4	50.5	34.9	31.6	47.7
Get a job	70.1	69.4	21.6	18.8	6.2	8.2	2.1	3.5
Be liked	9.3	4.5	27.8	12.5	45.4	40.9	17.5	42.0
Live in Brussels	42.9	12.8	37.8	32.6	14.3	33.7	5.1	20.9
Bring up children	12.5	8.0	42.7	25.3	33.3	34.5	11.5	32.2
Go shopping	29.6	5.7	38.8	12.5	24.5	55.7	7.1	26.1
Make phone calls	19.4	5.7	33.7	26.4	34.7	33.3	12.2	34.5
Pass exams	14.3	14.8	30.6	30.7	36.7	33.0	18.4	21.6
Be accepted in the community	26.8	14.8	51.5	35.2	10.3	33.0	11.3	17.0
Talk to friends at university	4.1	4.5	13.3	20.5	49.0	40.9	33.7	34.1
Talk to people out of university	17.5	5.2	36.1	26.0	36.1	41.6	10.3	27.3

it comes down to employment, as it is common knowledge that to get a job at whatever level in Brussels, one is expected to know at least both official languages, French and Dutch.

These results about language use and the importance of the L2 for the students involved in this study confirm the situation presented in the introduction. Firstly, it is obvious that Brussels is a dominant French-speaking city where Dutch is in most situations considered as unimportant, except in the context of employment. Secondly, it emphasises the fact that both linguistic communities in Brussels live side by side, having hardly any contact with each other and each other's language, impairing thus the development of a positive attitude to each other's community and language.

Attitudes towards Dutch, French and English in Brussels

According to the common framework of analyses (see Introduction), three variables were computed on the basis of a 10-item battery for each language: language attitudes towards L1 (Dutch or French according to the educational system), language attitudes towards L2 (French or Dutch) and language attitudes towards L3 (English). The Cronbach α tests as well as complementary factor analyses of our data indicated that the reliability of the batteries could be improved by removing some items and/or clustering them differently. However so as to ensure comparisons with the other regions taking part in this project, we decided to keep the variables as they are, knowing these variables and the interpretation of the results have to be considered carefully.

Before starting the analyses of variance used throughout the different cases in this research project, the means for the attitudes to L1, L2 and L3 (the languages depend on the educational system) are displayed in Figures 5.4–5.6. They have been split up into three main categories: unfavourable, neutral and favourable. Without alluding to statistical differences, these means already indicate the general attitudinal trends: the attitude to English is very positive, at least as positive as the attitude to the L1 and far more positive than the attitude to French or Dutch as an L2.

Following the common analytical procedure of the larger comparative research project, the three dependent variables (attitudes to L1, L2 and English) were analysed by means of one-way ANOVAs, together with *post hoc* tests when relevant, with the following background elements as independent variables: educational system (French medium versus Dutch medium), home language, gender, socioeconomical status, region, knowledge of other languages, age starting to learn the L2, age starting to learn English, watching TV in English and stay in an English-speaking country. Table 5.10 indicates per attitudinal variable whether the

Table 5.9 Percentages of students considering L2 in Brussels as important and rather important, split up according to home language

Importance of L2 in Brussels	Dutch speakers (n =98)	French speakers (n =91)	French +other (n =26)
Get a job (%)	91	89	92
Live in the city (%)	81	47	37
Go shopping (%)	68	30	29
Be part of the community (%)	78	51	56

differences between the groups are significant or not ($p < 0.05$) whereas Table 5.11 summarises the direction of the significant differences.

These results indicate that the differences in attitudes can mainly be interpreted according to the language community the students belong to. The fact that the student is a member of the French-speaking community or the Dutch-speaking community is determined by his or her home language, the region he or she comes from and hence the educational system he or she is involved in. The results of the *post hoc* tests demonstrate this phenomenon clearly, as the results for these three independent variables follow in the same direction. They indicate that the Dutch speakers in the Dutch-medium education coming from Flanders and the Flemish surroundings of Brussels (Vlaams Brabant) have more positive attitudes to their L1 but also to their L2 than the students involved in French-medium education, whether they only speak French at home or not, originating from Brussels or Wallonia. This last group of students actually shows more positive attitudes towards English than those from the Dutch-speaking community, as

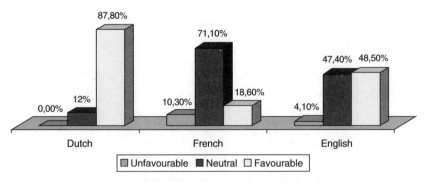

Figure 5.4 Attitudes towards the three languages in Dutch-medium education (L1 = Dutch)

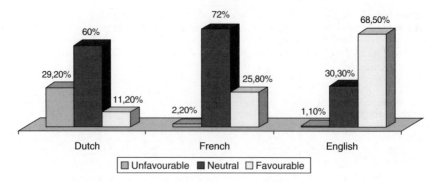

Figure 5.5 Attitudes towards the three languages in French-medium education (L1 = French)

illustrated in Figure 5.4 and Figure 5.5. These results match previous findings, revealing that French speakers do not perceive Dutch positively and favour English. The same effect can be noticed for the Dutch speakers but the difference between French and English is less important, as they have rather neutral attitudes towards French. Furthermore it is striking to notice that the students having both French and a migrant language as home languages and who are involved in the French-medium education follow the same attitudinal pattern as the French speakers, showing greater positiveness towards English than to Dutch. Yet they show a more neutral attitude towards French.

Except for these community-based variables, the analyses show that students who started studying the L2 before primary school are more favourable towards the latter than those who started after the age of 6. The knowledge of more than one language also seems to have a positive effect on attitudes, indicating that multilingualism goes along with

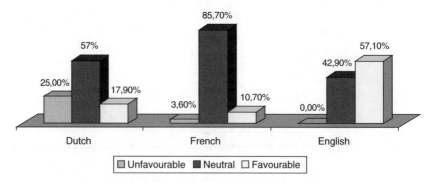

Figure 5.6 Attitudes towards the three languages in French-medium education (L1 = French + immigrant language)

Table 5.10 Results of one-way ANOVAs for attitudes to L1, L2 and English

	Attitude to L1	*Attitude to L2*	*Attitude to English*
Educational system	F 215.171 *** df (1, 237)	F 17.191 *** df (1, 235)	F 5.749 * df (1, 236)
Home language	F 45.178 *** df (4, 231)	F 5.892 *** df (4, 229)	F 4.989 ** df (4, 230)
Gender	n.s.	n.s.	n.s.
Socioeconomical status	F 215.171 *** df (2, 206)	n.s.	n.s.
Region	F 51.885 *** df (3, 223)	F 4.180 ** df (3, 221)	F 2.882 * df (3, 222)
Knowledge of other languages	F 3.331 * df (3, 235)	F 10.081 *** df (3, 233)	F 5.594 ** df (3, 234)
Age learning L2	–	F 3.072 * df (3, 223)	–
Age learning English	–	–	n.s.
Watching TV in English	–	–	F 4.595 ** df (3, 234)
Stay in English-sp. country	–	–	F 8.625 ** df (1, 229)

positive attitudes to second and/or foreign languages. A last set of significant differences indicate that students who have ever been to an English-speaking country or who watch English-spoken programmes on TV regularly, or even only once in a while, show more positive attitudes towards English than those who have never been to an English-speaking country or never watch TV in English. These findings were predictable, but question once again the causal relationship between practising or being in contact with a language and the attitudes towards that language. It is indeed hard to assess whether students never watch TV in English because they have negative feelings towards the language or whether it is because students have not been in contact or even been to an English-speaking country that they did not develop positive attitudes towards English.

To find out whether there is a relationship between the attitudes towards L1, L2 and English and the self-perceived competence in those languages, correlation analyses were performed for the entire group of informants. The results of the Pearson's correlation index indicate only

Table 5.11 Direction of significant differences for attitudes to L1, L2 and English (*post hoc* Tukey)

	Attitude to L1	*Attitude to L2*	*Attitude to English*
Educational system	Dutch-medium > French-medium	Dutch-medium > French-medium	French-medium > Dutch-medium
Home language	Dutch-sp. > others	Dutch-sp. > French-sp.	French-sp. > Dutch-sp.
Gender	n.s.	n.s.	n.s.
Socioeconomical status	Middle > lower	n.s.	n.s.
Region	Vlaams Brabant, Flanders > Brussels, Wallonia	Vlaams Brabant > Wallonia	Wallonia > Vlaams Brabant
Knowledge of other languages	1 lang. < 3 lang.	1 lang. < more lang.	1 & 2 lang. < 3 &4 lang.
Age learning L2	–	6 or younger > 6+	–
Age learning English	–	–	n.s.
Watching TV in English	–	–	Never < once a week or more
Stay in English-sp. country	–	–	Never < ever

weak positive correlations for the L2 and L3 and none for the L1 (L1*att L1: $r = -0.126$; L2*att L2: $r = 0.512***$; L3*att L3: $r = 0.350***$). Analyses per home language group (speakers of Dutch, French and French+ another language) did not reveal any significant correlations at all. These results indicate that there is only a very tenuous link between the attitudes, as measured and defined in the present study, and the self-evaluation of the students.

Discussion

Urban bilingualism can only be understood by taking into account the historical perspective and current role both languages play in their specific context. For Brussels, a majority/minority approach is a too narrow framework for this purpose. It mainly refers to the numeric presence of its native speakers while the case of English clearly shows that the function of a language itself determines its status and importance. In this respect, all three languages, Dutch, French and English, play their role in Brussels. This implies that if Dutch is the L1 of the respondent, the function of his or her L2 will differ from the function a French speaker gives to his or her L2. Even the relation with L3 differs: in some circumstances English is used where French was the obvious choice before, where it seldom replaces Dutch. Moreover, for about one third of its population, neither Dutch nor French can be considered as their mother tongue, while in this research project they will be considered as having French as their L1. L1 as well as L2 and L3 cover a diverse but complex content.

The linguistic divide, as referred to in the introductory part of this chapter, created a segregated educational landscape where teachers are skilled to function within one particular language segment. In bilingual Brussels, neither students nor teachers are trained to become bilingual but in the same way as in the corresponding monolingual areas. What is more, education is one of the domains in Brussels where highly educated employees, in contradiction to the private sector, work in a monolingual environment. Even the L2 and L3 is taught by a language teacher who is not a native speaker but has the same L1 as his or her students. Language teachers who are native speakers of the L2 are often discouraged by the tough examination they have to pass, proving their knowledge not of the language they will teach, but of the language of the school system they will work for. As a consequence, bilingual and native-speaker language teachers are very exceptional. If our respondents do not opt for L2 or L3 as their subject, language courses are only a minimal part of their curriculum in higher education or will even be absent. This is just one example where the educational model contradicts the actual situation in the classrooms. While education in Brussels is characterised by the linguistic diversity of its pupils, teacher training is similar to that in a monolingual environment.

The above situation is reflected in the results of this study. The analyses of the attitudes towards Dutch, French and English measured amongst students involved in teacher training programmes in Brussels have shown that attitudes to English are much more favourable than attitudes to the L2, which is perfectly in line with previous research (see above). Moreover the differences in attitudes can predominantly be explained in terms of the French- versus the Dutch-speaking community. The influence of social, political and historical factors together with the results on language use and importance of the L2 emphasise the lack of contact and the ignorance of both linguistic communities. Negative attitudes towards the 'other' language and potentially to its speakers are thereby favoured and hence increase the gap between the French- and

Dutch-speaking communities, living side by side in the officially bilingual city of Brussels.

Learning a language as such is not sufficient to develop a positive attitude towards its speakers. Even after 10 years of language training in the L2, students assess their linguistic competence as rather shaky, especially those who attended French-medium education. However the higher they rate their competence, the more positive their attitude. Especially intensive contacts improve their rating of the L2. Students from traditional bilingual families have a more positive attitude towards both L1 and L2, even if in daily life they prefer to use one above the other. Also the few Francophone crossovers, attending a Dutch-medium school, show a much more positive attitude towards Dutch. But these are mere side effects of a given situation or based on the personal decision of the persons involved rather than the result of a well considered educational policy.

After all, one has to be very careful with the interpretation of these results. It is obvious that positive attitudes towards a particular language are not a matter of training. Political, social and cultural factors seem at least as important as linguistic skills. The students for which neither Dutch nor French is their mother tongue perfectly illustrate this conclusion: they have a positive attitude towards L3 but the tensions between both traditional language groups result in their rather weak attitude towards both L1 and L2, even if one of these languages is a home language for them as well. On the one hand, the impact of the context outside the educational system makes it very hard to compare different cities and regions; on the other hand it forms the base for an appealing future project where this can be compared with the current educational policy not restricted to teacher training but concentrated on different language/ethnic groups in a multilingual and multicultural urban setting. Educational policy within such an environment is one of the key challenges European cities face today.

References

Ackaert, L. and Deschouwer, K. (1999) De relatie tussen taal en identiteit bij de Brusselse migranten. In M. Swyngedouw, K. Phalet and K. Deschouwer (eds) *Minderheden in Brussel. Sociopolitieke houdingen en gedragingen* (pp. 215–244). Brussels: VUB Press.

Baker, C. (2001) *Foundations of Bilingualism and Bilingual Education* (3rd edn). Clevedon: Multilingual Matters.

Dewaele, J.-M. (2005) Sociodemographic, psychological and politico-cultural correlates in Flemish students' attitudes towards French and English. *Journal of Multilingual and Multicultural Development* 26(2), 118–137.

Housen, A., Janssens, S. and Pierrard, M. (2000) *Frans en Engels als vreemde talen in Vlaanderen. Een vergelijkend onderzoek.* Brussels: VUB Press.

Housen, A., Mettewie, L. and Pierrard, M. (2002) Rapport Beleidsgericht onderzoek PBO/98/2/36. Taalvaardigheid en attitudes van Nederlandstalige en Franstalige leerlingen in het secundair onderwijs in Brussel. (Research report). Brussels: Centrum voor Linguïstiek – Vrije Universiteit Brussel.

Housen, A. and Pierrard, M. (2004) Meertaligheid in Nederlandstalig secundair onderwijs in Brussel: verslag van een effectenstudie. In A. Housen, M. Pierrard and P. Van de Craen (eds) *Brusselse Thema's. Taal, Attitude en Onderwijs in Brussel* (Vol.12, pp. 9–33). Brussels: VUB Press.

Janssens, R. (2001) *Taalgebruik in Brussel: Taalverhoudingen, taalverschuivingen en taalidentiteit in een meertalig Brussel* (Vol.8). Brussels: VUB Press.

Lochtman, K., Lutjeharms, M. and Kermarrec, G. (2004) Duits en andere 'vreemde' talen in Brussel: een attitudeonderzoek bij Brusselse studenten uit een economische studierichting. In A. Housen, M. Pierrard and P. Van de Craen (eds) *Brusselse Thema's. Taal, Attitude en Onderwijs in Brussel* (Vol.12, pp. 209–239). Brussels: VUB Press.

Mettewie, L. (1998) Remmingen bij Franstaligen om het Nederlands te leren of de plaats van het Nederlands in hun waardensysteem/Blocages des Franco-phones face à l'apprentissage du néerlandais ou la place du néerlandais dans leur système de valeur. In A. Morelli, L. Dierickx and D. Lesage (eds) *Racisme: een element in het conflict tussen Franstaligen en Vlamingen/Racisme: un element dans le conflit entre francophones et Flamands* (pp. 144–145). Berchem/Bruxelles: EPO/Labor.

Mettewie, L. (2004) Attitudes en motivatie van taalleerders in België. Een sociaal-psychologisch onderzoek naar het verwerven van de eerste en tweede taal door Nederlandstalige, Franstalige en tweetalige leerlingen in het secundair onderwijs in Brussel. PhD dissertation, Vrije Universiteit Brussel, Brussels.

Mettewie, L., Housen, A. and Pierrard, M. (2004) Invloed van contact op taalattitudes en taalleermotivatie in het Nederlandstalig onderwijs in Brussel. In A. Housen, M. Pierrard and P. Van de Craen (eds) *Brusselse Thema's. Taal, Attitude en Onderwijs in Brussel* (Vol.12, pp. 35–65). Brussels: VUB Press.

Persoons, Y. (1988) Identity and projection: The projected attitudes of Flemish high school students in Brussels. In R. van Hout and U. Knops (eds) *Language Attitudes in the Dutch Language Area* (pp. 39–53). Dordrecht: Foris Publications.

Witte, E. and Van Velthoven, H. (1998) *Taal en politiek. De Belgische casus in een historisch perspectief*. Brussels: VUB Press.

Chapter 6
Language Use and Language Attitudes in Friesland

JEHANNES YTSMA

Sociolinguistic context

Friesland (Fryslân) is one of the 12 provinces in the Netherlands (Figure 6.1 and Figure 6.2). It is the only province that is officially bilingual, Friesland having been recognised as a bilingual territory in the 1970s (Commissie Friese-Taalpolitiek, 1970). The province of Friesland is located in the northern part of The Netherlands and currently has 642,066 inhabitants, 4% of the total population of the Netherlands (data 2004). The capital of Friesland is Leeuwarden (Ljouwert) which has 85,896 inhabitants (data 2004). From a large-scale language survey conducted in the 1990s it is known that of the provincial population, 94% can understand the minority language and 74% can speak it (Gorter & Jonkman, 1995: 8). The latter percentage implies an absolute number of roughly 400,000 speakers of Frisian, a fifth of these being second-language learners. Figures on literacy in Frisian are considerably lower: 65% are able to read Frisian and only 17% can write in the language. The finding that such a small proportion of the population is able to write in Frisian undoubtedly has to do with the weak position of the language within education (see further). It is also associated with the fact that writing ability in the minority language is of limited importance in the domain of work; this hardly motivates inhabitants of the province to acquire proficiency in writing Frisian.

Broadly speaking, the above-mentioned percentages on Frisian language proficiency have appeared to remain rather stable over the last few decades, although there is a slow decline in speaking ability and a minor growth in writing skills. A worrying development for the future of the Frisian language is the indication from a recent language survey among young parents that Frisian is losing ground among the youngest generation (Foekema, 2004). Of the current generation of young parents (with children 0–12 years), 40% always spoke Frisian at home when they were a child themselves whereas only 29% of these parents now (always) speak Frisian at home with their children. These two percentages signify a loss of 11% within one generation.

Figure 6.1 The Netherlands in Europe

Research conducted in the 1990s indicated that about half the total population of the province spoke Frisian at home (55%), a third spoke Dutch at home (34%) and the remaining 10% of the inhabitants used another variety as their home language (Gorter & Jonkman, 1995). It should be noted that, although distances between social groups have levelled out to a considerable extent in modern times, Frisian speakers are still somewhat over-represented at lower educational levels, whereas Dutch-speaking people are slightly over-represented at higher levels of schooling (see Ytsma & De Jong, 1993).

As regards the position of Frisian in the media, it is worth mentioning that Omrop Fryslân broadcasts Frisian language radio and television programmes on a daily basis. In general, these programmes are popular among the inhabitants; there is a daily audience of 150,000 listeners and a daily viewing audience of 93,000. However, the use of the minority language in both provincial newspapers – the Leeuwarder Courant and the Friesch Dagblad – is quite minimal. It has been estimated for each of the two regional newspapers that approximately 5% of the text appears in Frisian, whilst a remarkable phenomenon is that articles written in

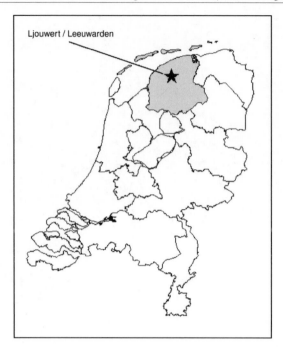

Figure 6.2 Friesland in the Netherlands

Dutch frequently quote Frisian-speaking people in their own language. Lastly, as regards written Frisian, book production in the minority language is relevant. In this respect it is significant to note that every year several publishing companies publish a total of about 100 books in Frisian, and over 60,000 people purchase 90,000 Frisian books.

Since the 1970s Frisian has, next to Dutch, enjoyed the formal status of an official language within the province. Nevertheless, its social prestige undoubtedly lies beneath that of standard Dutch. The difference in status between Frisian and Dutch is clear to such a degree that primary-school children in Friesland evaluate Dutch significantly higher than Frisian as to language status (Ytsma, 1990, 1995). The social prestige of Frisian is associated with the attitude of both Frisians and non-Frisians towards the language. In general Frisians reveal relatively positive attitudes towards their own language, while the attitudes of non-Frisian speakers are neutral or rather negative (see Section 3).

Despite the everyday prevalence of Frisian and Dutch throughout the province, English nevertheless holds a certain position in a number of formal domains within Dutch (and Frisian) society. That is to say that the foreign language performs an active function in 'modern' domains such as media and business. For example, there is extensive exposure to

English in the mass media. De Bot (1994) remarked that 40–60% of television programmes screened in the Netherlands are in English (all subtitled in Dutch). Moreover, English is increasingly used in commercial advertising. Gerritsen (1996) has pointed out that almost a fifth of the pages in Dutch newspapers and magazines contain English-language advertisements. However, there are no signs that English is intruding on the informal, core domain of the family. In this sense it indeed remains a 'foreign' language. By contrast, there are signs indicating the increasing importance of English in the domain of schooling. Noteworthy in this respect is that in the school year 2004–2005 the first secondary school in Friesland began a bilingual (Dutch/English) stream and other secondary schools intend to follow this approach in the years to come. This development is in line with the general trend of Friesland becoming more multilingual than bilingual (see Gorter, 2005). In respect of this development, a telling finding has been that primary-school children living in the capital city of Leeuwarden/Ljouwert (and surroundings) had over 60 different home languages (Extra & Kloprogge, 2000).

As already stated, the Frisian language received official recognition by the Dutch State in the 1970s. Official recognition of Frisian led to prudent 'promotion' of the minority language by the Dutch State. This was laid down in an administrative arrangement between the Dutch State and the provincial government in 2001 (see Gorter *et al.*, 2001). The covenant on the Frisian language and culture follows the same structure as the European Charter for Regional and Minority Languages, which has been ratified by the Dutch State and came into force in 1998. The covenant between state and provincial government encompasses provisions for media, education, culture and scientific research, as well as for public administration and the use of Frisian in the courts.

As regards linguistic distance it should be noted that Frisian, Dutch and English are typologically related languages; all three varieties belong to the branch of Germanic languages. Frisian has even been called the 'little sister' language of English, as there was a close affinity between Old English and Old Frisian (predating 1550). The close linguistic relationship between Frisian and Dutch without doubt explains why the vast majority of provincial inhabitants claim to be able to understand Frisian (see earlier). It should be remarked that Frisian forms a quite homogeneous speech community wherein all varieties of dialect are mutually understandable. The three major dialects often distinguished are Súd-Westhoeksk ('South-West Corner', spoken in the south-west), Wâldfrysk ('Wood Frisian', spoken in the north-west) and Klaaifrysk ('Clay Frisian', spoken in the east). However, it should be emphasised that the linguistic differences between the said dialects are confined for the greater part to phonological differences. In view of codification of the minority language, it is worth noting that written Frisian is fully standardised through the official 'provincial spelling', dating back to 1980.

The Frisian Educational System

In 1980 Frisian became an approved medium of instruction in all grades, and an obligatory subject throughout primary school. Moreover, the Dutch Ministry of Education in 1993 set attainment targets for the teaching of Frisian. These 'core objectives' describe which language skills the pupils have to attain by the end of primary school. Frisian attainment targets are exactly identical to those for Dutch. In theory this means that the curriculum of all primary schools in the province ($n = 495$ in 2000) should aim at full bilingualism in terms of the four basic language abilities (understanding, speaking, reading and writing). In practice, however, a majority of primary schools spend no more than one lesson per week on Frisian, and Frisian is actually used as a medium of instruction to a widely varying degree. Some primary schools use Frisian as medium of instruction for the greater part of teaching time (especially in the lower grades); other schools do not use the language as medium of instruction at all. Generally speaking, the degree to which the minority language is used as a vehicle of instruction depends on the linguistic constellation of the school population; the more Frisian-speaking children the school population includes, the more Frisian is used to teach other subjects. Note, however, that there is no single Frisian-medium primary school in which all lessons are taught in the minority language.

Given the above data on the position of Frisian at primary level, it is unsurprising that research has shown scholastic achievement in Frisian lagging behind, especially as far as writing Frisian is concerned, and regarding speaking ability among L1 Dutch schoolchildren (De Jong & Riemersma, 1994). In the light of these results many schools complain that the attainment targets for Frisian are set too high. Consequently, there are plans to somewhat reduce attainment targets for Frisian.

Since 1986 English has been an obligatory subject at primary level. English is mostly taught for one lesson per week in the upper grades only (that is Grades 7 and 8, which means from the age of 10 onwards). The English language is hardly ever used as a medium of instruction in primary schools. The attainment targets set for the teaching of English are confined to understanding, speaking and reading, and the general aim of foreign-language teaching is to obtain a basic communicative competence in English. Worthy of mention here is a project on trilingual primary schooling in Friesland, in which seven small, rural 'project' schools are experimenting with a trilingual model. In this innovative educational model, Frisian, Dutch and English are taught as school subjects and concurrently used as medium of instruction (see Ytsma, 2000a, 2000b).

The subdivision of teaching time within the trilingual model is 50% Frisian and 50% Dutch in Grades 1 to 6. In the upper grades (7 and 8), the division is 40% in Frisian, 40% in Dutch and the remaining 20% (two afternoons per week) in English. Interim results of the trilingual project are encouraging. The results thus far (re: Grades 3 to 6) generally show some improvement in children's command of Frisian in the project schools, whereas their command of Dutch is comparable to Dutch language proficiency measured among children attending control schools (Deelstra & Ytsma, 2005).

Since 1993 Frisian has been an obligatory subject in the lower grades of secondary education, and it has also become permissible to teach through the medium of Frisian in secondary schools. However, Frisian has been developed only poorly as a school subject at secondary level. In practice, many secondary schools fail to offer Frisian lessons to their students and the schools offering Frisian lessons mostly do so only in Grade 1. In practice, this boils down to some 40 Frisian lessons during first grade. As for the use of Frisian as medium of instruction, a study by the Inspectorate showed that in 1999 only 1% of all secondary schools regularly used Frisian as a medium of instruction. Thirty percent used it every now and then, and 69% never used Frisian to teach other subjects (Inspectie van het Onderwijs, 1999). The situation has probably not improved since then. A relatively favourable development has been that Frisian may be chosen as an examination subject in 11 (out of 49 in 2000) secondary schools in the school year 2004–2005. But the total number of students choosing Frisian as an examination subject is fairly modest (about 100). It seems a safe guess to argue that this low uptake has to do with the limited instrumental value of Frisian in the domain of work. Compared to Frisian, the position of English at secondary level is much more favourable, as (almost) every student attends English lessons for several hours per week and chooses to be examined on the subject.

Teacher training for primary level is provided by two educational institutes in the province: the Christelijke Hogeschool Noord-Nederland (CHN) and the Noordelijke Hogeschool Leeuwarden (NHL). Teacher training for primary level is basically conducted in Dutch; this applies to both CHN and NHL. Both teacher-training colleges offer Frisian courses to their students in Grades 1–3, and a majority of students attend these courses, in this way becoming formally qualified to teach Frisian. Only the NHL provides teacher training for secondary level and the number of students on this initial training course is low (some 15).

Lastly, it should be noted that Frisian language and literature can be studied at university level. The universities of Amsterdam, Groningen and Leiden, all located outside the province of Friesland, offer courses in Frisian.

Previous Studies on Language Attitudes in Friesland

Pietersen (1974) conducted a study into the language attitudes of teacher-training college students in Fryslân. In fact, Pietersen investigated what he called 'language engagement' amongst these future teachers. It turned out that there were no important age and gender differences as regards students' language engagement. However, there was a significant engagement difference related to 'origin' of the student concerned. It emerged that 47% of students born within the province of Friesland displayed a fairly strong engagement with the Frisian language, whereas no more than 11% of students born outside the province did so.

In the 1990s, De Goede *et al.* (1994) investigated, among other things, the attitudes of youngsters (16–26 years) living in Friesland. The authors concluded that the attitude towards Frisian measured among these young people was 'reasonably positive'. This is probably in line with the general feeling of current inhabitants of the province. But there are definitely demonstrable differences in the attitude towards Frisian between distinct sections of the population. Nowadays, by far the most important factor influencing provincial inhabitants' attitudes towards Frisian is their mother tongue. Tellingly, a large-scale and representative language survey conducted in the 1990s revealed that 87% of respondents with Frisian as their first language reported that the Frisian language meant 'a lot' to them, whereas the corresponding figure for those respondents with Dutch as their mother tongue was only 34% (Gorter & Jonkman, 1995: 35). The same pattern of Frisian speakers displaying far more positive attitudes towards Frisian than do Dutch speakers has been found among a sample of MDGO students (MDGO: senior secondary personal and social services and health care education) (Lutje Spelberg & Postma, 1995) and among a sample of primary-school children (Ytsma, 1995). Ytsma (1995: 129) reported a 'moderately positive' attitude of Frisian-speaking primary school children towards Frisian, whereas Dutch children's attitude could be described as 'fairly negative'. Furthermore, a matched-guise test in the same author's study revealed that Frisian children tended to prefer Frisian in terms of the 'solidarity' dimension, whereas Dutch children judged the solidarity value of Dutch somewhat more favourably (Ytsma, 1995: 132). Notably, a comparison of Dutch parents' attitude towards Frisian with the attitudes of their own (primary-school) children revealed that parental attitudes did not meaningfully deviate from the attitudes of their children (Ytsma, 1995: 137). The author concluded that 8% of variance in Dutch children's attitudes to Frisian could be assigned to parental impetus (Ytsma, 1995: 137), suggesting that parental attitudes partially mould the attitudes of their children.

Another factor that has been reported to relate to attitudes towards Frisian is socioeconomic status. Gorter and Ytsma (1988), for example, demonstrated a generally less positive orientation towards the Frisian language on the part of persons of higher socioeconomic status. Furthermore, it has been noted that attitudes towards Frisian are related to age, younger people showing a less positive language attitude (Gorter *et al.*, 1984). Finally, Benedictus (2005) recently noted in her undergraduate thesis that (second-year) CHN and NHL teacher-training student attitudes were not related to gender, whereas L1 Frisian students displayed significantly more positive attitudes towards Frisian than did L1 Dutch students. Moreover, middle-class students had a more favourable attitude towards Frisian than did students with a higher socioeconomic background. Interestingly, it was found that L1 Frisian students were more positively orientated towards trilingualism than were L1 Dutch students.

The Study

The sample

The students participating in the current study were in the first year of their teacher-training programme at the Christelijke Hogeschool Noord Nederland (CHN) in Leeuwarden/Ljouwert. A total of 99 teacher-training students completed the questionnaire. The said number of students means that well over half of the first-year students enrolled at the CHN teacher training college participated in the research. Frisian is an optional part of the students' training programme during the first three years (of four) of their training (one course per year). Except for voluntary Frisian courses, the medium of instruction for students during their training programme is almost entirely Dutch. Having followed the three Frisian courses, students are formally qualified to teach Frisian at primary level. At the time of completing the questionnaires the students were not yet attending any course in Frisian as part of their training programme. The mean age of informants was 18.7 years old. The majority of the students ($n = 84$) were female, so only 15 students were males. The strong numerical over-representation of female students in the sample is in keeping with the general gender distribution among teacher-training college students at CHN (and other teacher-training colleges). The distribution of the students according to mother tongue is depicted in Figure 6.3.

As regards linguistic background, 52 students had Frisian as their mother tongue (53%), 27 students had Dutch as their mother tongue (27%), 17 students had a bilingual (Dutch/Frisian) background (17%) and the remaining three students had 'another' linguistic background (3%). As to parents' socioprofessional status, 8.2% had high status, 57.8% were middle class and 34% belonged to the lower class.

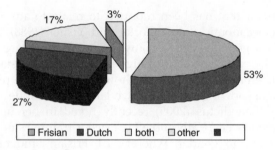

Figure 6.3 The students' L1

Regarding foreign language, 16.3% had started to learn English before the age of eight, and the remaining 83.7% at the age of ten or later (i.e. from Grade 7 PE onwards). As for informal contact with the English language, 58.6% had been to an English-speaking country. Moreover, it turned out that 33.7% never (6.1%) or hardly ever (27.6%) watched TV in English, whereas 29.6% watched it once or twice a week, 17.3% three to five times a week and 19.4% on a daily basis.

The instrument and the procedure

The instrument and procedure applied in this research were identical to those used by the other contributors to this volume, as stated in the opening chapter. The questionnaire was in the Dutch language, as the national language was presumably the most 'neutral' for the students. The future teachers completed the questionnaire in September 2004; that is, at the very beginning of the academic year. The students voluntarily filled in the questionnaire after their periods of instruction (at home or at college).

Results

The students were asked to estimate their own language proficiency in Frisian, Dutch and English. It should come as no surprise that the results obtained proved that nearly every student was fully competent in Dutch. This is certainly not the case as far as Frisian and English language proficiency is concerned. Reading and especially writing in Frisian seemed to be difficult for many students. It turned out that 38% of the students could not (6%) or hardly ('a little', 32%) read Frisian. The corresponding figures in respect of Frisian writing ability were 26% ('not') and 52% ('a little'). Speaking and writing in English was hard for a considerable proportion of the students. As to speaking ability, it was found that 3% could not speak English and 47% could speak it 'a little'. Regarding writing ability, it appeared that 3% could not write in English and 43% could hardly write in English ('a little'). However, a majority of the students reported that they could understand and read English '(very) well'. All in all, it could be concluded on the basis of the data reported that students' passive knowledge of English evidently exceeded their active English-language proficiency.

In addition to students' self-perceived language ability in terms of the four basic language skills, students were asked to estimate their general language proficiency in Frisian, Dutch and English. The results are graphically depicted in Figure 6.4.

From Figure 6.4 it may be seen that students' self-reported Dutch language proficiency is (very) good in almost every case. As regards Frisian, there is a considerable group of students with only little (24.2%) or no (4.2%) proficiency in the minority language. English language proficiency is mostly judged as being moderate ('a little': 45.7%) or good (47.9%).

Table 6.1 indicates language usage patterns amongst these future teachers. It was found that a majority of the students spoke Frisian at home (with father/mother/brothers and sisters) or with their neighbours, whereas the language used within the educational setting (friends in the classroom and especially teachers) frequently shifted to Dutch.

In addition, we asked the students which language they used in four distinct means of communication. Table 6.2 presents the outcomes obtained. The figures given indicate the Dutch language as being by far the most prominent in every means of communication listed. The relatively most favourable figures for Frisian are associated with watching TV. Namely, it was found that 27.1% of the students 'always' (17.7%) or 'more often than in Dutch' (9.4%) watched Frisian-language TV programmes.

Lastly, the future teachers were asked to estimate the importance attached to the Frisian language for people involved in a number of

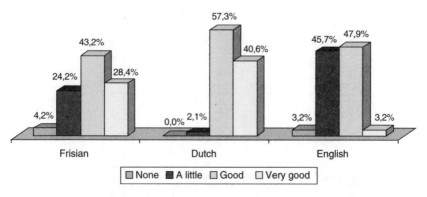

Figure 6.4 General language proficiency in Frisian, Dutch and English

Table 6.1 Language used when talking to the following people

	Always in Frisian (%)	In Frisian more often than Dutch (%)	In Frisian and Dutch about equally (%)	In Dutch more often than Frisian (%)	Always in Dutch (%)
Father	65.3	1.0	0.0	4.1	29.6
Mother	68.4	1.0	2.0	2.0	26.5
Brothers and sisters	64.6	2.0	1.0	3.0	29.3
Friends in the classroom	5.1	38.4	17.2	14.1	25.3
Friends outside school	19.2	35.4	9.1	8.1	28.3
Teachers	1.0	13.1	20.2	33.3	32.3
Neighbours	43.4	20.2	6.1	3.0	27.3

Table 6.2 Means of communication and language used

	Always in Frisian (%)	In Frisian more often than Dutch (%)	In Frisian and Dutch about equally (%)	In Dutch more often than Frisian (%)	Always in Dutch (%)
Watching TV	17.7	9.4	8.3	31.3	33.3
The press	10.4	6.3	6.3	28.1	49.0
Music	10.5	7.4	8.4	29.5	44.2
Listening to the radio	10.5	8.4	7.4	33.7	40.0

Table 6.3 Importance attached to the Frisian language in the following activities

For people to:	Important (%)	A little important (%)	Relatively unimportant (%)	Unimportant (%)
Make friends	24.2	35.4	28.3	12.1
Read	5.1	26.3	58.6	10.1
Write	5.1	23.2	57.6	14.1
Watch TV	2.0	20.2	63.6	14.1
Get a job	15.3	41.8	39.8	3.1
Be liked	5.1	20.2	45.5	29.3
Live in Friesland	50.5	37.4	12.1	0.0
Bring up children	34.3	40.4	17.2	8.1
Go shopping	9.1	16.2	49.5	25.3
Make phone calls	13.1	26.3	43.4	17.2
Pass exams	3.0	15.2	51.5	30.3
Be accepted in the community	16.2	29.3	41.4	13.1
Talk to friends at college	16.2	28.3	41.4	14.1
Talk to teachers at college	7.1	29.3	42.4	21.2
Talk to people out of college	15.2	29.3	36.4	19.2

activities. Table 6.3 gives an overview of the results. A striking result here is that, as a whole, the students attach little importance to the Frisian language for a great number of activities. The most negative result is found for the importance attached to Frisian for passing exams. It seems a safe guess that this reflects the low position of Frisian in the domain of education (see pp. 148ff.). Yet there are four activities in which Frisian is observed as being important: making friends, getting a job, bringing up children and, most markedly, living in Friesland. The latter presumably signifies that Frisian is seen as functional in terms of the broader society.

Up until now we have dealt with students' self-reported language proficiency and language use. We now direct our attention to students' attitudes towards the three languages at issue. To begin with, Figure 6.5 depicts the attitudes of the future teachers towards Frisian, Dutch and English. From Figure 6.5 it may be concluded that unfavourable attitudes towards the three languages are rare. As regards the Dutch language, it was even found that no students at all held negative opinions towards the dominant language. In this sense it may be stated that the national language of the Netherlands is 'undisputed'. As regards the attitudes towards Frisian and Dutch, it may be observed that the future teachers' attitudes were (mostly) favourable or neutral. Regarding English, we note that most students (58.6%) are neutrally orientated towards the foreign language. A good third of the students (34.3%) was favourably orientated towards English.

Relating a number of independent variables to students' attitudes towards the three languages under scrutiny, the first finding was that gender exerted no statistically significant influence on students' attitudes towards Frisian ($t = -1.005$, $p = 0.318$) and English ($t = 0.243$, $p = 0.808$). However, male students were significantly more positively orientated towards Dutch than were female students ($t = 1.995$, $p = 0.049$).

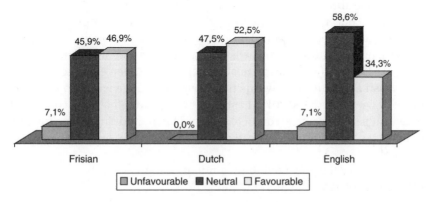

Figure 6.5 Attitudes towards the three languages

In relation to the students' socioprofessional status,[1] no significant group differences were found in attitudes towards Frisian ($t = -1.458$, $p = 0.148$), Dutch ($t = 0.870$, $p = 0.387$) or English ($t = 1.048$, $p = 0.297$). We therefore conclude that there is no significant relationship between socioprofessional status and attitude towards the three languages.

By contrast, the students' first language did have a notable influence upon their attitudes towards the three languages. The strongest influence of students' L1 was found in relation to attitudes towards the minority language ($F2, 94 = 32.884, p = 0.000$).[2] Scheffe multiple comparison testing proved that L1 Frisian students had more favourable attitudes towards Frisian than did bilingual (Frisian/Dutch) and L1 Dutch students, whereas the bilingual students had more positive attitudes than did L1 Dutch students. There was also a clear L1-based difference in the attitudes towards Dutch ($F2, 95 = 19.245$, $p = 0.000$). There was a significant contrast between the (less favourable) attitudes of the L1 Frisian students and the (more favourable) attitudes of L1 Dutch and bilingual students. Note that attitudes towards Dutch were not statistically different between the latter two groups. Lastly, we found a significant L1 effect on attitudes towards the foreign language ($F2, 95 = 3.824$, $p = 0.025$). Multiple comparison testing revealed a significant difference between the attitudes to English of only L1 Dutch and L1 Frisian students, the former being more positively orientated towards English.

Worthy of mention here is that neither age at which these future teachers began learning English, nor whether they had ever visited an English-speaking country had any effect on their attitudes towards English. Similarly, neither the age at which learning English began, nor having visited an English-speaking country could be related to students' self-perceived competence in English.

Finally, it was investigated whether students' self-perceived competence in the three languages was linked to their attitudes towards the languages concerned. It turned out that there was a significant correlation in each case. The correlation between self-perceived competence in Frisian and attitudes towards Frisian turned out to be the highest ($R2 = 0.645, p < 0.001$). The correlation between self-perceived competence in English and attitude towards the foreign language was also relatively high ($R2 = 0.575$, $p < 0.001$). Lastly, it was found that the correlation between self-perceived competence in Dutch and attitudes towards Dutch was, although statistically significant, much lower ($R2 = 0.219$, $p < 0.04$).

To wind up this last section on students' language attitudes, Table 6.4 briefly summarises the aforementioned outcomes.

Table 6.4 Overview of influential variables on language attitudes and self-perceived competence in English

Independent variable	Attitudes towards Frisian	Attitudes towards Dutch	Attitudes towards English	Competence in English
Gender	n.s.	Male > female	n.s.	—
L1	Frisian > bilingual Bilingual > Dutch	Frisian < bilingual/ Dutch	Dutch > Frisian	—
Socioprofessional status	n.s.	n.s.	n.s.	—
Age at which began to learn English	—	—	n.s.	n.s.
Ever visited an English-speaking country	—	—	n.s.	n.s.

Summary and Discussion

As far as Frisian language proficiency is concerned, the research findings reported in this contribution indicate that reading, and especially writing in Frisian, seems to present difficulties for many future teachers. It goes without saying that this results from the weak position of Frisian in primary and secondary schooling (see Section 2). It should also be borne in mind that these students are able to choose to learn Frisian orthography during their second year of study. Most students do so, as writing ability is a requirement for formal qualification to teach the minority language in Frisian primary schools. Regarding English language proficiency, a majority of students reported an ability to understand and read English '(very) well'. The fact that English is typologically related to these students' mother tongue (Frisian or Dutch) is probably beneficial in this regard. But the finding might also be mentioned here that many students (66%) regularly (i.e. at least once or twice a week) watched TV in English. However, students' active knowledge of English was far less developed. A small proportion of the future teachers (3%) even claimed to be unable to speak English, and 47% said they could speak English only at a low level ('a little'). Comparable figures were found as regards writing ability in English (3% 'not' and 43% 'a little'). It is far from easy to explain students' low active knowledge of English, but it seems not unlikely that the educational background of the current students plays a role here. This in the sense that nowadays a considerable proportion of students enrolled at teacher-training colleges in the Netherlands (for CHN about 40%) have previously completed a course of study in secondary vocational education (MBO) during which relatively little attention is paid to foreign-language teaching.

Given that these future teachers will have to teach English at primary level, the above-mentioned statistics on students' self-perceived English-language proficiency are rather worrying. In view of this it is pretty remarkable that over two thirds of the students (68%) *did not agree* with the statement worded 'CHN teacher-training college should be partially in English'. Evidently, many students do not see the need to further improve their foreign-language proficiency through an English-language immersion programme.

Regarding language use, it was found that a majority of the students spoke Frisian in informal settings (at home or with neighbours) whereas the language used in the more formal setting of education frequently shifted to Dutch. In view of this pattern of language use it is remarkable that a relatively large number of students were in favour of the use of Frisian as the medium of instruction during their training programme. It turned out, namely, that 63% of the students *agreed* with the statement 'CHN teacher-training college should be partially in Frisian'. This is, in our opinion, certainly something to be taken into account if CHN wants to improve Frisian-language ability among its teacher-training college students. There would seem to be a basis, as far as students are concerned, for the use of Frisian as vehicle of instruction during teacher-training courses.

Rather negative findings were observed in connection with the use of Frisian in various means of communication, and in relation to the importance attached to Frisian. Dutch was shown to be by far the more prominent language in each of the four means of communication presented to the students (radio, TV, newspapers/magazines and music). Likewise, it was demonstrated that the students attached little importance to the Frisian language in relation to a great number of activities. Nevertheless, there were a number of activities in which Frisian was observed to be important. A vast majority of the students felt that Frisian was important for people to live in Friesland. In all likelihood this signifies that the minority language is viewed as functional within the broader society.

Looking at students' language attitudes, we found no students holding negative attitudes towards Dutch. The future teachers' attitudes towards Frisian and Dutch were (mostly) favourable or neutral. As far as English was concerned, a majority of students was neutrally oriented towards the foreign language, and a good third favourably oriented towards English. However, the students did not respond positively to every single item concerning the English language. A clear example here was the item worded 'I prefer to be taught in English'. Over two thirds of the students (70%) disagreed with this.

An interesting point of concern is whether students' attitudes towards Frisian, Dutch and English are influenced by factors such as gender, first language and (socioprofessional) status, or whether the attitudes are in fact fairly stable personal attributes. The outcomes revealed that gender did not exert a significant influence upon students' attitudes towards Frisian and English. This is in line with recent outcomes reported by Benedictus (2005). However, it was found in our study that male students were more positively orientated towards Dutch than were female students, so it cannot be concluded that gender entirely fails to influence students' language attitudes.

Benedictus (2005) recently observed that teacher-training college students' attitudes towards Frisian were linked to their social status in the sense that high-status students showed less positive attitudes towards Frisian. This finding is in keeping with the general pattern observed within Friesland, namely that positive attitudes towards Frisian decrease as social status increases (see Gorter *et al.*, 1984; Gorter & Ytsma, 1988). In this respect it is remarkable that the current study revealed no status-based attitudinal differences whatsoever.

The crucial factor influencing future teachers' attitudes towards Frisian, Dutch and English is their first language. Students evidently prefer their own language. For L1 Frisian students this implies that they have more positive attitudes towards Frisian than do L1 Dutch students. Similarly, L1 Dutch students display more positive attitudes towards Dutch than do L1 Frisian students. Finally, it was shown that L1 Dutch students were more positively orientated towards English than L1 Frisian students.

The fact that we found considerable L1-based differences in students' attitudes towards the three languages investigated, combined with the fact that these three languages form an integral part of the school curriculum at primary level, argues in favour of a language-awareness programme at CHN teacher-training college. An earlier study conducted among teacher training students in The Netherlands showed that changing language attitudes within education was indeed attainable (Münstermann, 1988). Interestingly, Münstermann's research pointed out that a combination of two strategies – persuasive communication (on Dutch dialect) and active participation (in dialect experiences) – had an effect on the measured attitudes of teacher-training college students' attitudes towards dialect. Lastly, it is worthy of mention that a study by Gorter and Ytsma (1988) indicated, in line with Münstermann's study, that it was possible to induce a shift in (vocational-school) students' attitudes towards Frisian. The Frisian study demonstrated that the linguistic background of the students was related to the process of change in language attitude. The (more positive) language attitude of Frisian-speaking students shifted in a (even more) positive direction, while the (less positive) language attitude of non-Frisian-speaking students did not. Such outcomes warn us against too much optimism when it comes to the mutability of language attitudes.

Notes

1. For numerical reasons (*n* per group) two status groups were distinguished here (in contrast to the tripartite distinction in Section 4.1): high status (categories 1–3) versus medium–low status (the other categories).
2. Note that the size of the three groups distinguished differed considerably (see the second part of Section 4), which may somewhat complicate interpretation of the findings of the ANOVA conducted.

References

Benedictus, J. (2005) *Over Fries gesproken... Een onderzoek naar taalhouding en drietaligheid bij Pabo-studenten in Friesland*. Doctoraalscriptie, Rijksuniversiteit Groningen.

Commissie Friese-Taalpolitiek (1970) *Rapport van de Commissie Friese-Taalpolitiek*. Den Haag: Ministerie van Cultuur, Recreatie en Maatschappelijk werk.

De Bot, C.J. (1994) *Waarom deze rede niet in het Engels is*. Nijmegen: Hertogenbosch.

Deelstra, H. and Ytsma, J. (2005) Onderzoeksresultaten groep 3 en 4 project Drietalige Basisschool/Onderzoeksresultaten groep 5 en 6 project Drietalige Basisschool. Fryske Akademy, unpublished manuscripts.

De Goede, M.P.M., Jansma, L.G., Van Ophem, J.A.C. and Verhaar, C.H.A. (1994) *Jongeren in Friesland.* Ljouwert/Leeuwarden: Fryske Akademy.

De Jong, S. and Riemersma, A.M.J. (1994) *Taalpeiling in Fryslân. Onderzoek naar de beheersing van het Fries en het Nederlands aan het einde van de basisschool.* Ljouwert: Fryske Akademy.

Extra, G. and Kloprogge, J. (2000) *Meertaligheid in Leeuwarden. De status van allochtone talen thuis en op school.* Tilburg/Utrecht: Babylon/Sardes.

Foekema, H. (2004) *Overdracht van de Friese taal.* Amsterdam: TNS/NIPO.

Gerritsen, M. (1996) Engelstalige productadvertenties in Nederland: Onbemind en onbegrepen. In R. van Hout and J. Kruijsen (eds) *Taalvariaties. Toonzettingen en modulaties op een thema* (pp. 67–83). Dordrecht: Foris Publications.

Gorter, D. (2005) Three languages of instruction in Fryslân. *International Journal of the Sociology of Language* 171, 57–73.

Gorter, D. and Jonkman, R.J. (1995) *Taal yn Fryslân op 'e nij besjoen.* Ljouwert: Fryske Akademy.

Gorter, D. and Ytsma, J. (1988) Social factors and language attitudes in Friesland. In R. Van Hout and U. Knops (eds) *Language Attitudes in the Dutch Language Area* (pp. 59–72). Dordrecht: Foris Publications.

Gorter, D., Jelsma, G., Van der Plank, P. and De Vos, K. (1984) *Taal yn Fryslân.* Ljouwert: Fryske Akademy.

Gorter, D., Riemersma, A. and Ytsma, J. (2001) Frisian in the Netherlands. In G. Extra and D. Gorter (eds) *The Other Languages of Europe* (pp. 103–118). Clevedon: Multilingual Matters.

Inspectie van het Onderwijs (1999) *Fries in de basisvorming. Evaluatie van de eerste vijf jaar.* Utrecht: Inspectie van het Onderwijs.

Lutje Spelberg, H.C. and Postma, B. (1995) Taalattitudes in een tweetalige situatie. *It Beaken* 57 (1), 30–43.

Münstermann, H. (1988) Changing language attitudes in education. In R. van Hout and U. Knops (eds) *Language Attitudes in the Dutch Language Area* (pp. 73–84). Dordrecht: Foris.

Pietersen, L. (1974) *De toekomstige leerkrachten en het Fries: een onderzoek op de pedagogische academies en de opleidingsscholen voor kleuterleidsters in Friesland.* Ljouwert/Leeuwarden: Fryske Akademy.

Ytsma, J. (1990) Taalattitudes op de basisschool in Friesland. *GRAMMA* 14 (2), 169–183.

Ytsma, J. (1995) *Frisian as First and Second Language. Sociolinguistic and Socio-psychological Aspects of the Acquisition of Frisian among Frisian and Dutch Primary School Children.* Ljouwert/Leeuwarden: Fryske Akademy.

Ytsma, J. (2000a) Trilingual primary education in Friesland. In J. Cenoz and U. Jessner (eds) *English in Europe. The Acquisition of a Third Language* (pp. 222–235). Clevedon: Multilingual Matters.

Ytsma, J. (2000b) A trilingual project in primary education in The Netherlands. *The EuroCLIC* 7, 6–7.

Ytsma, J. and De Jong, S. (1993) Frisian. In G. Extra and L. Verhoeven (eds) *Community Languages in The Netherlands* (pp. 29–49). Amsterdam: Swets & Zeitlinger.

Chapter 7
Language Use and Language Attitudes in Ireland

MUIRIS Ó LAOIRE

Introduction

While Ireland is almost universally English speaking, a proportion of the population (currently estimated at 3%) are native balanced bilinguals, speaking Irish (Gaelic) as well as English, residing mainly in the *Gaeltachtaí* (the Irish-language speech community). A further 10% of the population could be described as balanced but secondary bilinguals, now referred to as neospeakers of Gaelic located mainly outside the Irish language speech community (for detailed statistics on the use of Irish, see the Report of the 2002 National Census at www.cso.ie). For historical reasons, outlined below, Irish is enshrined in the constitution as the first official and national language, with English designated as the second official language.

The sociolinguistic situation with regard to the Irish language has been treated exhaustively elsewhere (Ó hUallacháin, 1994; Ó Laoire, 1996; Ó Riagáin, 1997) to require a long rehearsal here. In brief, Irish belongs to the Celtic branch of the Indo-European family and is estimated to have been brought to Ireland between 500 and 300 BC by invading Celts (Ó Siadhail, 1989: 1). By the end of the 11th century AD, Irish was the primary language of Ireland and Scotland. While some shift to French and English occurred during the Anglo-Norman invasions and colonisations of the 12th and 13th centuries (Risk, 1968; Picard, 2003); this linguistic impact was at first absorbed and a predominantly Irish-speaking Ireland emerged with its cultural traditions remaining distinctive and viable until the Tudor conquests in the 17th century. These conquests led to the dispossession of the native aristocracy and to the demise of the native social, political and cultural institutions. Following the demise of the native cultural institutions, the gradual Anglicisation of the Irish-speaking middle classes followed. The shift to English was particularly rapid during the decades following the Great Famine of 1845–1858. The post-famine percentages for Irish speakers (i.e. 5.33%) have predominantly represented the size of the Irish language speech community to this day. The retreat of the *Gaeltacht* speech community to

Figure 7.1 Map indicating location of *Gaeltachtaí* 2005

a scattering of separate areas predominantly around the Western seaboard (see Figure 7.1) was already determined in these percentages.

After independence in 1922, there were some state corpus planning initiatives, mainly comprising a dual policy of maintenance and restoration, i.e. maintenance of the spoken language in the Gaeltachtaí and its restoration or regeneration through reversal of language shift in all other areas. The latter involved in particular a reintroduction of the language into domains where it had been excluded since the 17th century (Ó Laoire, 2005 forthcoming). The education system was designated as the major institutional means by which such a reversal would be achieved. In fact, the education system became a cornerstone of the movement for the revival and regeneration of Irish in the English-speaking regions. In fact, the espoused planning policies for a language restoration devolved almost entirely on the schools. The government's aim for the immediate inclusion of Irish as a core curriculum subject, simply stated, was to gradually replace English with Irish as the sole medium of instruction in all subjects (Ó Buachalla, 1984; 1988; Ó Domhnalláin, 1977). This meant that Irish in primary and postprimary education became what Flynn (1993: 79) has termed, a 'politically-based curriculum subject', i.e. a subject taught to bolster the government's aim of fostering an Irish-speaking identity on behalf of the nation.

The leaders of the separatist Irish-Ireland (Ó Laoire, 1999) movement propagated the view that Irish, being the ancestral language of the country, was *ipso facto*, the most distinctive mark of Irish ethnicity. The language was also projected significantly as belonging predominantly to parts of rural Ireland and appeared to be dislocated from the growing urban consciousness of the 1960s, 1970s and 1980s. This was the predominant essentialist view that fuelled the revitalisation movement.

The dual policy of restoration mainly through the education system and of maintenance of the language as a spoken language in the *Gaeltachtaí* was subject to considerable modification as its implementation was pursued with a considerable deal of determination and commitment and with varying degrees of success. The overall result of this status and acquisition planning was an increase in the ration of Irish speakers outside the Gaeltacht and a decrease in the indigenous Irish speakers and users in the Irish-speaking regions. To speak about results in terms of increase and decrease, however, is an oversimplification masking important spatial and social shifts in the designation of what was to constitute an Irish-language speech community. The sociopolitical contextualisation of efforts of Irish-language maintenance and regeneration competing against the predominance of English has formed the general discourse for language planning in Ireland.

Successive surveys since the mid-1970s continue to show a considerable majority of respondents favouring the use of Irish and the provision for the language in education, and significantly, with 65%+ of the population regarding Irish as essential to the maintenance of a distinctive cultural identity.

The current state of the language provides some grounds for a cautious optimism about its survival in the 21st century. Over the last decades, the shift of emphasis has been from a language revival to a language survival in the new millennium (Ó hÉallaithe, 2004). The establishment of an Irish-channel TV, TG4 in 1997 (Watson, 2003), has contributed to a rejuvenation of the image of the language, particularly among young people. Over 270,000 (6.75%) people, for example, watch *Ros na Rún*, TG4's popular soap opera, on any given week. The Official Languages Act was singed into law in 2003. The Act is the first piece of legislation to provide a statutory framework for the delivery of services through the Irish language. There are concerns, however, regarding the language's ultimate survival. While returns from census and surveys of Irish speakers tend to be interpreted polemically, the fact that school-going children continue to conflate percentages of users shows the shaky precarious position of Irish bilingualism. While some shift to Irish has occurred as a result of a language-in-education policy and planning, it has not secured home bilingual reproduction and intergenerational transmission to any considerable extent. Favourable attitudes towards the language do not appear to translate into motivation for active use or for deliberate language shift in the home domain. In spite of the positive attitudes to the language and the momentum of individuals, families and voluntary organisations involved in the language movement, home bilingualism does not appear to be gaining ground. In recent times, the state's reactive response to language pressure or lobbying groups mark a new devolvement of central responsibility. Here the state may have more success by cooperating with grassroots movements rather than opposing them. It is only in recent times that the languages of minorities are becoming legitimated and institutionalised in the public domain (May, 2001) and it is in local decisions that planning has its ultimate impact (Kaplan & Baldauf, 1997).

It has been commented on recently that the only true bilingual areas are the Gaeltacht (Ó hÉallaithe, 2004) and that the concept of a language revival outside the Gaeltacht is illusory. Here the language along with the new immigrant home languages may only in time have a ritual function in what may be a continuing long-term *durée*. Future status planning may be driven more by an ecological desire to maintain an important place for Irish in the linguistic diversity of a multicultural Ireland. It is likely in a broader global context that efforts at language revitalisation focusing on language rights and human development will continue to coexist and survive more easily with globalisation than with national states (Wright, 2004); hence, the recreation of identity and the motivation (Ager, 2001) to chart language planning for Irish in this changing context for many years to come.

The Irish Education System

Overall responsibility for most aspects of the education system lies with the Department of Education and Science. Primary education comprises eight years with both English and Irish viewed as core curriculum subjects. A characteristic feature of the Irish primary and postprimary school system is that the curriculum can be mediated in two languages, Irish and English. The choice of language as the medium of instruction is contingent, variously, on location, linguistic experience, cultural history, and the cultural aspiration of parents and the community (Ó Murchú, 2001).

In terms of language, there are three types of school within the system of education at both primary and postprimary levels:

(1) schools in which English is the medium of instruction,
(2) schools in English-speaking areas of the country in which Irish is the medium of instruction, which are termed *Gaelscoileanna* (all-Irish medium schools), and

(3) schools in Gaeltacht areas in which Irish is the medium of
    instruction.

Such a configuration of provision raises significant issues and challenges for language teaching and learning and for curriculum development in the language.

A revised curriculum for Irish as an L2 was introduced in Irish
secondary schools in the 1990s and in primary schools in 2000. This
curriculum was based on new insights into language development, with
implications for the design of new courses and materials. This was to
counteract unsatisfactory findings with regard to the syllabi then in
place. The traditional grammar translation method, which became
synonymous with the direct method, characterised the teaching of Irish
for many years. In the 1970s, these methods were supplanted by the
structuralist and behaviourist-orientated audiolingual method. The Irish
curriculum was often criticised at the beginning of the 1980s. The aims of
Irish courses were found too be vague and unrealistic, with no graded
objectives. Fluency was expected at all stages of schooling. There was
also concern expressed about the deterioration in the standard of Irish
including an overemphasis on literature in the syllabus and unsatisfactory teaching practices encouraged by the examination system (CEB,
1985). Dissatisfaction was also directed at the excessive prominence of
reading and writing. Students and teachers were said to be 'frustrated'
by a syllabus that did not facilitate development of oral competency
(CEB, 1985: 29).

Most of the 1980s and 1990s were taken up, therefore, with syllabus
reform to make the language more accessible and relevant to all students
and to lower the rates of failure. The adoption of communicative-type
syllabi in both junior and senior cycle programmes was undertaken
deliberately by the National Council for Curriculum and Assessment
(NCCA) with this background of malaise and with the objectives of
accessibility and relevance in mind.The Irish-language speech communities (*Pobal na Gaeilge*) include both the territorially defined *Gaeltachtaí*
(Irish speaking regions), as well as a growing number of networks of Irish
outside these regions. Unlike the *Gaeltacht* where the student of Irish, who
may have the support mechanism and neighbourhood domains in
sustaining his proficiency through daily use of the language, the school
alone, for the learner of Irish as L2 outside the *Gaeltacht*, may indeed be the
only source of language learning and interlanguage development.
Learning Irish in school all too often is not reinforced by participation
in, and integration into, the speech community. Irish-speaking networks
outside *Gaeltacht* have never been sufficiently numerous to form a readily
identifiable and easily visible speech community.

The shift to communicative language teaching has been by and large useful in language instruction for bilingualism but the underlying potential to foster bilingualism in the English-speaking areas has been untapped to a considerable extent (Ó Laoire, 2005). The implementation of a communicative syllabus involved a transition from 'school Irish' to everyday Irish. The term 'school Irish' denotes a certain type of attenuated and oversimplified language unrelated to a large extent to the Irish of everyday use. It is, nonetheless, the type of Irish that one encounters regularly in situations where the Irish language is used outside the *Gaeltacht*. With the introduction of the new communicative-type syllabus, perhaps there was a new expectation that the second-level syllabus somehow would teach students to speak everyday Irish and that this would in turn lead to an extension of bilingualism outside the *Gaeltacht*. There is no evidence, however, that this has occurred.

A third language is not generally included in the primary curriculum. A recent pilot initiative has resulted, however, in other European languages (mainly French, German, Italian and Spanish) being taught at primary level. An initiative introduced in 1997 to teach another European language other than Irish and English in primary school was the first official attempt by the Department of Education and Science to integrate L3 into the learning experience of children at that level. Attention had focused through the 1990s on research (e.g. Singleton, 1992) that suggested that instruction in second language be initiated as early as material, social and educational conditions were such as to favour a positive, enjoyable and nonthreatening experience. As well as stressing the metalinguistic, cognitive, educational and cultural benefits of learning a foreign language in primary school, it was hoped to address glaring inequalities in the system where only a minority of primary-school children benefited from the provision of an L3, often determined by an ability to pay for it. A survey conducted by the Irish Primary Teachers Association (INTO) in 1991 showed that 23.8% of all primary schools had made 'private' provision for the teaching of an L3 with instruction taking place in the majority of cases (65.6%) outside school hours on a fee-paying basis. In 1997, 270 schools were selected from over 1300 applicant primary schools to participate in what is known as the Pilot Project for Modern Languages in Primary Schools. In the interest of language diversification, schools were given the option of choosing Italian, Spanish, German or French for 1.5 h/week. There is a sustained growth in the number of schools participating in what is now called an initiative. In 2001, 299 schools were involved and this has risen to 377 in the current academic year (2003), with 53 schools (14.5%) offering Spanish, 91 schools (24.1%) offering German and 0.4% offering Italian, with French being taught in over half of schools, 216 (57.3%). At present the pedagogical applications of the initiative include a cross-curricular approach with several sets of learning and teaching aims within

Table 7.1 Exposure to languages within the Irish education system

	Hours primary	*Hours postprimary*	*Total hours*
English 13 years	1480	648	2128
Irish 13 years	1480	648	2128
Other languages 3–5 years		377	377

a single cross-curricular activity (Furlong & Moran, 2001). An evaluation report for the first two years of the pilot project has been recently published (Harris & Conway, 2003) and the NCCA, on the basis of this report, will assess the feasibility of introducing an L3 at primary level on a national basis.

At postprimary level, students continue with their study of Irish and English and generally one or two European languages for a further three to five years. Thus students have exposure to language within the education context as shown in Table 7.1.

English, however, is the medium of instruction for all subjects except in the Irish-medium schools. Generally speaking the percentages of students who study the different languages can be gleaned from the examination performance statistics published annually by the Department of Education and Science. In 2001, an analysis of the Junior Certificate level, a proficiency examination taken after three years at postprimary school, shows the percentage of students presenting for languages in terms of a percentage of the overall examination cohort (Table 7.2). These figures show that the vast majority of students at junior cycle, postprimary are exposed to L2 and L3.

In the final examination, the Leaving Certificate, for which candidates present after a further two years of study and on which entry into tertiary level largely depends, the situation is as shown in Table 7.3. Apart from a slight drop in the numbers presenting for an L3, the proportions remain stable, indicating an overall preference for French, which may have as much or indeed more to do with the wide availability of subject and tradition in schools than with student choice. In the examination of that year, it is interesting to note that 0.25% presented for Arabic with numbers under 10 presenting for Dutch, Portuguese, Swedish, Japanese, Finnish and Hebrew. The Department of Education and Science, through a recent initiative, are committed to the desirability of greater diversification in the foreign languages on offer in the curriculum.

Table 7.2 Percentages of students studying languages at Junior Certificate level 2001

N = 60,124 students
69.4% French
21.6% German
3.1% Spanish
1.27% Italian
92.9% Irish
98.9% English

Table 7.3 Percentages of students studying languages for Leaving Certificate 2001

N = 51,935 students
65% French
18% German
2.9% Spanish
0.27% Italian
97.8% Irish

Surveys of Language Attitudes

The Committee on Irish Language Attitudes Research (CILAR) was established in 1972 at a time when issues relating to the extension of bilingualism were being considered at a policy level (Ó Murchú, 1970). The aim of CILAR's work was to survey and investigate attitudes towards the Irish language and towards efforts to restore it as a general means of communication. Secondly it sought to examine the extent to which the public would support policy development aimed at restoring Irish as a general means of communication. This was the first large-scale systematic assessment of public attitudes towards Irish. As well as collecting data on language attitudes, it also surveyed language competence and language use in the population, with a separate survey testing language attitudes in the Gaeltacht areas. Since the publication of the final report in 1975, there has been relatively prolific macrosociolinguistic and microlinguistic research on the Irish language.

The study was replicated, with some new questions added in the early 1980s and 1990s as part of an overall approach to regular monitoring of trends in language attitudes and behaviour.

As regards attitudes, the studies found that the average person placed considerable value on the symbolic role of Irish in ethnic identification and as a cultural value in itself.

A majority in each survey, but by no means an overwhelming one (1973: 72%; 1983: 73%; 1993: 66%), agreed that no real Irish person can be against the revival of the language. Some 70% of the respondents declared themselves in favour of an Irish–English bilingualism with the same amount again in favour of the language. There were consider-able variations in attitude, however. The attitudes of persons living in the *Gaeltachtaí* or Gaelic-speaking regions were more favourable than the majority living in English-speaking Ireland. The data in the 1983 and 1993 survey reveal that attitudinal patters changed very little in the course of 20 years. The 1993 data record some appreciable shifts to a more positive stance in some items.

The correlation, however, between favourable language attitudes and language use remains low, i.e. positive attitudes do not necessarily translate into extended use of the language. The context of networks, social pressures and accepted behaviours must be taken into account in order to predict language use more accurately rather than relying on data on declared attitudes.

The current study of Irish students' attitudes to Irish and to the L3 they have studied is located within this general national context described above.

The Irish Study

The sample

The participants in the study were 120 first-year college students enrolled in an education and arts degree programme. The mean age of the subjects was 19 years and 2 months and they were predominantly (92.8%) in the 17–21 age range. The vast majority of students were female (73.5%). The distribution of English to Irish speakers was exactly in a 4:1 ratio (Figure 7.2). One fifth of all the participants had recorded Irish as their L1. But it must be pointed out that these Irish L1 speakers are bilingual, as is the situation in the case of all L1 Irish speakers.

13.3% of students recorded their parental occupation as a manager director or owner of business or company with more than 25 workers, 27.5% were middle class and 42.5% came from working-class families. 80.2% had started to learn Irish as an L2 before the age of eight and 84.1% (101 subjects) embarked on learning the L3 by the age of 11 or 12, with 12.5% (15 subjects) beginning the study of an L3 before the age of 11. As

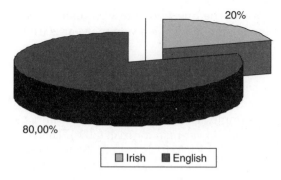

20%

80,00%

☐ Irish   ■ English

Figure 7.2 Language background of respondents

Table 7.4 Percentages of different L3s being studied

Language	%
French	54.6
German	17.5
Spanish	8.3
Other	10.4

indicated above, Irish students generally tend to study French, German or Spanish or Italian as an L3. The vast majority of students study French as the main L3. This is reflected in the responses of students here. The proportion of students studying the different L3s available in the Irish education system, therefore, is as shown in Table 7.4.

As for contact with the L3, well over half of all students had been to the country where the L3 was spoken, although it is unclear what exposure they had to speaking or using the language, nor was the length of exposure specified. Students in secondary schools in Ireland often tend to visit the country of their L3 (generally France, Belgium or Germany) as part of an annual school tour, where the emphasis tends to be on cultural rather than linguistic exposure. Less than 3% reported always watching TV in French, Spanish or German. This is a surprisingly low finding given that satellite and digital TV is available with stations available through the foreign languages in question in this survey. The extent of their competence emerged, however, from the data in response to self-report on language proficiency below.

The instrument and the procedure

The instrument and the procedure used in this study were the same as those followed by all the contributors to this volume, as explained in the introductory chapter. The questionnaire was distributed to two tertiary institutions at the beginning of the academic year 2004 in English.

Results

The data on self-reported level of competence (Figure 7.3) yielded some interesting findings. The number of students who classified themselves, for example, as having a very good competence in English (15%) was significantly lower than for Irish (30%). This may be due to the fact that students whose L1 is Irish are taught the same curriculum as Irish L2 students, often achieving very high grades. The achievement of high grades might be due to the fact that students are tested in aural and reading comprehension, both components for which there is a significant weighting of marks. This may have given rise to the perception that Irish is, in fact, an 'easier' subject in which one can achieve high grades. Also, the proportion of respondents who rated themselves as being good in the L3 (78.1%) is remarkably high. The respondents had an opportunity to study a foreign language to academic BA level and sometimes to MA level as part of their teacher education. The informants were obviously following these L3 programmes and thus figures appear somewhat inflated.

The pattern of language use shows that English is the dominant language of most of the respondents both in home, college and neigh-bourhood domains. The results here point to the limited use of the Irish language in the home domain.

From Table 7.4, the pattern of language use indicating minimal linguistic interaction in Irish is evident. In general, 70.6% of the informants always use English in the home domain, as against 4.28% who use Irish. The ratio of Irish use is lower in the case of language use with friends: 1.6% ($n = 2$) compared to 90.1% in the case of English. The fact that 40.4% respondents use Irish by contract in contact with teachers indicates the school- or

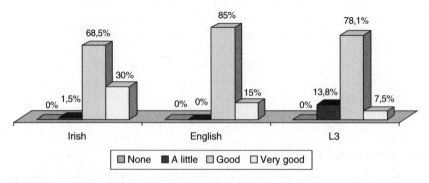

Figure 7.3 Level of competence in the three languages

education-orientated use of the language. The percentage diminishes again in relation to the use of Irish (always in Irish or Irish more than English) in the neighbourhood domain, i.e. 3.9%, which is higher than, but still consistent with, the percentage reported in the use of Irish among friends. This indicates that the use of the Irish language decreases very significantly outside the school sphere (Table 7.5). This reflects the commentary in the opening section on the use of Irish in sociolinguistic contexts, indicating a need to promote the use of Irish in youth friendship networks and youth culture as well as the assertion that Irish has mainly been and continues to be a school activity. The home and neighbourhood domains are crucial contexts for intergenerational transmission, and if the language is contracted in these contexts, as it appears to be from these figures, it does not augur well for language maintenance, regeneration and revitalisation.

Similar to Basque (see Lasagabaster, this volume), the Irish-only means of communication (see Table 7.6) appears also to be minimal among the future teachers, again with a predominance of English very noticeable.

It is significant that between one-fifth and a quarter of all respondents report watching Irish-medium and English-medium TV in equal measure. This reflects a growing interest in the Irish-medium TV, TG4. This channel, initially called *Teilifís na Gaeilge*, started broadcasting in 1996. Unlike Raidió na Gaeltachta (all-Irish radio station), the Irish-medium radio channel, which primarily targets the Gaeltacht audience, the TV channel, now called TG4, sought and continues to seek a share of the national audience, claiming in its website that around 20% of viewers tune in to the station at some point each day. With a strong commitment to quality production and entertainment, the station aims to serve the interests and needs of all groups with some knowledge of Irish. The TV medium appears to be more attractive than the print media, however, with significantly less numbers here accessing knowledge and entertainment. Here too attention is drawn to the fact that English predominates in pop music with 83.3% listening to music through English and 0% of respondents listening to music through the medium of Irish.

However, if all the percentages corresponding to the five different categories are added up, the percentages of use of the Irish language is low: 6.68% (always in Irish) and 14.9% (nearly always in Irish).

As far as the importance attached to the Irish language is concerned (see Table 7.7), Irish is not considered important to go shopping 90%, with 90% considering it unimportant when it comes to being liked and 91% considering the language unimportant when one has to make phone calls. So Irish is not important when it comes to carrying out everyday activities and significantly in creating networks and friendships.

On the other hand, the activities in which Irish is perceived to be important concern more utilitarian motivations in student life, i.e. passing

Table 7.5 Language used when talking to the following people

	Always in Irish (%)	In Irish more often than English (%)	In Irish and English about equally (%)	In English more often than Irish (%)	Always in English (%)
Father	4.16	4.16	5.0	5.0	70.3
Mother	6.6	4.16	5.0	10.0	68.5
Brothers and sisters	2.1	4.5	4.16	15	73
Friends in the classroom	1.6	1.6	0.83	12.3	74
Friends outside school	0.83	0.83	0.83	0.83	90.1
Teachers	30.1	10.3	10.6	30.1	17.7
Neighbours	1.6	3.3	3.3	10	75.8

Table 7.6 Means of communication and language used

	Always in Irish (%)	In Irish more often than English (%)	In Irish and English about equally (%)	In English more often than Irish (%)	Always in English (%)
Watching TV	0.83	7.5	23.6	58.3	8.3
The press	0	1.6	2.5	17.5	80.5
Music	0	0	0	17.5	83.3
Listening to the radio	5.8	5.8	1.6	19.8	18.9

Table 7.7 Importance attached to Irish in daily usage

For people to:	Important (%)	A little important (%)	A little unimportant (%)	Unimportant (%)
Make friends	10.1	8.2	38.4	42.0
Read	12.0	6.9	20.4	55.5
Write	10.1	1.8	30.5	48.5
Watch TV	1.6	5.5	28.0	59.0
Get a job	76.1	15.8	7.2	0.9
Be liked	3.2	3.2	39.5	45.7
Live in Ireland	55.1	28.5	10.6	1.6
Bring up children	34.6	20.1	10.6	15.5
Go shopping	1.6	1.6	30.5	59.5
Make phone calls	1.6	6.4	45.5	45.5
Pass exams	70.5	20.2	3.6	0
Be accepted in the community	9.5	20.1	42.9	28.5
Talk to friends at university	30.1	29	25.0	15.0
Talk to teachers at university	45.5	20.5	18.6	13.0
Talk to people out of university	6.5	6.5	55.3	20.5

exams (90.7%), talking to teachers 59% and getting a job (91.9%). Participants agree then on the important utilitarian role that the Irish language plays in their lives as students hoping to enter teaching and perhaps other professions where knowledge of the language is a prerequisite to securing employment.When analysing the attitudes towards the three languages in contact at school (Figure 7.4), one notices that students' L1 appears to have most impact on their attitudes to the L3 (Table 7.8).

As in the case of the Basque context, unfavourable attitudes towards English (the L3) being most prominent among the Basque-speaking respondents, here too unfavourable attitudes to the L3 are to be found more among Irish as L1 students. 23.5% of Irish as L1 speakers display a less than positive attitude both to English and the L3. In the case of attitudes among English as L1 students, the attitudes appear to be more positive with as low as 2.5% showing unfavourable attitudes. The attitude of Irish as L1 students towards Irish were of course more favourable to Irish than the English as L1 students ($F = 9.869$; $p < 0.001$). As regards attitudes to the L3, those with English as an L1 were more favourably disposed also towards the L3 ($F = 2.13$; $p < 0.020$). This reflects a finding of an earlier study (Lasagabaster & Ó Laoire, forthcoming). This study showed that a high proportion of Irish as L1 students of L3 displayed significant negative (nonintegrative type) attitudes to the L3. The same held true for the Basque situation to lead the authors to remark: 'This may be due to strong attachment and commitment that these students have to the language. It is as if "they have no room for any other language" in an attitude underscored by passionate motivation. ... There is no doubt that these results should make the people in the Basque Country and Ireland think about why these students show such a *protective* attitude. The sociolinguistic situation in both contexts, where the minority language is

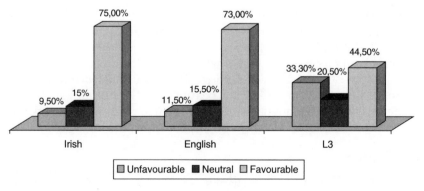

Figure 7.4 Attitudes towards the three languages

Table 7.8 Summary of the most influential variables on language attitudes

Independent variable	Attitudes towards Irish	Attitudes towards English	Attitudes towards L3
Gender	n.s.	n.s.	n.s.
L1	Irish > English	Irish > English	Irish > English
Socioprofessional status	n.s.	n.s	n.s.
Age at which they started to learn L3	n.s	n.s	n.s.
Ever visited an English-speaking country			Yes > no
Knowledge of other foreign languages			Yes > no
Language competence	Irish > English		Irish > English

improving its situation but still lags clearly behind the majority language (Spanish and English respectively) may be the reason behind these results'.

Some of the more salient findings here are:

	Irish as L1	English as L1
I like hearing L3 spoken	SA: 29% (7/24)	SA: 58% (50/86)
L3 should be taught to all	SD: 25% (6/24)	SD: 6.9% (6/84)
I prefer to be taught in L3	SD: 87.5 (21/34)	SD: 6.9% (6/84)

The age at which the students set out to learn L3 did not appear to have an effect on their attitudes towards the foreign language. Those who had visited the L3 country had an impact on their attitudes, with these students being more favourable towards the L3 than those who had not ($F = 9.869$; $p < 0.001$). The self-reported level of competence in the Irish language seemed also to have a bearing on the attitudes to the L3. Students whose first language was Irish or who had self-reported high competence were not as favourably disposed towards the L3 ($p < 0.001$).

Discussion

The main objective of this chapter was to examine the language use and language attitudes of university students who were perhaps embarking on careers as teachers. This study, in line with the findings on language attitudes in the national surveys (CILAR, 1975; Ó Riagáin & Ó Gliasáin, 1983, 1993), reveals that a majority of the student teachers surveyed revealed positive attitudes to the Irish language. The positive utilitarian-type attitude here, however, is linked to the prospect of securing employment. The vast majority (91.9%) sees Irish as being very important or a little important in getting a job (Table 7.7). This is not surprising, as student teachers are expected to have a reasonably high competence in Irish to qualify to work as a teacher in a primary school and to work as a subject teacher of Irish in a secondary school.

Further glimpses into the pragmatic or utilitarian nature of their attitudes towards the language can be gleaned from the data. Irish is regarded as very important in passing examinations (90.7%) and in talking to teachers (59%). It is significant however that 83.6% of respondents also judged a knowledge of Irish to be very important or important to live in Ireland. This finding would appear to confirm the statistical data of the three national surveys (CILAR, 1975; Ó Riagáin & Ó Gliasáin, 1983, 1993), where over 75% of respondents expressed support for and positive attitudes towards the societal presence of the Irish language.

The symbolic role of the Irish language in ethnic identification continues to constitute an important element in attitudes to Irish. This seemingly strong belief, however, may constitute more of a passive stance rather than a proactive attitude. The results here show clearly that the favourable attitude does not translate into active language use. The pattern of language use shows clearly that English is the dominant language of most of the respondents both in home, college and neighbourhood domains and illustrates that Irish is not considered important when it comes to carrying out the everyday activities and significantly in creating networks and friendships. English predominates in pop music with 83.3% listening to music through English. The fact that almost a quarter of respondents state that they watch Irish language TV is a testament to the growing influence of the Irish-language media in effecting change in Irish people's language behaviour. TV can transmit positive attitudes to Irish through youthful vibrant imagery and discourses and ensures that the home is no longer the sole domain of English; nevertheless, no one realistically expects that a family will change its language simply by watching Irish language programmes. It may not initially alter the language of the home domain, as it operates chiefly in activating or reactivating the receptive (understanding) rather than the productive (speaking) skills, but over time it could cause changes in attitudes (see Ó Laoire, 2001).

The attitudinal measurement here was componential and a more revealing picture of the type and extent of attitudes emerges within a range of more specific items relating to the attitudes to the third language. While attitudes to the L3 (French, German or Spanish) were generally positive, unfavourable attitudes towards the L3 are to be found more among Irish as L1 students. 23.5% of Irish as L1 speakers display a less than positive attitude both to English and the L3. In the case of attitudes among English as L1 students, the attitudes appear to be more positive, with only a very small percentage, 2.5%, showing unfavourable attitudes. When it comes to analysing the effect of the different independent variables, it was observed that the only variable that was definitive was the language background of the informants. Those whose L1 is Irish and whose attitude to Irish is positive do not appear to transfer this positive attitude to the L3. This may well be due to a heightened sense of loyalty to the minority Irish language and to a sense of protectionism against the other wider languages of communication they encounter in the education system (English, French, Spanish and German). Further qualitative-type ethnographic direct studies are required to explore this 'hostility' factor further.

This study uncovers a strong link between linguistic attitudes and behaviours in the home and in school. It shows clearly that while there is strong support for the Irish language generally, there is no evidence of increasing use of Irish in the home domain, with the exception of significantly growing numbers watching Irish-medium television. Academic performance and employment prerequisites underscore the importance of Irish for this young generation of well educated students who within a short period of time will exert an important influence as teachers on their students' attitudes to language. The fact, however, that the use of Irish in everyday domains and the fact that positive attitudes are not being converted into language use continues to pose a serious challenge to language planners and educators in Ireland.

References

Ager, D. (2001) *Motivation in Language Planning and Language Policy.* Clevedon: Multilingual Matters.

Committee on Irish Language Attitudes Research (CILAR) (1975) *Report.* Dublin: The Stationery Office.

Flynn, D. (1993) Irish in the school curriculum: A matter of politics. *The Irish Review* 14, 74–80.

Furlong, Á. and Moran, M. (2001) Policy and pedagogy in planning for the pilot project for modern languages in primary schools in Ireland. Paper read at IRAAL Conference: Language Education in Ireland: Current Practice and Future Trends. Language Centre, Maynooth, October 2001.

Harris, J. and Conway, M. (2003) *Teaching Foreign Languages in the Primary School.* Dublin: ITÉ.

Kaplan, R. and Baldauf, R. (1997) *Language Planning: From Practice to Theory.* Clevedon: Multilingual Matters.

Lasagabaster, D. and Ó Laoire, M. (forthcoming) Attitudes towards trilingualism: A comparison between the Basque and Irish contexts. To appear in *Teanga*. IRAAL, Dublin.

May, S. (2001) *Language and Minority Rights*. Harlow: Pearson.

Ó Buachalla, S. (1984) Educational policy and the role of the Irish language from 1831 to 1981. *European Journal of Education* 19 (1), 75–92.

Ó Buachalla, S. (1988) *Education Policy in Twentieth Century Ireland*. Dublin: Wolfhound Press.

Ó Domhnalláin, T. (1977) Ireland: The Irish language in education. *Language Problems and Language Planning* 1, 83–96.

Ó hÉallaithe, D. (2004) From language revival to language survival. In C. Mac Murchaidh (ed.) Who Needs Irish?: *Reflections on the Importance of the Irish Language Today* (pp. 159–192). Dublin: Veritas.

Ó Huallacháin, C. (1994) *The Irish and Irish: A Sociolinguistic Analysis of the Relationship Between a People and Their Language*. Dublin: Irish Franciscan Provincial Office.

Ó Laoire, M. (1996) An historical perspective on the revival of Irish outside the Gaeltacht 1880–1930, with reference to the revival of Hebrew. In S. Wright (ed.) *Language and The State* (pp. 51–63). Clevedon: Multilingual Matters.

Ó Laoire, M. (1999) *Athbheochan na hEabhraise: Ceacht don Ghaeilge?* Dublin: An Clóchomhar.

Ó Laoire, M. (2001) Language policy and the broadcast media. In H. Kelly Holmes (ed.) *Minority Language Broadcasting* (pp. 63–69). Clevedon: Multilingual Matters.

Ó Laoire, M. (forthcoming) Language planning in Ireland. Monograph in R. Kaplan and R. Baldauf (eds) *Current Issues in Language Planning series*. Clevedon: Multilingual Matters.

Ó Murchú, M. (1970) *Language and Community*. Dublin: Comhairle na Gaeilge.

Ó Murchú, H. (2001) Irish: *The Irish Language in Education in The Republic of Ireland*. Ljouwert/Leeuwarden: Mercator Education.

Ó Riagáin, P. (1997) *Language Policy and Social Reproduction: Ireland 1893–1993*. Oxford: Clarendon Press.

Ó Siadhail, M. (1989) *Modern Irish*. Cambridge: Cambridge University Press.

Picard, J.M. (2003) The Latin language in early medieval Ireland. In M. Cronin and C. Ó Cuilleanáin (eds) *The Languages of Ireland* (pp. 57–77). Dublin: Four Courts.

Risk, H. (1968) French loan-words in Irish. *Études Celtiques* 12, 585–655.

Singleton, D. (1992) Second language instruction: The when and how. In J. Matter (ed.) *AILA Review 9: Language Teaching in the Twenty-first Century* 46–54.

Watson, I. (2003) *Broadcasting in Irish: Minority Language, Radio, Television and Identity*. Dublin: Four Courts.

Wright, S. (2004) *Language Policy and Language Planning: From Nationalism to Globalisation*. Hampshire: Palgrave MacMillan.

Chapter 8
Language Use and Language Attitudes in Malta

SANDRO CARUANA

Sociolinguistic Context

Malta, a small island in the Mediterranean, covering an area of around 316 km^2 (Figure 8.1 and Figure 8.2), with a population of almost 400,000 inhabitants, has a rich and varied history, which has inevitably influenced the languages used on the island throughout the course of the years. Currently Maltese and English are actively used both in their spoken and written forms.

Maltese, a Semitic language, owes its origins to the period of time (870–1090) when the Arabs took over Malta, seemingly in a violent manner, and thereby introduced their own vernacular, which eventually took over any pre-existing language (Brincat, 1995; 2003). Successive colonisers, most notably the Normans (1091–1194), reintroduced contacts with the Romance world and Italian gradually gained a major role in Malta and was especially used as a written medium alongside Latin (Cassola, 1998). However, the situation was to change drastically during the British colonial period (1800–1964) when English was introduced slowly but surely in Malta and eventually replaced Italian as the country's official language after a lengthy struggle known as the 'language question' (Hull, 1993). As time passed, the status of Maltese improved and from an exclusively spoken variety the language acquired its written form. While in the 1930s it was still defined as *il-lingwa tal-kcina*, 'the language of the kitchen', it is now a fully fledged language, which is used regularly by speakers pertaining to all social classes and has recently been recognised as one of the official languages of the European Union, following Malta's accession in 2004. Presently Maltese is considered to be the national language of Malta whereas both Maltese and English are official languages.

A closer look at the current sociolinguistic situation in Malta reveals that Maltese is very widespread as a spoken variety but that it is used to a lesser extent as a written medium. In fact, Maltese can be said to be the language used to communicate orally in most circumstances. It is the language that is used almost exclusively on local television and radio stations and it is used regularly in most churches, in the law courts and

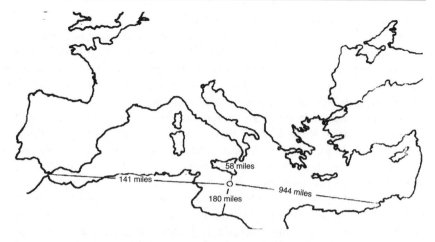

Figure 8.1 The geographical position of the Maltese islands

in parliament. English, on the other hand, is mainly used in writing. The most popular local daily newspaper is in English and so are most textbooks used in schools. Official governmental and legal documentation is normally written both in English and in Maltese.

Maltese is the mother tongue of the vast majority of the population, but a substantial number of Maltese people also claim that either English, or Maltese and English simultaneously, are their first language. In this respect data included in studies vary quite considerably and are inevitably influenced by the nature and social background of the respondents taken into consideration. A recent study by Sciriha and Vassallo (2001), however, indicates that a staggering 98.6% of a large and varied sample made up of

Figure 8.2 The Maltese islands

500 respondents from different social background state that Maltese is their native language. Only 1.2% of respondents state that English is their mother tongue and another 1.2% affirm that both English and Maltese are their first language. These figures confirm those obtained by Borg *et al.* in a 1992 study, as reported in Camilleri (1995: 96), wherein from a sample of 186 informants 96% used mainly Maltese at home.

Language use also reveals a person's underlying culture and background and in this sense Malta is no exception. At times Maltese nationals who speak in English are perceived as *tal-pepè* 'snobs' or *qziez* 'show-offs'. On the other hand, in certain circumstances, these English speakers are also prejudiced towards those who find difficulty in expressing themselves in English or are unable to do so, as they automatically consider them to be uneducated or pertaining to a low socioeconomic group. Still, even those who claim to use exclusively Maltese or English at all times are likely to use forms of codeswitching or codemixing, as, whichever the mother tongue, one is inevitably conditioned into using the languages one is regularly in contact with. As Berruto (1998: 16) claims, in a bilingual context codeswitching and codemixing are always present, whether to a greater or to a lesser extent, and Malta is no exception to this.

In this respect, it is necessary to point out that regular use of English in Malta, especially as a spoken medium, is often associated with families pertaining to a higher socioeconomic class. English also gains ground over Maltese in certain contexts, including studies at higher or at tertiary level. Textbooks used in the vast majority of university courses are in English and therefore the knowledge of both spoken and written English constitutes an advantage to those students who pursue studies at this level.

Though the Maltese society may be defined as bilingual, the linguistic situation on the island is more complex than this definition may suggest as Italian also has a significant role in Malta. In fact, Italian television channels, received in Malta via antenna or via satellite, are quite popular amongst Maltese of all ages (Caruana, 2003; in press). To a lesser extent, Italian music, radio channels, magazines and newspapers have also played a significant role in making Italian more widespread in Malta throughout the last two or three decades. The fact that in Malta many individuals have been exposed regularly to Italian via the media seems enough to justify the fact that nowadays a number of Maltese understand Italian well, and possibly also speak the language fluently enough. Generally, Maltese have a positive perception of Italian and are often pleased enough to use the language if the opportunity arises. There are regular cases of Italian tourists who visit Malta to learn English but who are disillusioned by the fact that most Maltese speak to them, or try to speak to them, in Italian as soon as they make out their nationality!

The presence of the Italian media in Malta was especially influential up to the early 1990s. In fact, up to 1993 there was only one local state-owned television channel alongside which a large number of Italian channels could be received via antenna. These included the Italian state-run channels as well as a large number of private channels.

In 1993 the introduction of cable television as well as transmissions from local private television channels started to change the nature of linguistic exposure via the media. Some households also installed satellite television thus gaining access to channels transmitting from all over the world. In fact, from an almost total dominance of Italian channels via antenna, there was a gradual but constant increase of people who installed cable or satellite television and therefore gained access to English-language channels. Official data from the company that provides cable television service in Malta indicate that this service is now available in over 75% of Maltese households, whilst according to a survey on ICT use in Malta by the National Statistics Office (2003), around 15% of the population receives television channels via satellite. Furthermore, local channels increased in popularity and gnawed at the viewership of Italian channels, especially due to two stations owned by the major political parties. This is confirmed by the regular surveys carried out by the Broadcasting Authority (2004), which reveal that the share of Italian channels today varies between 15% to 20% of viewership, whilst that of local channels almost reaches 70%.

Maltese is used by most presenters and disc jockeys on radio channels, however songs played are almost exclusively in English. Songs in Italian and in Maltese tend to be few and far between. As stated earlier, most reading material is in English, including newspapers, magazines, books and especially textbooks. However, though the most widespread newspaper is in English, two daily newspapers published in Maltese also have a considerable circulation. Furthermore, the past years have witnessed a considerable increase of publications in Maltese. Italian, on the other hand, is limited to a few magazines that are popular amongst a rather small number of people.

The above situation is clearly confirmed by the data resulting from a survey carried out by the National Statistics Office (2002) among a sample of 800 subjects representative of the target population of Maltese aged 16 years and over. The data for this survey were collected in November 2000. Results confirm that Maltese is the language that is used as the spoken vernacular of the population, with 86.2% of the subjects stating that they opt for Maltese during daily conversation.

The results of this representative sample show that 70.9% of Maltese nationals prefer reading magazines in English, 22.7% prefer reading magazines in Maltese and 6.5% choose to read them in Italian. As far as books are concerned, the percentage increases substantially for Maltese

(35.8%), and decreases for Italian (3.1%) and English (61.1%), although the latter language is still the most popular. With respect to radio programmes, the vast majority of Maltese (82.4%) prefer to listen to programmes in Maltese. Again the situation changes when the subjects were asked to report their preferences regarding listening to songs. In this case almost 58.3% of the Maltese population prefers to listen to songs in English, 30.5% enjoys listening to songs in Maltese, with the remaining 11.2% opting for songs in Italian. As regards watching television, 44.9% of the population prefers following programmes in Maltese. In this sphere, according to the National Statistics Office (2002), Italian obtains 29.6% of the preferences, thereby surpassing English, which obtains 25.5% of preferences.

One must also consider the fact that the use of the Internet in Malta is on the increase and is now available in over 30% of households (National Statistics Office, 2003). The use of the Internet is much more widespread among the younger generations and offers considerable exposure to English, although Maltese is used quite extensively both in order to send e-mails and to chat.

The Maltese Educational System

As far as schooling is concerned, Maltese and English are both obligatory subjects from the start of primary schooling. At secondary level, students start learning one or two other languages, and may generally choose between Arabic, French, German, Italian and Spanish. However, as reported by Zammit (1999: 34), there are also two Church schools and three independent private schools in which Italian or French are taught at primary level. In these cases, the attitudes towards these foreign languages are positive both among parents and among the students.

Maltese and English are studied by all students at both primary and secondary level. As far as the other languages are concerned, Italian is the most popular in state schools (frequented by most Maltese students) and is studied by about 70% of students, followed by French and German. In some local private and Church schools Italian is an obligatory subject in secondary schools whereas others offer students the option of studying both Italian and French in the first years of secondary school, but students are then asked to choose one of these two languages in order to study it more in depth during the final years of secondary schooling.

The above considerations indicate that the linguistic situation in Malta is complex indeed and relies heavily on the heritage of the historical and political permutations of the past. In view of this in the Maltese context it is rather difficult to apply the terms 'minority' and 'majority' language because Malta is essentially bilingual and both languages are used regularly by most of the population. Maltese is the mother tongue of practically all the Maltese and English is a second language. On the other hand, Maltese is used mainly orally while at a written/reading level English is used much more. The use of Maltese is therefore limited as far as higher education is concerned and a sound knowledge of English is important in order to form part of the higher strata of society. Therefore, in this study Maltese cannot really be considered to be a 'minority' language in the same terms as Basque or Catalan in Spain or as Irish in the Republic of Ireland. In fact, Maltese can only be considered to be a 'minority' language if one considers it within a much more global context, which goes well beyond the Maltese shores. Such a context would imply that English is a 'majority' language only on the grounds that a sound knowledge of it can further the opportunities of the Maltese both in local academic spheres and of course internationally. Italian, on the other hand, is clearly the island's third language as it is associated mainly with means of communication and it is not spoken locally although exposure to it is still significant and a considerable number of Maltese can also comprehend this language well.

A number of studies on the bilingual situation in Malta are mainly concerned with investigating issues related to codeswitching and codemixing. These include research by Ellul (1978) and by Camilleri (1995). Ellul (1978) studied instances of codeswitching between parents and preschool children and affirms that 'it can be argued that children will not be considered educated until they are bilingual, in the sense that they are equally proficient in English and in Maltese' (Ellul, 1978: 31). Camilleri (1995: 154–160) provides a detailed account of codeswitching between Maltese and English as used in local secondary schools. Teacher–student interactions that took place in a number of lessons were registered, transcribed and analysed. As stated earlier, in Maltese schools, though most textbooks are in English, lessons are often carried out in Maltese. This is mainly the case in state schools, as in private schools, normally frequented by students coming from a high socio-economic background, English is used more frequently. One of Camilleri's (1995) most significant findings is the fact that 'switching from Maltese to English is mainly accounted for by the use of English technical terms and phrases (77.8% of code-switching units)' (Camilleri, 1995: 216, *brackets in the original*). Consequently, in classes where Maltese is used frequently, English is resorted to whenever a teacher includes aspects related to the content of a subject in his/her explanation. This is illustrated by the following example taken from a mathematics lesson, followed by my translation:

> **Teacher:** mela naghtu kaz tinsa l-**formula** tar-**rate** tinsiha ghal xi raguni jew ohra… tinqeda bil-formula originali (*writes on blackboard*)

i equals p r t over hundred... tajjeb... issa mela ghandek **two two five** veru?... l-**interest is two two five** hawnhekk... il-**principle** huwa... **two five o o**... ir-**rate**... x'se nnizzel? (Camilleri, 1995: 159, bold, italics and brackets included in the original)

Teacher: So, for example, you forget the formula for the rate, you forget it for some reason. You use the original formula (writes on blackboard) I equals p r t over hundred, right? Now, so two two five, true? The interest is two two five here, the principle is two five o o, the rate, what am I going to write down?

It is therefore clear that within Maltese state schools, Maltese is generally perceived as necessary for most informal communication, whereas English is generally the language of instruction mainly used in order to refer to content-related terms. In this respect, it is also necessary to observe that in Malta second-language teaching occurs in the language being taught as teachers are encouraged to use Italian to teach the Italian language, French to teach the French language and so on. However, even in these cases it is far from unlikely for exchanges to occur in Maltese or in English throughout these lessons.

Previous Studies on Language Attitudes Carried Out in Malta

Research studies on language attitudes carried out in Malta have become more numerous in recent years. This is possibly due to an increasing awareness amongst the Maltese of the importance of being proficient in a number of languages. In fact, in the past, languages were mainly deemed useful in order to communicate with tourists visiting our shores, whereas now there is a growing awareness of their importance even in order to further one's opportunities by studying or working abroad. This is also confirmed in a number of considerations included in the studies mentioned hereunder.

Said (1991) investigates the attitudes towards Maltese and English of 400 students aged between 14 and 16, frequenting either Church schools or local Junior Lyceums (high achievers' schools). In this study none of the participants express negative attitudes towards the two languages in question, but there is a clear tendency for students from professional and middle classes to express a more positive attitude towards English when compared to students from skilled manual and unskilled manual working classes. Within the schools considered in this research, there is a clear perception that English is more important than Maltese for study purposes.

A study carried out by Zammit (1999) reveals that in the five primary schools in which Italian or French are taught alongside English and

Maltese, the students expressed positive attitudes towards the foreign language they are learning. These positive attitudes were also expressed by teachers and parents, although concern was also expressed because of the fact that in certain cases the school curriculum was too heavily loaded. In these schools English is often used as a language of instruction even to teach these foreign languages and this is undoubtedly due to the fact that the schools in question are either Church or private schools, in which the tendency to use English rather than Maltese as a language of instruction in all subjects is very widespread.

Sciriha's study (2001) on trilingualism in Malta provides an interesting insight especially with regards to attitudes towards Arabic, a language which is typologically close to Maltese, but which is not widespread at all on the island. The reactions to a hypothetical introduction of Arabic as a compulsory subject in Secondary schools were negative among the 500 subjects aged between 11 and 24 included in this study. In fact, only 11% of respondents were pleased with the idea and the reasons given to motivate the negative responses include a number of considerations which reveal that most Maltese do not associate themselves with this language. The reason for this negative response may also be attributed to the fact that in the 1980s the Maltese government had close ties with the Libyan government and this led to the introduction of Arabic, which became obligatory in secondary schools. This administrative decision encountered great resistance in many sectors of Maltese society. On the other hand, Italian is viewed in a favourable light, as only 19% of the respondents for whom Italian is a compulsory subject at school claim that they do not appreciate the language. Sciriha's (2001) data also reveal that the respondents are aware of the importance of being trilingual. In fact 94% of the subjects claim that being trilingual is indeed positive and that it is mainly useful in order to interact with people of different nationalities. Results also show that within the local context, Maltese is perceived as the most important language followed by English, Italian and French. On the other hand, when languages are ranked according to their worldwide importance, English is rated most highly, followed by French and German.

In Sciriha and Vassallo's (2001) linguistic survey, a number of interesting aspects emerge regarding language use in Malta. The vast sample of this survey ($n = 500$) provided a significant cross-section of the population and included subjects of different ages (the youngest being 15 and the oldest over 55) and different walks of life (including self-employed, managers, nonmanual and manual workers, and housewives). As stated earlier, 98.6% of these respondents claimed that Maltese is their first language; 87% of the sample claimed to possess a good knowledge of English, 70% of Italian, 17.2% of French and 4.6% of German.

Maltese is mainly used in familiar domains such as at work, and to communicate with family members and with friends. English and other foreign languages are mainly used to watch films, to watch television, to listen to the radio and to read books, newspapers and magazines. Interestingly enough, Sciriha and Vassallo's study (2001) reveals that on average the Maltese state that they use Italian as much as they use English – this is undoubtedly due to the influence of Italian TV channels, as Italian is a much sought-after language especially in the field of entertainment, including sports.

As in the case of other studies referred to above, the knowledge of foreign languages is considered to be very useful by the majority of the subjects and is often linked to better working possibilities and opportunities. In this study very positive attitudes emerge with regards to foreign-language learning, mainly because of the fact that locals are conscious of the fact that Maltese cannot be useful once they are away from the island or in order to communicate with foreigners. As such, English, as well as other foreign languages, are generally pictured in a positive light.

Micheli's (2001) study mainly focuses on the distinction between instrumental and integrative attitudes. The authors findings highlight the fact that attitudes towards English in Malta are mainly instrumental, that is, they are linked with the motivation to learn the language for useful and utilitarian purposes. On the other hand, attitudes towards Maltese are integrative as they are related to the desire to identify with one's culture or language group.

Sciriha's (2004) research on the sociolinguistics of mobile telephony in Malta also provides interesting insight. When asked what language the respondent uses when the addressee of a call on the mobile phone answers in English, 20.8% of a sample of 500 subjects responded that they would use Maltese anyway, whereas 11% would codeswitch between English and Maltese. Amongst those who would use Maltese (amounting to 159 subjects), a significant 33.3% affirm that they are unable to communicate in English, whereas 27% responded that as they are Maltese they feel inclined to speak in the native language, irrespective of the response received from their interlocutor. The latter aspect substantiates the observation that some Maltese speakers do not perceive the use of English positively as they feel that the Maltese language is very much part of their identity whereas English is not. In the case of short text messages (SMS), English is used by 27.3% of respondents, whilst Maltese follows closely at 22.9%. In other cases respondents state that they use both languages. This result is not surprising considering the fact that English is very widespread when writing is concerned. Furthermore, as Sciriha (2004: 98) herself points out, mobile phones in Malta have in-built English dictionaries whilst no similar service is available for Maltese.

As stated earlier, Italian has an important role in Malta and it is certainly more widespread than other foreign languages, including French and German. Up to the early 1990s, Italian was so popular in Malta that the extent of spontaneous acquisition of the language was very significant indeed. Studies carried out by Brincat (1998) and by Caruana (2003; in press) generally demonstrate that the attitude towards Italian in Malta is highly positive, as it is often associated with television. Italian is often perceived as an 'easy' language to learn and sometimes students in Maltese opt to learn French or German at school, instead of Italian, as they are convinced that they can learn Italian by watching television or by means of a short course which can be frequented after school hours. The knowledge of Maltese also facilitates the comprehension of Italian as, despite being a Semitic language, 48% of Maltese vocabulary derives from Italian or from Italian dialects, especially Sicilian (Brincat, 2003: 360). On the other hand, French and especially German are perceived as harder languages to learn. This situation is also confirmed in the choice of languages in state schools. Students in Malta sit for an examination at the end of primary schooling and according to the results they achieve they are placed in Junior Lyceums (high achievers) or in Area Secondary Schools (low achievers). Italian is much more popular in the schools frequented by low achievers and even in Junior Lyceum it is normally chosen by students who, despite being high achievers, obtain the lower marks in the end-of-primary-schooling examination, as shown by Farrugia (2004).

The Study

The sample

The data collection of this study was carried out in October and November 2004, that is at the start of the academic year 2004–2005. All the data were collected from first-year students frequenting the University of Malta. Data were collected from students enrolled in the Faculty of Education and the Faculty of Arts. Students of the Faculty of Education included both students specialising in Pedagogy/Teaching Methodology as well as others majoring in Psychology. It must be pointed out that the latter will not necessarily pursue the teaching profession but some of the modules they will be completing at university are educationally related. The students specialising in teaching methodology as well as students frequenting the Faculty of Arts also included those studying Maltese, English and Italian. This was necessary, as Humanities students choose to specialise in two areas and if students studying languages were not included in the study, the sample would have inevitably been small. Furthermore, one must observe that students of the Faculty of Arts do not specialise in teaching methodology as they major in the content of the subjects they choose to study. However, these students also have the option of following a one-year Post Graduate Certificate in Education at the end of their course or they can pursue their studies Master's level – either option presently enables them to obtain a teacher's warrant.

Questionnaires were distributed to 365 students and a total of 189 (52%) of these questionnaires were gathered. Ninety-six (51%) questionnaires were completed by students of the Faculty of Education who were specialising in Pedagogy and Teaching Methodology, 73 (39%) question-naires were collected from students frequenting the Faculty of Arts and the remaining 20 (10%) questionnaires were filled in by students of the Faculty of Education who are specialising in Psychology or Psychology-related areas. Among these students 24 (13%) were studying Maltese at university, 20 (11%) were studying English and 30 (16%) were studying Italian. Ten of these students were studying a combination of two of these languages, as most students studying in the secondary education area are asked to select two areas of specialisation. This aspect is to be taken into account when the results of the questionnaire are analysed, as these students' attitudes towards the languages they are specialising in are inevitably highly positive.

Among the respondents, 32 (17%) are specialising in Primary Educa-tion, 106 (56%) in Secondary Education and 10 (5%) in Physical Education. The remaining 41 (22%) respondents included the 20 students specialising in Psychology and students specialising in Social Education, including students from the Faculty of Arts majoring in Sociology or students of Personal and Social Education from the Faculty of Education.

It is also necessary to point out that out of the 189 subjects included in this study, only 27 subjects (14%) were studying at university in order to become teachers of Mathematics, Computing or of other Science subjects. Again, the fact that this percentage is rather low is to be given due importance when considering the results of this study, as the attitudes of these students could differ from those studying languages or the social sciences.

The average age of the respondents was just over 19 years. The youngest students who responded to the questionnaire were 17 years old whereas the oldest respondents were two mature students aged 43. A total of 114 (60%) respondents were 18 year olds. Twenty-six subjects (14%) were aged 19 and 25 subjects (13.5%) were 17 years old. The remaining 24 (12.5%) respondents were over 20 years of age.

The prevalence of female respondents over male respondents is particularly noteworthy, with 141 (75%) female respondents and 48 (25%) males. This is also due to the fact that the Faculty of Arts and the Faculty of Education both have a large presence of female students.

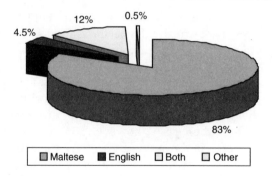

Figure 8.3 The students' L1

One hundred and fifty-seven (83%) of the respondents affirmed that Maltese is their mother tongue. This figure is very much in line with those reported in previous studies, to which reference has been made above. Only 8 (4.5%) respondents stated that English is their first language whereas 23 (12%) respondents stated that Maltese and English were acquired simultaneously as their first languages. One student (0.5%) claimed that his/her mother tongue was neither Maltese nor English (Figure 8.3).

The parents' occupation of 22 (12%) subjects pertains to a high socioeconomic status group, whereas the parents' occupation of 68 (37%) subjects pertains to a middle socioeconomic group. The remaining 93 (51%) subjects who responded to this question form part of families that are of low socioprofessional status.

Results

The results regarding the subjects' self-evaluation of their general competence in the three languages are represented in Figure 8.4. It is evident that a large majority of candidates (81%) claim to have a very good

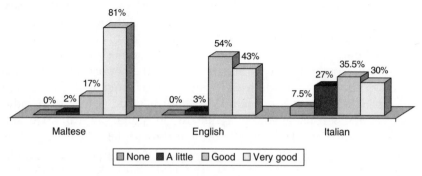

Figure 8.4 Level of competence in three languages

knowledge of Maltese. This figure drops to 43% for English and to 30% for Italian. However, it is noteworthy that as far as English is concerned only 3% of subjects claim to have a poor competence in the language. On the other hand, the subjects' competence is considerably lower in Italian.

It is worth pointing out that 109 subjects (58%) also claim to be proficient in a second foreign language. The vast majority of these subjects know French whereas few subjects state that they are competent in either German or Spanish. In these cases, however, 53% of the subjects claim to have a little competence in the language. Only 12 subjects (6%) claim that they are also competent in a second foreign language. Interestingly enough, not a single subject claimed to be competent in Arabic, despite its typological proximity with the Maltese language.

In Table 8.1 data regarding the use of the two official languages in social interactions are presented. Maltese is used almost exclusively when the subjects interact within the family and with neighbours. Within school, English is used more extensively, especially in student–teacher interactions. This result is a logical consequence of the fact that in Malta most textbooks are in English and therefore English is often used as a language of instruction. It is also noteworthy that in interaction with friends (both at school and outside school) both English and Maltese are used quite extensively.

The results reported in Table 8.2 illustrate the presence of the three languages in relation to means of communication. Due to the Maltese sociolinguistic situation (as explained in Section 1), in this table it was deemed necessary to include considerations regarding input from means of communication that do not transmit exclusively in Maltese or in English. Consequently, in the table below, subjects were provided the option included in the column 'in other languages', which gives a clear indication of the number of individuals who are not solely exposed to the two official languages via the media. In fact, in this case the importance of Maltese decreases considerably when compared to English and Italian. As far as watching television is concerned, 58% of the subjects follow television programmes in English and Maltese, but the remaining 42% watch programmes in other languages – in the case, on the strength of results of past research, it can be safely said that most of these subjects watch television in Italian. On the other hand, the importance of English is noteworthy when reading newspapers and listening to music are concerned. Maltese gains ground on English when listening to radio programmes is considered. Consequently, in Malta, one can state that exposure to all three languages is present through television, English is by far the most popular language to read newspapers and to listen to music, whereas radio programmes are mainly followed in Maltese and English, but not in Italian.

Table 8.1 Language used when talking to the following people

	Always in Maltese (%)	In Maltese more often than English (%)	In Maltese and English about equally (%)	In English more often than Maltese (%)	Always in English (%)
Father	85	7	2	4	2
Mother	79	10	6	3	2
Brothers and sisters	75	11	9	2	3
Friends in the classroom	40	41	12	5	2
Friends outside school	49	31	11	6	3
Teachers	31	28	15	20	6
Neighbours	80	11	1	5	2

Table 8.2 Means of communication and language used

	Always in Maltese (%)	In Maltese more often than English (%)	In Maltese and English about equally (%)	In English more often than Maltese (%)	Always in English (%)	In other languages i.e. not in Maltese or in English (%)
Watching TV	5	10	18	15	10	42
The press	10	16	21	24	25	4
Music	2	3	6	30	52	7
Listening to the radio	21	23	22	17	15	2

In Table 8.3 the importance attributed to Maltese is considered. The results generally confirm the tendencies already evident in the Table 8.1 and Table 8.2. In fact, Maltese is considered to be highly important in order to interact socially, especially to make friends, to live in Malta and to read and write. On the other hand it is considered to be less important in order to interact with teachers and friends at university. It is also considered to have a limited role when watching television is concerned, and the importance of Maltese does not seem to relate significantly to whether a person is liked or not by others. Interestingly enough Maltese is considered to be important to pass exams by 47% of the subjects. This is probably related to the fact that the importance of Maltese as an academic subject has increased over the past years and it is necessary to obtain a basic qualification in Maltese in order to pursue one's studies. Quite a large number of subjects consider Maltese to have little importance when other social activities (such as going shopping, making phone calls and being accepted in the community) are concerned. This is possibly due to the fact that during these activities interactions are carried out both in Maltese and in English, and codeswitching and codemixing are often present in these instances.

The attitudes expressed by the subjects towards Maltese, English and Italian are illustrated in Figure 8.5. Attitudes towards Maltese are more favourable than attitudes towards English and Italian. Very few subjects express unfavourable attitudes towards Maltese and English. On the other hand, 65% of subjects have a neutral attitude towards Italian and 12% of the subjects express a negative attitude towards this language. This is possibly due to the fact that the subjects' competence in Italian is generally lower than that in Maltese and in English. However, the unfavourable attitude towards the language may also be due to the fact that this small number of subjects may have a general feeling of aversion towards Italian lifestyle and culture.The data collected with regards to the subjects' attitudes towards the three languages represent the dependent variable of the study and therefore the relationship with the other variables of the study was examined.

The attitude of male subjects towards Maltese is significantly more favourable than that of female subjects [$F1, 187 = 6.53$ ($p = 0.011$)]. On the other hand, no significant differences were registered between males' and females' attitudes towards English and Italian. Highly significant differences were registered when the subjects' mother tongues were taken into consideration. In fact, subjects who have Maltese as a mother tongue expressed a much more favourable attitude towards Maltese itself, when compared to subjects with either English [$F2, 163 = 4.576$ ($p < 0.001$)] or both Maltese and English [$F2, 178 = 3.342$ ($p = 0.001$)] as mother tongue. No statistically significant differences, regarding

Table 8.3 Importance attached to the Maltese language to do the following activities

For people to:	Important (%)	A little important (%)	A little unimportant (%)	Unimportant (%)
Make friends	66	23	3	8
Read	68	23	7	2
Write	70	21	7	2
Watch TV	30	43	15	12
Get a job	56	32	11	1
Be liked	31	35	14	20
Live in Malta	68	23	4	5
Bring up children	63	26	5	6
Go shopping	41	35	13	11
Make phone calls	44	33	15	8
Pass exams	47	30	15	8
Be accepted in the community	42	39	11	8
Talk to friends at university	36	40	19	5
Talk to teachers at university	26	40	23	11
Talk to people out of university	50	34	9	7

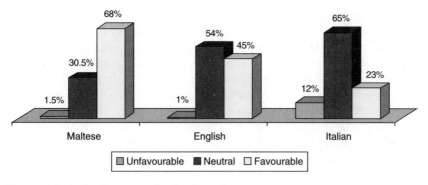

Figure 8.5 Attitudes towards the three languages

attitudes towards the Maltese language, emerge between the English L1 and the Maltese/English L1 groups.

All eight subjects with English L1 have a favourable attitude towards English. This group is very small and this inevitably also must be accounted for, especially when considering the differences that emerge when comparing these subjects to Maltese L1 and Maltese/English L1 groups. In fact, attitudes towards English are much more favourable among the English L1 group when compared both to the Maltese L1 group [$F2, 163 = 4.214$ ($p < 0.001$)] and to the Maltese/English L1 group [$F2, 29 = 2.937$ ($p = 0.006$)]. Subjects with Maltese/English L1 also have a more favourable attitude towards English than subjects with Maltese L1 [$F2, 178 = 3.973$ ($p = 0.004$)]. No statistically significant differences are registered in the relation between subjects' mother tongue and their attitude towards Italian.

The socioeconomic status of the subjects' families also yields statistically significant results. In fact, the attitude towards Maltese is significantly more favourable among subjects coming from families in the lower socioeconomic bracket when compared to subjects coming from the higher socioeconomic status group [$F2, 113 = 5.293$ ($p < 0.001$)]. In this respect only 27% of the subjects from families of high socioeconomic status express favourable attitudes towards Maltese whereas the percentage increases to 78.5% in the case of subjects from the lower bracket. Socioeconomic status, on the other hand, also affects the attitudes towards English and in this case results are in contrast with those registered for Maltese, as favourable attitudes towards English are more favourable among subjects with high socioeconomic status when compared to subjects from lower status groups [$F2, 113 = 2.535$ ($p = 0.013$)]. In fact, only 34% of those from lower socioeconomic status families express positive attitudes towards English. Attitudes towards Italian, on the other hand are not affected by socioeconomic status.

As predictable, in Malta the size of one's hometown does not yield statistically significant differences towards attitudes. This is due to the fact that, being a small country, the population in most Maltese hometowns does not vary considerably. On the other hand, the language spoken in the subjects' community does lead to significant differences as subjects who live within Maltese-speaking communities have a more positive attitude towards Maltese [$F1$, $185 = 3.34$ ($p = 0.001$)], whereas subjects living in English-speaking communities have a more positive attitude towards English [$F1$, $185 = 2.914$ ($p = 0.004$)].

As far as Italian in Malta is concerned, significant differences emerge when the age at which one starts learning the language is taken into consideration. Results indicate that subjects who start learning Italian before they are 8 years old develop a more favourable attitude towards the language [$F1$, $165 = 2.553$ ($p = 0.016$)]. However, no statistically significant differences emerge when one's proficiency in the language is taken into consideration. This is undoubtedly due to the fact that Italian in Malta is introduced in secondary schools, when students are 11 years of age. Therefore the subjects who claimed that they started learning Italian at a younger age than 11 were those who were exposed to the language via television. It is therefore not surprising that the attitude of these subjects towards the language is highly favourable.

Results are highly significant when one considers whether subjects have ever visited Italy, with a clear predominance of favourable attitudes among those who did visit Italy [$F1$, $184 = 3.178$ ($p = 0.002$)]. On the other hand, one's proficiency in Italian is not affected by this aspect. One's attitude towards Italian is also significantly related to watching television. In fact 35.5% of subjects who watch Italian television daily have a favourable attitude towards Italian, whereas this figure is significantly lower among subjects who do not follow television programmes in Italian so regularly [$F4$, $184 = 5.365$ ($p < 0.001$)]. One's competence in Italian is also related to the amount of television one watches, with almost 50% of subjects who watch Italian daily claiming that they have a very good knowledge of the language [$F4$, $184 = 5.751$ ($p < 0.001$)]. Conversely, attitudes and proficiency in Italian are not affected by one's competence in an additional foreign language.

Finally, it must be observed that in the cases of all three languages, Maltese [$R^2 = 0.271$ ($p < 0.01$)], English [$R^2 = 0.41$ ($p < 0.01$)] and Italian [$R^2 = 0.578$ ($p < 0.01$)], there is a significant correlation between the students' self-perceived language competence and their attitudes towards each of the three languages. This shows that there is a relation between the subjects' proficiency in the three languages and their attitude towards them. Subjects who rate themselves as being proficient in Maltese, English and Italian have a more favourable attitude towards the respective languages. Subjects who rate themselves highly proficient in all three languages generally have a highly favourable attitude towards Maltese. Favourable attitudes towards English are mainly limited to subjects who rate themselves highly proficient in English itself. On the other hand, subjects who rate themselves to be highly proficient in both Maltese and Italian have a less favourable attitude towards English. The results discussed in this section are summarised in Table 8.4.

Discussion

The results clearly reveal that most subjects included in the study have a favourable attitude towards languages. In fact, unfavourable attitudes are registered only in very few cases, thereby confirming the outcome of other studies carried out in Malta (Micheli, 2001; Said, 1991; Sciriha, 2001). This result is encouraging as it shows that future teachers are aware of the fact that knowing languages other than Maltese will allow one to further one's opportunities both locally and overseas.

The use of Maltese is much more widespread than the use of English among the potential teachers included in the study. In fact, Maltese is used much more frequently in day-to-day interactions with family and acquaintances. Furthermore, the number of subjects who claim to be highly proficient in Maltese is much higher than those who claim to be highly competent in English or in Italian. Consequently, this confirms the indication that the distinction between Maltese and English in terms of minority and majority languages is not as distinct as it may be with other languages within the European context.

The use of English gains ground in educationally related spheres, especially in interactions with teachers or with fellow university students. This is clearly determined by the fact that English is still very important as a written medium and it is also important to gain access to university. Micheli's (2001) findings are therefore confirmed by this outcome, as attitudes towards English in Malta are mainly instrumental, whereas attitudes towards Maltese are integrative.

Interestingly enough, however, when the subjects were asked to rate the importance they give to Maltese when carrying out a series of activities (Table 8.3), 70% of them considered Maltese to be important even to write. This shows that a number of future teachers do think that Maltese is not only important as an oral medium, but also as a written variety. This result is probably also influenced by the fact that Primary Education future teachers included in the sample are aware of the fact that they need to have a good command of the language even in its written form as they will be teaching it in local primary schools in the future.

Table 8.4 Summary of the most influential variables on language attitudes

Independent variable	Attitudes towards Maltese	Attitudes towards English	Attitudes towards Italian	Competence in Italian
Gender	Males > females	n.s.	n.s.	—
L1	Maltese > English/both	English > Maltese/both	n.s.	—
	—	Both > Maltese	—	—
				—
Socioprofessional status	Low > high	High > low	n.s.	—
Age at which subjects started to learn Italian	—	—	Before 8 > at or after 8	n.s.
Ever visited an Italian-speaking country	—	—	Yes > no	n.s.
Knowledge of other foreign languages	—	—	n.s.	n.s.
Watching television	—	—	Watching Italian TV daily > not watching Italian TV daily	Watching Italian TV daily > not watching Italian TV daily
Size of hometown	n.s.	n.s.	n.s.	—
Predominant language in hometown	Maltese > English	English > Maltese	n.s.	—

Attitudes towards Maltese and English are influenced by mother tongue and by the language spoken in one's community. The relation between the socioprofessional status of the subjects' parents and attitudes towards languages does persist, even though differences in social classes are certainly much less evident than they were in the past. Still, attitudes towards Maltese tend to be more positive among those subjects with parents forming part of the lower socioeconomic groups. Another important factor that determines attitudes is the language spoken in one's community. On the other hand, other variables, which in the past could have been considered as influential in determining language attitudes, did not have significant effects. The most noteworthy among these is schooling – in fact, in the past there was a clear divide in Malta between public and Church/private schooling, as the latter were normally considered to be the domain of students with an English-speaking background, as confirmed by a number of studies carried out in Malta referred to by Camilleri (1995: 90–97). However, this divide is not so evident among university students who may become teachers in the future, as no significant differences emerge in their attitudes towards the three languages, irrespective of the secondary school they attended.

Despite the above, results indicate clearly that subjects who have a high proficiency in English and who have a favourable attitude towards this language, are generally less 'tolerant' towards other languages and often do not have favourable attitudes not only towards Maltese, but also towards Italian. This aspect is particularly evident among the eight subjects whose L1 is English, although any consideration in this respect must take account of the very small number of English L1 speakers included in this sample. Still, in these cases it seems that these respondents are content to have a sound knowledge of English and they often deem that this is enough to help them get along with their studies and their career. Furthermore, it seems that they do not associate the Maltese language with their identity of Maltese nationals, an aspect which is normally of great importance for Maltese L1 speakers.

Results also confirm the endemic link between Italian in Malta and television viewing, thereby confirming past findings (Brincat, 1998; Caruana, 2003). In fact, one notes that attitudes towards Italian are not conditioned by the variables that influence attitudes towards Maltese and English such as mother tongue, socioeconomic status or the language that is prevalently spoken in the community in which one lives. On the other hand, favourable attitudes are registered mainly among subjects' who follow Italian television programmes daily, among those who have visited Italy and among those students who started learning Italian before they were 8 years old. These therefore include those subjects who acquired Italian spontaneously through television, as the subject is only introduced in secondary schools, at age 11. As such, even though Italian television programmes have decreased their viewership in Malta over the past 10 years, that is since the introduction of pluralism and of cable or satellite television, they still hold an important role within the Maltese society.

As stated in the first part of Section 4, the 189 subjects of this study also included a number of students studying Maltese, English and Italian. As expected, these respondents all expressed favourable attitudes towards the languages they are studying. However, the trends reported in this study were all confirmed even when these students were excluded from the relations between variables that were examined. On the other hand, the number of subjects studying science or computing-related subjects was rather limited, as it amounted to only 14% of the sample. The attitudes of these subjects towards languages did not affect the outcome significantly. Further investigation in this respect would be necessary in order to investigate whether there are significant differences in Humanities and Science future teachers' attitudes towards the three languages.

Malta's position in the centre of the Mediterranean has always led to many cross-cultural influences. The present situation and the attitudes that future teachers show towards the three languages they are in contact with is undoubtedly the result of these influences. Maltese is now firmly established and it is now an important part of the Maltese identity. This language has certainly gone a long way over the past century. Besides achieving its standardisation, it is now part of all realms of local cultural, social and political walks of life. English still maintains an important role and it is positive to see that university students are aware of its significance. Over the past years there has been a growing concern regarding the level of English in Malta and it is beyond doubt that future primary school teachers not only ought to have an adequate proficiency in the language, but should also strive to help their students gain awareness regarding the importance of English worldwide. Certain prejudices towards English as the language of the 'snobbish' upper classes also emerged in the response to the questionnaire, but these were rather few and far between. Most future teachers seem to be aware that these attitudes are not beneficial and while stressing their Maltese identity most subjects also expressed positive attitudes towards English. Within this context, the Italian language has maintained its role as a third language. Most subjects express neutral or favourable attitudes towards it, and knowledge of it is certainly viewed as enriching and valuable. The acquisition of Italian in Malta demonstrates the importance of input via television in language learning and how languages are learnt if one takes an interest in the cultural and social context in which they are used.

References

Berruto, G. (1998) Situazioni di plurilinguismo, commutazione di codice e mescolanza di sistemi. *Babylonia* 6, 16–21.

Brincat, J. (1995) *Malta 870-1054 Al-Himyari's Account and its Linguistic Implications.* Valletta: Said International.

Brincat, J. (1998) A Malta l'italiano lo insegna la televisione. *Italiano e oltre* 13, 52–58.

Brincat, J. (2003) *Malta. Una storia linguistica.* Genova: Le Mani.

Broadcasting Authority Malta (2004) *Continuous radio and television audience assessment. June–December 2004.* Malta. On WWW, 12th March 2005, at http://www.ba-malta.org/.

Camilleri, A. (1995) *Bilingualism in Education, the Maltese Experience.* Heidelberg: Julius Groos Verlag.

Caruana, S. (2003) *Mezzi di comunicazione e input linguistico. L'acquisizione dell'italiano L2 a Malta.* Milano: Franco Angeli.

Caruana, S. (2006) Trilingualism in Malta. Maltese, English and 'italiano televisivo'. *International Journal of Multilingualism* 3 (3).

Cassola, A. (1998) *L'italiano a Malta.* Malta: MUP.

Ellul, S. (1978) *A Case Study in Bilingualism, Code-switching Between Parents and their Pre-school Children in Malta.* Cambridge: Huntington.

Farrugia, A. (2004) Gli studenti della prima media e la competenza in italiano L2. Unpublished B.Ed. (Hons.) dissertation, University of Malta.

Hull, G. (1993) *The Malta Language Question: A Case History in Cultural Imperialism.* Valletta: Said International.

Micheli, S. (2001) Language attitudes of the young generation in Malta. Unpublished M.Phil. thesis, University of Vienna.

National Statistics Office (2002) *Kultura 2000 a survey on cultural participation.* Valletta: NSO.

National Statistics Office (2003) *Culture Statistics 2000.* Valletta: NSO.

Said, L. (1991) Attitudes towards Maltese and English. Unpublished B.Ed. (Hons.) dissertation, University of Malta.

Sciriha, L. (2001) Trilingualism in Malta: Social and educational perspectives. *International Journal of Bilingualism and Bilingual Education* 4, 23–37.

Sciriha, L. (2004) *Keeping in Touch. The Sociolinguistics of Mobile Telephony in Malta.* Malta: Agenda.

Sciriha, L. and Vassallo, M. (2001) *Malta – A Linguistic Landscape.* Malta: Caxton.

Zammit, M. (1999) Attitudes towards the teaching and learning of modern languages in the Maltese Primary school. Unpublished B.Ed. (Hons.) dissertation, University of Malta.

Chapter 9

Language Use and Language Attitudes in Wales

JANET LAUGHARNE

The Sociolinguistic Context

In Wales there is a strong and lively tradition of a power struggle between two languages, Welsh and English. As can be seen from Figure 9.1, Wales is located in the South-Western part of the UK, sharing its boundaries with England. Together with Northern Ireland and Scotland these regions make up the UK. The population of Wales is around 5.2 million and that of its closest neighbour, England, 56 million. This relative size and neighbouring location has accounted in the past for the encyclopaedia entry which read 'for Wales, see England'.

The Welsh language shares Celtic roots with Breton in Northern France and Cornish in the South of England. According to the last census in 2001, the number of Welsh speakers in Wales was around 22% of the population, that is around 1.2 million. There are also Welsh speakers living outside Wales, notably in Patagonia, but also across the world, and the Internet has become an increasing domain for talking the language (Petre, 1997).

The history of Welsh, from the 19th until the last 40 years of the 20th century, was one of decline westwards, with a corresponding increase in the use of English. For example, the 1901 census showed that 50% of the population could speak Welsh; 30% of these were monolingual Welsh speakers. By the 1991 census there were 18.6% Welsh speakers, with over 55% of these living in the two most concentrated Welsh-speaking areas, Gwynedd and Dyfed in North and West Wales respectively (Jenkins & Williams, 2000). This situation has been represented as a broad twofold division (Aitchison & Carter, 2004) as can be seen in Figure 9.2. Areas in the North-East and South-East particularly, Cluster 1, showed wide-spread loss of Welsh, while in the shaded area, Cluster 2, a greater proportion of the population spoke Welsh. The situation was complicated by the fact of economic decline in the Welsh-speaking 'heartland' and a consequent loss of young people from these areas. In these circumstances, one might expect Welsh to have long since died. Yet the story of Welsh as a minority European language is one of successful language survival.

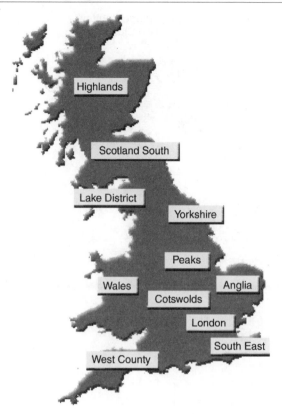

Figure 9.1 Map of Wales in the UK

The 1991 census showed, for the first time, a slowing down in the overall decline in numbers of speakers and even a growth in some areas, in the younger population. Key reasons for this change from decline to growth have been identified as an increasing awareness of the crisis of incipient language death and consequent political activity, both in parliament and by lobby groups. Other factors have been the growth of Welsh-medium education from the 1970s; and the establishment of the Welsh-medium radio in 1977 and the television channel, S4C (Sianel 4 Cymraeg), in 1982.

Interestingly, areas of greatest language loss, such as South-East Wales, were areas of proportionately greatest growth in the 1991 census. This effect was most evident in the youngest part of the population, in 5–15 years olds. By the 2001 census, there was an overall increase in numbers of speakers from 18.6% to 20.5% and a continuing trend of growth in the youngest age groups. The Welsh Language Board (2004a) reported that the highest percentages of Welsh speakers were in the 5–15 age group at 40.8%.

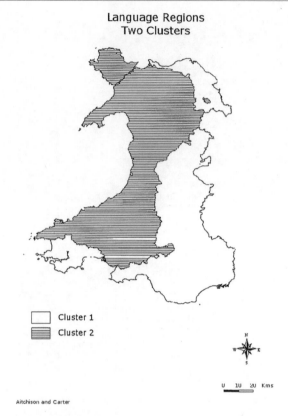

Figure 9.2 Linguistic distribution of Welsh-speaking areas in Wales
Source: Aitchison & Carter (2004)

Devolution and the introduction of the National Assembly for Wales, in 1999, have focused further the agenda for Welsh language planning into the 21st century. The policy document *Iaith Pawb* (Everyone's Language) (National Assembly for Wales, 2003) aims for an increase of 5% in the numbers of Welsh speakers by 2011, the next census. This would bring the numbers to around 26% of the population. Following on from the success of Welsh-medium education and the increase of Welsh spoken by young people, the focus has been on language transfer from one generation to the next and on using Welsh in domains beyond the home and school. There is also an aim to increase Welsh language education provision for the post-16 phase. These aims reflect the classic point made by Fishman (1985: 370) about the 'primary reward systems above and beyond the school', which must be in place if a minority language is to flourish in the community as a whole.

Wales in the UK

Several points are clear about Wales in the UK. First is its geographical closeness to England. This means that many people in Wales have English as their first language or they are fluently bilingual, with English as their second language. This is different from, for instance, Catalonia, where English would be the third or fourth language learned. The close proximity of England, the use of English by the vast majority of the population in the UK and its influence as a world language have a strong impact on language learning, as is reflected in the findings of these data. It is to be noted that all the participants could speak English. Indeed, 97% said they spoke good or very good English. Secondly, bilingualism in Wales is well established in policy and practice. Williams (2000: 656) identified a five-tier model of language survival that can be used as a measure here:

> idealism – 'vision'
> protest – 'mobilising'
> legitimacy – 'acceptance in some domains'
> institutionalisation – 'representing the language strategically'
> normalisation – 'extending to optimum range of social situations'.

In Wales at the beginning of the 21st century, it is the last two, 'institutionalisation' and 'normalisation' that represent the stage of language survival on Williams' model.

To this end, The Welsh Language Act (1993) was a significant milestone, as it laid the requirement for bilingual provision in all institutions, private and commercial, in Wales. Following this, too, there have been developments, such as *Mentrau Iaith* (Language Initiatives), to engage more local communities in using Welsh, especially in areas that have traditionally been strongly Welsh speaking. There are incentives to businesses to offer bilingual materials and there is increased visibility of Welsh on the Internet. Williams (2000: 677) notes there have been significant increases in the number of domains in which Welsh is used in the last three decades of the 20th century.

The focus has shifted, it is true to say, from seeing Welsh in polar opposition to English to a more integrated bilingual one: thus the word itself 'bilingual' is in common use and one most people are aware of in Wales. By implication, what this means in Wales is the existence of both the English and Welsh languages.

Beyond Bilingualism: Wales in Europe

The idea of 'beyond bilingualism', and learning European languages, causes some hiccups in Wales, as so much energy and resources have been put into establishing mechanisms to maintain and increase Welsh and make Wales a bilingual country. The term 'trilingualism' is relatively unfamiliar in Wales, whereas the term 'bilingualism' is becoming quite established. Yet, of course, there are trilingual speakers in Wales, coming from many parts of the world. Some come from the group under scrutiny, particularly speakers of French, German and Spanish. There are also trilingual speakers of other languages, notably Somali, Vietnamese, Cantonese, Bengali, Gujarati, Punjabi, Arabic and Urdu. The main point to note here, though, is that the teaching of Modern Foreign Languages (MFL) in the UK, and in this instance in Wales, has not thrived for some time. The decrease in take-up of MFL in secondary schools was noted by Estyn (2004b: 12), the Welsh school inspectorate, as 'a disturbing trend'.

The issue of European language learning is a UK-wide one and a government-funded study, the Nuffield Commission, was undertaken in 2000 to investigate the problem. Following this, initiatives were started across the UK as a whole to introduce MFL to children at a younger age. The value of speaking languages was stressed, for example LLAS (Language, Linguistics and Area Studies) published *Seven Hundred Reasons for Studying Languages* in 2004. In Wales, the NAW asked the newly formed CILT Cymru (Centre for Information on Language Teaching and Research) Wales to produce a policy document on MFL. This document, called *Languages Count*, produced in 2002, identified the importance of European languages to Wales for business, culture and citizenship.

MFL (generally French, German and Spanish) are to be introduced into primary schools in Wales from 2011. It will be interesting to see how this initiative is received, particularly by parents, and whether they will see MFL as competitive or additive. In the past, parents have been polarised in their views, some arguing for Welsh in preference to MFL, while others have argued the opposite, saying that teaching Welsh takes away time, money and opportunity for learning a European language in the curriculum.

Finally, definitions of bilingual and trilingual in Wales, with reference to European languages, are all to an extent influenced by the factor of English as one of the languages of the UK. Because it has such power and status as a common world language, it inevitably appears as one language in bi- or trilingual combinations of languages. Therefore, there is a distinction to be made between policy and practice in trilingualism in the UK. *Languages Count* (NAW, 2002b) is aspirational and looking to the future. In practice, the situation of MFL contrasts strongly with that of English and Welsh in Wales. The reasons for this are clear, but the challenge is nevertheless to achieve a greater degree of trilingualism than has existed in the past.

The Welsh Educational System

Welsh in education

In 1988 the Education Reform Act ruled that Welsh could be a medium of instruction for schools and, in addition, that Welsh should be taught as a subject in all state schools in Wales for pupils up to the age of 14. A cross-curricular dimension called the Curriculum Cymraeg was also required in the National Curriculum for Wales. This is the dimension that represents the cultural, historical and social aspects of Wales in the UK.

'Welsh-speaking schools' (NAW, 2004) are offered, where the medium of education is entirely, or largely, Welsh and where English is studied as a subject rather than the medium of education. Currently, around 31.9% of children are educated in Welsh-speaking schools (NAW, 2004). This represents about 1 in 5 children of school age. There are 448 Welsh-speaking primary schools and 54 Welsh-speaking secondary schools, with a total school population of 91,300 children (NAW, 2004). This situation follows on from a 40-year growth of Welsh-medium education in Wales. Analysis of performance in national tests has indicated that pupils perform well in Welsh-medium schools and that their level of English competence does not suffer (Reynolds *et al.*, 1998; Welsh Language Board, 2004b). The demand for Welsh-medium education is increasing across Wales. It is to be noted that much of the demand comes from parents who do not speak Welsh themselves. The areas of least naturally occurring Welsh in the community have been ones of particular growth in Welsh-medium provision and this has contributed substantially to the increase of Welsh speakers in the younger population.

The Mudiad Ysgolion Meithrin (MYM) (Nursery School Movement), established in 1971, was the bedrock upon which Welsh-medium education developed. The MYM is a flourishing Welsh-medium nursery provision throughout Wales for preschool children, which continues to grow strongly. It is organised on a regional basis, independently from the maintained school sector.

It has been recognised that there is a less satisfactory provision for Welsh-medium education between the ages of 16 and 21 than in earlier phases (Estyn, 2004a). Lack of suitably qualified staff and appropriate resources are two main reasons for this difficulty. The government policy document, *Iaith Pawb* (NAW, 2003), has an aim to increase the amount of Welsh language provision post-16 and in the university sector. Welsh-medium provision is less available in further and technical education, and in the sciences, and more available in the arts and humanities university departments (Estyn, 2004a). At the other end of educational provision, with the creation of a new Foundation Phase in Wales (NAW, 2004), which covers ages 3–7, there is an increased focus on bilingualism for the youngest ages and more children will be introduced to both Welsh and English.

So the overall picture is one of growth. There will be a continuing need to train more bilingual teachers as Welsh-medium provision is offered from the early years through to higher education. One finding of the current research is the high levels of competence of the participants in both Welsh and English. As over 97% were training to be teachers, this is heartening for future provision.

MFL in education

Unlike the healthy growth of Welsh in Wales, the uptake of MFL, mainly French, German or Spanish, has been in steady decline in schools over the last 10 years (CILT, 2005; Estyn, 2004b). These languages are begun in secondary school for the majority of pupils, after the age of 11. A further MFL can be added after the age of 13 or 14. In effect, pupils only learn a European language for three years, from the age of 11 to 14, when they can drop it in favour of other curriculum choices. This is clearly not likely to be successful as a language-learning strategy.

The uptake shows a trend shared by other noncompulsory subjects in a curriculum where there has been an increased focus on the basic skills of literacy, numeracy and information technology (IT). Not surprisingly, subjects that are seen as easier, more enjoyable, or ones that will lead to future employment, are chosen over MFL, which has been traditionally seen as 'difficult' and where many pupils do not achieve fluency comparable to their European counterparts in English (Lee *et al.*, 1998).

The aspect of crowding of the curriculum also contributes to the problem. There is pressure for schools to deliver on assessed standards for subjects and also on cross-curricular dimensions, such as citizenship, health education and, in Wales, the Curriculum Cymraeg. In response to the above difficulties the Welsh Baccalaureate has been piloted in several schools across Wales. It has a unit called Wales and Europe with a language module at levels from beginner to skilled, where Welsh and another European language are required (Welsh Baccalaureate, 2004).

Overall, then, it is clear that there is disharmony currently between bilingualism and trilingualism in Wales. As we have seen, two policy documents emerged within a year of each other from the National Assembly for Wales: *Iaith Pawb* (NAW, 2003) and *Languages Count* (NAW, 2002b). As yet, many more teachers are aware of the document that talks of bilingualism *Iaith Pawb*, than the one that talks of trilingualism, *Languages Count*.There are two main linguistic challenges in education in Wales:

(1) to maintain and expand the lesser used minority language, which will always be at risk against its globally spoken, Internet-friendly neighbour, English; and

(2) to succeed in turning around the decline in the number of pupils choosing to study European languages in school and university.

Ironically, these two challenges sit in a parallel and paradoxical way together: many of the fluent Welsh bilingual speakers in schools in Wales have come from English-speaking homes and are exactly the same sort of children who have been unsuccessful in learning a European language in the past and who avoid choosing it when options are available in the curriculum. Certainly, the relative lack of take-up of MFL in Wales, and the UK in general, has been seen as a threat to its future prosperity, as portrayed in a publicity campaign under the banner of *Languages Work* (Department for Education and Skills, 2004). The contrast with continental Europe can be seen clearly in the following quotation, where Cenoz (2003: 203) discusses the issue of trilingual speaking:

> Third language acquisition is becoming more widespread because of the trend to introduce a foreign language from an earlier age and a second foreign language at the end of primary school or in secondary school and because of the increasing use of minority languages in education.

This is not mirrored in Wales at the present time, but it might be, as the policies of *Languages Count* develop.

Previous Studies on Language Attitudes in Wales

Much research on language attitudes in Wales has taken place around education. Here the focus has been on the Welsh language, especially on its threatened survival, and research to find out the causes of language loss. A key question regarding attitude was the fall-off of use and less positive attitude towards Welsh in children around the age of 11–12 years old.

Several studies, between the 1950s and 1980s, asked school children their attitude to Welsh (see Jones, 1949, 1950; Sharp *et al.*, 1973; Lewis, 1975 in Baker, 1988). Baker found, in analysing these studies, that the question of why young people had a less favourable attitude to Welsh after the age of 11 was increasingly refined as research sought to locate the most influential variables on the effect. He concluded in his research that one strong influence was the nature of the 'active, participatory culture' (Baker, 1988: 124) young people engaged in and that this might require addressing within policies on language planning.

Attitudes to language have been explored via geolinguistics and language use, as in the work of Balsam (1985), Williams (1985, 1988) and Aitchison and Carter (1985, 1994, 2000, 2004). These mapped language use and attitude onto geographical areas. Balsom proposed a three Wales model within a discussion of politics in Wales. *Y Fro Cymraeg* was represented by North and West Wales. This area was strongly identified with Welsh culture and was Welsh speaking. *Welsh Wales* he described as South Wales, an area that was non-Welsh-speaking, but identifying with Wales and Welsh culture. *British Wales* he described as the remainder of Wales (near borders with England, apart from a small part of West Wales in Pembrokeshire). This area was non-Welsh-speaking and relatively more British-identifying in attitude.

Aitchison and Carter developed the idea of geolinguistics by relating it to census data and carrying out longitudinal survey work of language use in Wales. They particularly examined the shifts over time of language use in different regions, using a variety of factors, such as gender, age, education and social class. Because their work spans 20 years they offer a fine-grained level of detail regarding language use. They show, particularly, the population shifts in speakers of Welsh according to area and age as being one of an increase in young speakers in Balsom's *Welsh Wales* model and of loss in *Y Fro Cymraeg*.

Williams (1985) also explored the idea of geolinguistics, through concept mapping of the 'Welshness' associated with regions of Wales. This was a very interesting approach and a methodology that has been adopted in other studies, such as within the work of Garrett (2003). Garrett examined attitudes to accent and dialect in the English spoken by teenagers in schools throughout Wales. Indeed, Garrett *et al.* (2003: 20) make an important point when they say 'ethnolinguistic identity in Wales is as much bound up with use of the English language as with use of Welsh'. This line of research has linked fruitfully to other work on minority languages and attitude, for example research on language and attitude in Canada (Giles & Coupland, 1991).

Of course, attitudes are complex and subject to change. This is especially so with the political and social changes, which have happened since the 1990s in Wales, notably the establishment of the National Assembly for Wales in 1999. A poll carried out in 1996 for the Welsh Language Board, and discussed in Aitchison and Carter (2004: 21), reported over 90% agreement that the number of Welsh speakers should be increased and that there should be more opportunities to use Welsh (94% for Welsh speakers and 80% for non-Welsh speakers). The Welsh Language Board also carried out a survey with 815 adults in 1995, which was the first large-scale study on attitudes of that decade. It found 74% of the respondents described themselves as Welsh and 14% as British. Twenty-three percent strongly supported the use of Welsh in society, with a further 48% supporting it. Only 3% strongly opposed its use. Eighteen percent of the sample said they could speak Welsh fluently (Central Office of Information/WLB, 1995).

The attitude survey above was undertaken 10 years prior to the present study and there are broad points of similarity and difference to note. One similarity is the positive attitude towards Welsh. A difference is that there is a much higher percentage (69% as opposed to 18%) in numbers of self-reported fluent speakers in the current data. This might be in part because of the nature of the sample, who were mainly training to be teachers. However, the large difference in the percentages also reflects the gains over the last 10 years in numbers of speakers. This is supported by the finding of the General Teaching Council for Wales (GTCW, 2005: 8) that 35.4% of teachers in their first year of teaching were able to speak Welsh.

The National Assembly for Wales, since its establishment, has been instrumental in shaping attitudes to language, particularly through the Welsh Language Board and commissioned work. For example, there is the project 'Twf' which was started in 1999 to encourage intergenerational language transfer, reported by Edwards and Newcombe (2003), and the work on attitudes to Welsh and commerce (Welsh Consumer Council, 1996).

Finally, Baker's study, *Attitudes and Language* (1992), has proved to be an influential work, not only in Wales, but across the UK and internationally. This study brought together a number of novel aspects, including theory and research instruments from social psychology, an area that had previously been under-represented in research on bilingualism. One of its key findings, in a large-scale, longitudinal study with pupils between 11 and 16 years, showed the impact of popular culture to be high in predicting language attitudes. Baker (1992: 137) concluded:

> Whether a minority language lives or dies may be about its ability to give a life-saving injection to the culture of its teenagers.

This work, importantly, looked at attitudes to bilingualism as 'holistic, additive and organic' (Baker, 1992: 137). Much of the strategic development of the National Assembly for Wales in *Iaith Pawb* (2003) and the language planning of the Welsh Language Board arises from the knowledge created by Baker's research (1985, 1988, 1992, 1994, 2002) into bilingualism in and beyond Wales.

The Study: Sample and Results

The sample

Questionnaire responses were collected from higher education institutions (HEI) in mid and South Wales: Aberystwyth, Carmarthen, Swansea, Newport and Cardiff. Two hundred and three students took part. In terms of socioeconomic groups, 60.3% came from higher, 29.4% from middle and 9.8% from lower groups. This strongly underlines the economic factors that affect students' ability to take up university places. All students were in the first term of their first year of training.

The majority of the students (77%) were training for primary education (5–11 years) with 19% training for secondary education (11–18 years) and a small number studying psychology and early years education (3–5 years). Although all students were in their first year of training, there was a wide span of ages. The youngest was 18 and the oldest was 47. Seventy-two percent of the sample was in the age range 18–24 and, within this group, the average age was 20 years. Most of the sample (92.2%) came from Wales, 4.9% came from England and 0.5% from Ireland. None came from Scotland and 2.5% came from another country. Most (77.6%) came from a hometown of less than 100,000 inhabitants, while 22.1% came from larger towns; 6.4% did not respond, perhaps because they came from a rural community. 65.2% of the sample came from mainly English-speaking and 30.9% from mainly Welsh-speaking hometowns.

As can be seen from Figure 9.3, 46.6% said English was their first language. There were 3% who had a language other than English or Welsh as their mother tongue. Twenty-five percent said they had Welsh as their first language. These figures are higher than 2001 census returns (WLB, 2004a) and also the figure of 35.4% for those in their first year of teaching returned in a survey in 2004 by the General Teaching Council for Wales (GTCW, 2005). If this figure is added to those who say they have Welsh and English together as their mother tongue, this figure rises to 51%, which is a significant finding and one which will be returned to in the discussion later in the chapter.

The age at which most of the sample started learning MFL was 11 or 12 (63.2%). This is usual in the UK, at the start of secondary school. Despite three years' study of a MFL, 16.5% defined themselves as having no knowledge of a European language; 56.5% said they had a little knowledge and a surprising 26.5% (54 students) said they had good or very good knowledge; 66.8% had no knowledge of a second MFL, 22.6%

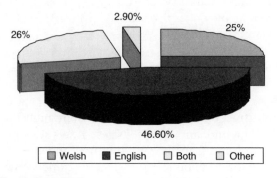

Figure 9.3 The students' L1

had a little knowledge and 10.5% said they had good or very good knowledge of a second MFL. Most of the respondents (77.5%) had visited a MFL-speaking country. The most striking feature of these figures overall for MFL is the number of students, over a quarter, who said they had a good or very good knowledge of a European language.

Procedure

The data were collected during the first two months of the academic year. Questionnaires were either collected by hand in the author's home institution with the help of other staff in the education and psychology departments, or by post from the four other education departments in West and South Wales whose senior managers agreed to take part in the research. The questionnaire was presented in English only for reasons of logistics and communication across several institutions and departments. No student was disadvantaged by this, since all had English as a first or second language. However, it is recognised that not offering the questionnaires in Welsh was a weakness in a study examining bi- and trilingualism. One error in adapting the questionnaire to the Wales context occurred for question 16c where the majority and minority languages were transposed. This resulted in responses being towards the majority language, English, rather than minority language, Welsh.

A strong feature of the study is the fact that responses were collected from five different HEIs. This represented a good spread, both geographically and in terms of the provision of education departments across Wales.

Results

As Figure 9.4 shows, it is clear that the greatest confidence is in English (82%) and the least in the third language (9%). This is not surprising in the general context discussed above. What is most striking is that 42% of the sample said their Welsh was very good and a further 27% said it was good. This figure is much higher than 2001 census figures for the general population and even those for the 5–15-year-old group, which were 40.8% (WLB, 2003). Regarding the third language taught in school, while there are 55% who say they had little knowledge of MFL, 26.5% (54) students say they had good or very good competence. This is again a surprising figure, and may relate to the benefits of bilingualism in helping to create confidence in learning subsequent languages.

The attitudes toward the three languages are demonstrated in Figure 9.5. From this it can be seen that the least unfavourable attitudes are towards Welsh (3.09%) and the most unfavourable are towards the MFL (13.97%), with English being closer to the percentage of Welsh (4.62%). The most favourable attitudes are towards Welsh (62.37%), with English

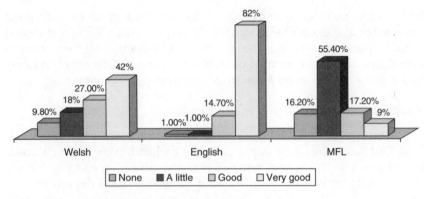

Figure 9.4 Level of competence in the three languages

and MFL together (50.89%) not equalling the degree of positive attitude shown towards it. The most neutral attitude is shown towards MFL at 68.16%, followed by English (58.46%) and Welsh (35%). It indicates that in the group as a whole there are strongly favourable attitudes shown towards Welsh, with only a small percentage of students who are neutral or unfavourable. This reflects similar trends found in other research in Wales (Baker, 1985, 1988, 1992; Central Office of Information/WLB, 1995; Williams & Morris, 2000; WLB, 2001).

There is a more neutral response for both English and MFL with the balance towards a more unfavourable attitude for MFL and a more favourable attitude for English. These figures must be seen in the context of self-reporting and of a questionnaire about Welsh and English to which many respondents would be sensitised in considering the 'right' or 'appropriate' response. However, it highlights the relative lack of positive attitude toward MFL quite starkly. Interestingly, it contrasts with

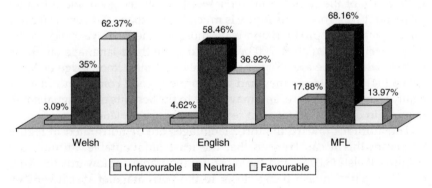

Figure 9.5 Attitudes towards the three languages

the 26.5% of students who said they had good or very good competence in MFL and this is a point that will be returned to later in the chapter.

From Table 9.1 it can be seen that the most consistent use of Welsh was within the family and that the highest use of 'always Welsh' was to teachers (27%). At the other end of the spectrum, 'always in English', the highest use was to father (57.4%) and then neighbours (55.7%). It is to be noted, regarding the aspect of friends outside school, that, although 64.6% either mainly or always spoke English, a further 29.6% either mainly or wholly spoke Welsh to friends outside school, with a further 14.7% saying they used both languages about equally. This is a very important point given the drive of NAW and the national language policy *Iaith Pawb* (NAW, 2003) to increase the use of Welsh outside the classroom and will be returned to in the conclusion.

In terms of proportions of numbers, the highest figures lie in the 'always in English' column with over 50% for three addressees and none less that 30%. The lowest figures lie in bilingual use in the home, which are all less than 5%, with the exception of the 'in English more than Welsh' category, which is more than 11%. Taken together, these figures reflect the importance of family and school for the use of Welsh and underline the continuing need to develop Welsh and bilingual provision in domains outside the immediate home and the classroom.

Table 9.2 gives the results for the languages used in various media activities. From this it can be seen that the most use of Welsh is for TV, with 62.8% using this medium for some form of Welsh viewing. This is very encouraging and reflects the impact of the Welsh channel S4C, which has been established since 1982. The next highest figure for Welsh is 43.1% for listening to the radio. The press and music are 39.7% and 36.4% respectively. Overall, these figures show that more than a third of the students use some form of Welsh for all four media activities. This finding indicates increasing bilingual use of the two languages in the media.

For Table 9.3, as explained in the procedure section of the study, the findings relate to the majority language, English. It can be seen that the three responses that are over 80% are for its importance for reading, writing and getting a job. Conversely, the four areas where English is seen as least important are for being liked (30.9%), for being accepted in the community (21.1%) and for living in Wales and bringing up children (14.2% each). Generally, there is a high consistency in the view that it is important to speak English, with most responses in the 'important' category being over 50%. However, there are also responses to the midway categories, indicating a gradation of agreement. In some ways this is quite surprising. The relativity in opinion, especially around language used socially, with children and in the community is an interesting finding on attitudes to English and Welsh.

Table 9.1 Language used when talking to the following people

	Always in Welsh (%)	In Welsh more often than English (%)	In Welsh and English about equally (%)	In English more often than Welsh (%)	Always in English (%)
Father	22.1	2.0	2.5	11.3	57.4
Mother	20.6	4.4	5.4	11.8	54.9
Brothers and sisters	23.	3.4	5.4	20.6	41.7
Friends in the classroom	13.2	17.6	15.7	18.1	33.3
Friends outside school	7.8	11.8	14.7	24	40.2
Teachers	27	18.6	7.8	8.8	36.3
Neighbours	11.3	11.3	6.4	11.3	55.9

Table 9.2 Means of communication and language used

	Always in Welsh (%)	In Welsh more often than English (%)	In Welsh and English about equally (%)	In English more often than Welsh (%)	Always in English (%)
Watching TV	26.5	19.1	7.4	9.8	35.3
The press	10.3	10.3	7.8	11.3	57.4
Music	1	1.5	7.4	26.5	61.3
Listening to the radio	1	2.9	9.3	29.9	54.4

Table 9.3 Importance attached to the English language to do the following activities

For people to:	Important (%)	A little important (%)	A little unimportant (%)	Unimportant (%)
Make friends	65.2	23	2.9	6.4
Read	86.3	8.3	0.5	2.5
Write	83.8	10.9	1.5	1.5
Watch TV	57.4	31.4	3.4	5.4
Get a job	81.9	10.9	1	2
Be liked	22.1	25	16.7	30.9
Live in Wales	35.8	34.8	11.3	14.2
Bring up children	47.5	25	9.8	14.2
Go shopping	39.7	31.9	10.8	13.2
Make phone calls	53.4	31.4	4.9	7.4
Pass exams	59.3	22.1	6.4	7.8
Be accepted in the community	31.4	26.6	16.2	21.1
Talk to friends at university	44.1	33.8	10.8	7.4
Talk to teachers at university	46.1	28.4	12.7	8.3
Talk to people out of university	45.1	31.9	8.8	8.3

With regard to other findings, for gender there was a statistically significant result in that men were more positive in attitude than women about both English [F (1, 191) 192 = 4.838, $p = 0.029$] and MFL [F (1, 175) = 8.120, $p = 0.005$]. There was no statistically significant result for Welsh, although the mean attitude showed a more positive attitude in women. For age, there was a significance value only for Welsh [F (23, 169) = 2.528, $p = 0.000$], with a generally positive attitude towards Welsh, but within that trend, the older the student the less positive they were in attitude. In socioeconomic groups, there were no statistically significant results for attitudes to any of the three languages.

An unexpected finding was that university training course revealed significant values for attitudes towards all three languages: for Welsh [F (3, 189) = 4.401, $p = 0.005$], for English [F (3, 190) = 2.890, $p = 0.037$] and for MFL [F (3, 174) = 4.921, $p = 0.003$]. Secondary education and social education students were more positive than primary and early years students about MFL, while primary and social education students were more positive about Welsh than secondary and early years students.

As for geographical factors, if the student had travelled abroad there was a more favourable attitude to MFL [F (4, 174) = 3.901, $p = 0.005$]. Size of hometown had a significance value for attitude to Welsh [T (180) = -2.574, $p = 0.011$], but not English or MFL. Those from towns of less than 100,000 inhabitants had a more favourable attitude towards Welsh than those from a town with more than 100,000 inhabitants. The language of hometown showed a statistically significant result for Welsh [F (1, 188) = 26.411, $p = 0.000$] and English [F (1, 185) = 9.996, $p = 0.000$], but not MFL. Those from mainly Welsh-speaking communities had a more favourable attitude to Welsh, while English-speaking communities had a more favourable attitude to English.

When linguistic factors were considered, students' first language showed a significant value for all three languages. For Welsh [F (3, 189) = 16.668, $p = 0.000$], those who had Welsh or both Welsh and English as a first language had a more positive attitude towards Welsh than those who had English. For English [F (3, 190) = 15.467, $p = 0.000$], those whose first language was English had the most positive attitude, followed by those who had Welsh and English together. Those who had Welsh only as their first language had the least positive attitude. For MFL [F (3, 174) = 2.891, $p = 0.038$], those with English, and both Welsh and English, as a first language(s) were more positive than those who had Welsh as a first language.

Regarding the age at which a language was learned, there were no significance values found for age of learning MFL or English, unlike Welsh where age of learning had a significant value for attitude to all three languages. For Welsh [F (19, 174) = 4.931, $p = 0.000$], the most favourable

Table 9.4 Summary of the most influential variables on language attitudes

Independent variable	Attitudes towards Welsh	Attitudes towards English	Attitudes towards MFL	Competence in MFL
Training	Primary and Social Education > EY and Secondary	EY > Social Education, Primary and Secondary Ed.	Social Education and Secondary > Primary and Early Years	
Gender	n.s.	Men > Women	Men > Women	
Size of hometown	−100,000 > + 100,000	n.s.	n.s.	
Language of hometown	Mainly Welsh speaking > Mainly English speaking	Mainly English speaking > Mainly Welsh speaking	n.s.	
Age at which they started to learn MFL	n.s.	n.s.	n.s.	Good and very good <7 and > 16 years old
Visited L3-speaking country			Visited > not visited	Visited > not visited
Age at which they started to learn Welsh	Younger > older	Older > younger	Older > younger	
L1	Welsh, both Welsh and English > English	English, > both English and Welsh and Welsh	English > English and Welsh and Welsh	

(Continued)

Table 9.4 (*Continued*)

Independent variable	Attitudes towards Welsh	Attitudes towards English	Attitudes towards MFL	Competence in MFL
Competence (+, good and very good; −, a little or none)				
Welsh	+ Welsh > − Welsh	− Welsh > + Welsh	− Welsh > + Welsh	
English	n.s.	+ English > − English	n.s.	
MFL	n.s.	− MFL > + MFL	Good MFL > v. good MFL	

attitude for this variable was shown if Welsh was learnt before the age of five, with a downward trend sharply dipping for those who learnt Welsh at age 12 and recovering upwards for those learning Welsh after the age of 13. For attitudes to English [F (19, 175) = 3.750, $p = 0.000$], related to the age of learning Welsh, mean scores show a rising trend of favourable attitude to English, with peaks at age 11 and 21 and a decline in positive attitude towards English for those learning Welsh after the age of 21. This broadly confirms previous studies on age and language attitude towards Welsh (Baker, 1988, 1992). For MFL [F (19, 159) = 2.139, $p = 0.000$], there was a rising trend so that those who learnt Welsh at an older age were generally more positive towards MFL than those who learnt Welsh at an earlier age.

Competence is, here, on a self-reported scale and, as such, is of course open to individual and subjective interpretation. However, it is un-doubtedly a very important variable to analyse in relation to questions of attitude towards language. Welsh competence gave a significance value for attitude to all three languages: Welsh [F (3, 182) = 50.226, $p = 0.000$], English [F (3, 183) = 16.538, $p = 0.000$] and MFL [F (3, 167) = 3.857, $p = 0.000$]. The higher the level of competence in Welsh the more positive the attitude towards that language, with a converse pattern for attitude to English. Those who spoke no Welsh had a much more positive attitude towards learning MFL than those who spoke Welsh. English competence only showed a significance value for attitude towards English [F (3, 188) = 3.743, $p = 0.012$], with the most favourable attitude in those who said they had very good English.

MFL competence gave a significance value for attitude towards MFL [F (3, 173) = 14.980, $p = 0.000$] and English [F (3, 187) = 3.763, $p = 0.012$], but not Welsh. Those who said they had 'very good' MFL had a less positive attitude towards this language group, curiously, than those who said they had 'good' competence. Those with little or no knowledge of MFL scored the most favourable attitude towards English. The age of learning MFL had a significance value [F (22, 177) = 3.486, $p = 0.000$] for competence. Interestingly, this contrasts with the nonsignificance value for this variable on attitude to MFL. The effect of visiting a L3 country on competence also gave a significance value [F (1, 173) = 6.574, $p = 0.011$].

Taken together, these findings about competence confirm key points about attitudes to the languages under consideration. Attitude to Welsh is shown to be a very sensitive variable and one which inter-related with many others, such as language of hometown, addressee, training phase, socioeconomic group as well as competence, first language and age of learning the language. There were often significance values for all three languages under consideration. This is helpful in pointing to future work, which would need to look further at these variables together.

Few variables gave a significance value for attitudes towards English. First language, competence, gender, training phase and language of hometown showed an effect but they were generally related to English only, rather than to Welsh and MFL as well. The data show the value attached to English, both as a global language and one spoken throughout the UK, including Wales. This is reflected in the number of nonsignificant variables found for English, together with the level of positive and neutral attitude scores for that language. In essence, this shows the lack of perceived threat to it by either Welsh or MFL. It should be noted that all the students in the sample spoke English and that there was a high level of self-reported good or very good competence in English (97%). However, it was interesting to note the relative unimportance ascribed to English for some items in the data, including 'being liked' (47.6%), 'living in Wales' (25.5%), 'being accepted in the community' (37.3%) and 'bringing up children' (24.0%).

For MFL the link between attitude and other factors is less sensitive than Welsh, but more so than English. There was significance value offered in several cases not only towards MFL, but also towards English and Welsh. Variables that gave significance values for MFL were first language, visiting a European country and whether the respondent spoke more than three languages.

Discussion

These data show Welsh linguistic vitality (Bourhis *et al.*, 1981) to be high and the aspiration for increasing numbers of bilingual speakers in Wales to be feasible. In the data there are 51% respondents who said Welsh was their first or equal second language. Taken together that is a higher figure than those who say that English alone was their first language. Even putting aside elements such as the nature of the group (education students) and the situation in which the data were collected (an attitude questionnaire), this is an exciting finding to report and underlines the continuing trend upwards in the younger part of the population in Wales. Also, Welsh competence is shown to be high and this again is a positive aspect to report relative to the future need for teachers who are able to speak Welsh.

An interesting trend is shown in these data between bilingual ability in Welsh and English and competence in MFL. Twenty-six percent of the sample said they had good or very good MFL, which is a higher than expected level of competence in the third language and is a significant finding. Generally, the link between being bilingual and competence in further languages is demonstrated in these findings. Therefore, even though attitudes towards MFL were neutral or negative in the data, this was contradicted in some measure by other responses that gave more positive opinions. For instance, there was general agreement that Welsh,

English and MFL were all 'easy languages to learn', which again reflects an underlying trend of confidence in the ability to learn languages.

For relative attitudes to the three language groups, attitude to Welsh was the most favourable score, with English next and then MFL. With regard to relative competence, English was the highest score, then Welsh and MFL. These figures reflect the growth in Welsh speakers and underline the aspect of bilingualism, with a very good degree of self-reported competence in both English and Welsh. This can, again, be seen as a mark of an increasingly linguistically able population.

The impact of the media is demonstrated in the 62.8% who view the Welsh television channel S4C using some degree of Welsh. This is a very encouraging sign regarding the use of this media in the development of bilingualism in Wales. The domains in which Welsh is spoken reflect previous findings, being mainly in education and the home (Baker, 1988, 1992; Welsh Language Board, 1995, 2003; Williams & Morris, 2000). However, the increased use of Welsh with friends, both in university and socially, is a trend worth noting.

In terms of the relative status and relationship to one another of Welsh, English and MFL, economic factors cannot be ignored and it is hard to imagine how English could cease to be a most powerful and persuasive language from the point of view of communication in a world context. From the point of view of culture and identity in Wales, the imperative is Welsh as well as English. The third language, whether it is French, German or Spanish, does not, currently, carry that imperative of economic power or cultural attachment. But, as these data show, although there is a fairly low level of positive attitude to MFL, there is a degree of confidence in self-reported competence towards European languages and also the perception that language learning is not difficult. These are optimistic signs.

Wales has traditionally been willing to be European in its approach to policy formation. For instance, the current implementation of the new curriculum 3–7 owes much to Italy and other European models of early years education. Wales, it would seem, needs now to become more European in its attitude to languages. Indeed, the fact of Wales striving to be recognised at many levels as a bilingual country paves the way for trilingualism. Making a bridge between the benefits of increased competence in other languages, which are offered from being bilingual, and a more positive attitude to more languages will be important in the future. Williams (2000: 681) said:

> The distinctly modern feature of bilingual identity in Wales is that it is based increasingly on contextualised individuality rather than on ethnic and ancestral affiliation.

This 'contextualised individuality' might well need to contain within it, as well as language use and attitudes to Welsh and English, the ability to use other languages locally, nationally and internationally. Then Wales will sit comfortably in the UK, in Europe and beyond.

References

Aitchison, J. and Carter, H. (1994) *A Geography of the Welsh Language*. Cardiff: University of Wales Press.

Aitchison, J. and Carter, H. (2000) *Language, Economy and Society: The Changing Fortunes of the Welsh Language in the Twentieth Century*. Cardiff: University of Wales Press.

Aitchison, J. and Carter, H. (2004) *Spreading the Word: The Welsh Language 2001*. Talybont: Y Lolfa.

Baker, C. (1985) *Aspects of Bilingualism in Wales*. Clevedon: Multilingual Matters.

Baker, C. (1988) *Key Issues in Bilingualism and Bilingual Education*. Clevedon: Multilingual Matters.

Baker, C. (1992) *Attitudes and Language*. Clevedon: Multilingual Matters.

Baker, C. (1994) *Foundations of Bilingual Education and Bilingualism*. Clevedon: Multilingual Matters.

Baker, C. (2002) *A Parents' and Teachers' Guide to Bilingualism*. Clevedon: Multilingual Matters.

Balsam, D. (1985) The three Wales model. In J. Osmond (ed.) *The National Question Again: Welsh Political Identity in the 1980s* (pp. 1–17). Llandysul: Gomer.

Bourhis, R.Y., Giles, H. and Rosenthal, D. (1981) Notes on the construction of a 'Subjective Vitality Questionnaire' for ethnolinguistic groups. *Journal of Multicultural and Multilingual Development* 2, 145–155.

Bwrdd yr Iaith Gymraeg (2001) The Use of the Welsh Language 2000 Welsh. Cardiff: The Welsh Language Board. On WWW at http://www.bwrdd-yr-iaith.org.uk. Accessed on 20th July 2005.

Bwrdd yr Iaith Gymraeg (2004a) Census 2001: Main Statistics about Welsh. Cardiff: The Welsh Language Board. On WWW at http://www.bwrdd-yr-iaith.org.uk. Accessed on 20th July 2005.

Bwrdd-yr-Iaith Gymraeg (2004b) A Bilingual Education for your Child: From Nursery to Primary School. Cardiff: The Welsh Language Board/NAW. On WWW at http://www.bwrdd-yr-iaith.org.uk. Accessed on 20th July 2005.

Cenoz, J. (2003) Teaching English as a third language: The effect of attitudes and motivation. In C. Hoffmann and J. Ytsma (eds) *Trilingualism in Family, School and Community* (pp. 202–218). Clevedon: Multilingual Matters.

Central Office of Information and the Welsh Language Board (1995) *Public Attitudes to the Welsh Language: A Research Report prepared by NOP Social and Political for the Central Office of Information and the Welsh Language Board*. London: NOP Social and Political.

The CILT Bulletin for Language Teaching and Research in Higher Education. London: CILT. On WWW at http://www.cilt.org.uk. Accessed on 26th July 2005.

Department of Education and Skills (2004) *Languages Work*. London: DfES.

Edwards, V. and Newcombe, L. (2003) Evaluation of the efficiency and effectiveness of the TWF project, which encourages parents to transmit the language to their children. Cardiff. The Welsh Language Board. On WWW at http://www.bwrdd-yr-iaith.org.uk. Accessed on 20th July 2005.

Estyn (2004a) The Welsh Language – Our language: its Future (Iaith Pawb). Advice to support the implementation of aspects of the Education and Lifelong learning Committee Policy review. Cardiff: Estyn. On WWW at http://www.estyn.gov.uk. Accessed on 26th July 2005.

Estyn (2004b) Modern Foreign Languages in Welsh-Medium Schools. Cardiff: Estyn. On WWW at http://www.estyn.gov.uk. Accessed on 26th July 2005.

Fishman, J.A. (1985) *The Rise and Fall of the Ethnic Revival: Perspectives on Language and Ethnicity.* New York: Moulton Publishers.

Garrett, P., Coupland, N. and Williams, A. (2003) *Investigating Language Attitudes: Social Meanings of Dialect, Ethnicity and Performance.* Cardiff: University of Wales Press.

General Teaching Council for Wales (GTCW) (2005) Wales' first inductees. *Teaching Council for Wales* 7, 8–9.

Giles, H. and Coupland, N. (1991) *Language: Contexts and Consequences.* Milton Keynes: Open University Press.

Jenkins, G.H. and Williams, M.A. (eds) (2000) *'Let's Do Our Best for the Ancient Tongue': The Welsh Language in the Twentieth Century.* Cardiff: University of Wales Press.

Jones, W.R. (1949) Attitude towards Welsh as a second language. A preliminary investigation. *British Journal of Educational Psychology* 19, 44–52.

Jones, W.R. (1950) Attitude towards Welsh as a second language. A further investigation. *British Journal of Educational Psychology* 20, 117–132.

Languages, Linguistics and Area Studies (LLAS) (2005) Seven hundred reasons for learning languages. On WWW at http://www.llas.soton.ac.uk. Accessed on 26th July 2005.

Lee, J., Buckland, D. and Shaw, G. (1998) *The Invisible Child: The Responses and Attitudes to the Learning of Modern Foreign Languages Shown by Year 9 Pupils of Average Ability.* London: CILT (Centre for Information on Language Teaching and Research).

Lewis, E.G. (1975) Attitude to language among bilingual children and adults in Wales. *International Journal of the Sociology of Language* 4, 103–121.

Petre, P. (1997) *Travels in an Old Tongue: Touring the World Speaking Welsh.* London: Harper Collins.

Reynolds, D., Bellin, W. and ab Ieuan, R. (1998) *A Competitive Edge: Why Welsh Medium Schools Perform Better.* Cardiff: Institute of Welsh Affairs.

Sharp, D., Thomas, B., Price, E., Francis, G. and Davies, I. (1973) *Attitudes to Welsh and English in the Schools of Wales.* Basingstoke/Cardiff: Macmillan/University of Wales Press.

The National Assembly for Wales (2002a) *Ein hiaith: ei dyfodol, Our Language: Its Future.* Cardiff: National Assembly for Wales.

The National Assembly for Wales/Centre for Languages Teaching and Research (CILT) Cymru (2002b) *Languages Count.* Cardiff: National Assembly for Wales.

The National Assembly for Wales (2003) *Iaith Pawb: A National Action Plan for a Bilingual Wales.* Cardiff: National Assembly for Wales

The National Assembly for Wales (2004) *School in Wales: General Statistics.* On WWW at www.wales.gov.uk. Accessed on 20th July 2005.

Welsh Baccalaureate (2004) Welsh Baccalaureate programme information. On WWW at http://www.wbq.org.uk. Accessed on 20th July 2005.

Welsh Consumer Council (1996) *Y Gymraeg fel pwnc defnyddwyr: papur polisi* [*Welsh as a Consumer Issue: A Policy Paper*]. Caerdydd: Cyngor Defnyddwyr Cymru.

Williams, C.H. (1985) On cultural space: perceptual culture regions in Wales. *Etudes Celtiques* 22, 273–295.

Williams, C.H. (2000) Restoring the language. In G.H Jenkins and M.A. Williams (eds) *"Let's Do Our Best for the Ancient Tongue": The Welsh Language in the Twentieth Century* (pp. 657–681). Cardiff: University of Wales Press.

Williams, G. and Morris, D. (2000) *Language Planning and Language Use: Welsh in a Global Age.* Cardiff: University of Wales Press.

Chapter 10

The Linguistic Issue in Some European Bilingual Contexts: Some Final Considerations

ÁNGEL HUGUET and DAVID LASAGABASTER

The European Union: Multilingualism for All

The European Union (EU) is clearly committed to a multilingual Europe in which all its educational systems are advised to include two Community languages. In 1995 the White Paper on education and training entitled *Teaching and Learning: Towards a Learning Society* proposed that EU citizens should be proficient in three European languages, that is to say, in their mother tongue and two other Community languages, in an attempt to keep multilingualism as one the main characteristics of Europe's identity. The concept of Community languages referred to the national languages of two other EU member-states, although in later European Commission documents this was specified in such a way that 'reference was made to one foreign language with high international status (English was deliberately not referred to) and one so-called "neighbouring language"' (Extra & Yagmur, 2004: 403).

Apart from being an added value when it comes to obtaining a job in today's European border-free single market, this multilingualism should help to promote tolerance and a better understanding amongst Europeans, to prepare people to live in a multicultural society, to equip citizens to participate in public life, to strengthen social cohesion and solidarity, while at the same time mitigating the spread of xenophobia and parochialism among current and future generations. It is therefore important that the learning of foreign languages does not become exclusive to just an elite or to those who, due to particular socio-geographical conditions, can afford it. Moreover, the special Eurobarometer Report 54, which was focused on the language skills of European citizens and their attitudes towards language learning, clearly shows that this idea is shared by the vast majority of Europeans, as 93% of parents considered it important for their children to learn other European languages, while 72% of Europeans believed that being able to speak foreign languages was/would be useful for them and almost the same proportion agreed that this should be English. In fact, English happens to be the most popular foreign language for European in-service training grants awarded under the Comenius action (Socrates programme), as 60% of the grants are aimed at courses taught in English, compared to only 14% in French and 5% in both German and Spanish. This report also demonstrates that, although much is said about linguistic and cultural diversity, languages other than English, French, German, Spanish and Russian are rarely learnt in European primary and secondary schools.

The EU considers that the best way to promote multilingualism relies on the early learning of the first foreign language (FL), which is why it is recommended to start at preschool level, whereas the second foreign language should be included in secondary education. The aforementioned White Paper proposes some measures to be taken in order to promote FL learning, such as the exchange of teaching materials and experiences, of teachers to teach their mother tongue in schools in another country, or the definition of a *European Quality Label* award to be given to those schools which meet certain criteria regarding the promotion of community language learning.

The result of this new multilingual educational landscape is that in all European bilingual contexts students will have to contend with four languages in the school curriculum: the two native languages plus two other European languages. Hence, in countries such as Spain, where till rather recently (the early 1980s) only the majority language – Spanish – could be used at school, the last few decades have witnessed a change from a monolingual school system into a multilingual one where the presence of more than two languages is a very common feature. The consequence of this situation is that English is becoming the L3 in many contexts (Cenoz & Jessner, 2000), as can be observed in this volume. Although it is universally understood in Ireland and Wales, having long been the dominant language, and very widespread in Malta, English represents the third language in the rest of the chapters that make up this volume, namely the Basque Country, Brussels (in most of the cases), Catalonia, Friesland, Galicia and the Valencian Community.

The social pressure to improve students' proficiency in foreign languages has led to the implementation of pilot projects in some Spanish communities, in which pupils start learning a foreign language – overwhelmingly English – before it becomes compulsory at the age of 8. In fact, Spain is the only European country where English as a foreign language is taught as early as the age of three or four (Eurydice, 2005).

Nevertheless, fulfilling the European Commission's objective of everyone having a grasp of two other community languages has a long way to go. According to the Eurobarometer Report 54 (2001), 53% of European citizens say they can speak at least one European language apart from their mother tongue and of those just half (26%) can speak two foreign languages. If we consider the results obtained amongst the future teachers included in this volume, this understanding of foreign languages shows a very heterogeneous picture, as those who perceive their command of the L3 as good or very good ranges from 80% in the Irish context to just a quarter (26%) in the Welsh context.

The Irish figures are strikingly high, but it has to be pointed out that in Ireland primary teachers can study a FL to academic BA level and sometimes to MA level as part of their teacher education. The informants seem to have been following these FL programmes and thus figures appear somewhat inflated (see Ó Laoire, this volume). Curiously enough, both extremes (Ireland and Wales) share the same majority language, English, and therefore when we refer to the L3 in these two contexts and Malta – where British colonial history has exerted a major role – the language concerned is either French, Spanish, Italian or German.

As can be seen in Figure 10.1, two main groups can be distinguished. The first one is made up of Ireland, Malta, Dutch-medium Brussels and Friesland, whose percentages of good competence in at least one foreign language are above 50%. The other group consists of French-medium Brussels, the four bilingual Spanish contexts, and Wales, where less than 50% of the future teachers consider their command to be good. At this stage it has to be remembered that Brussels is probably the most complex linguistic setting of those here analysed, as Mettewie and Janssens clearly depict in their chapter, which is why the data are divided into two sections: Dutch-medium and French-medium Brussels.

The data concerning Wales and the four bilingual areas in Spain are particularly worrying, as it is hard to imagine how (having less than a third of the would-be teachers capable of speaking an L3) the multilingual objectives set by the European Commission can be met.

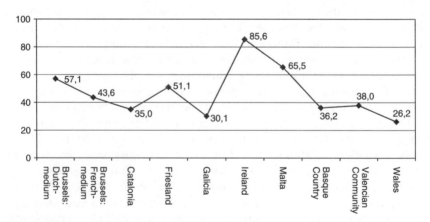

Figure 10.1 Percentage of preservice teachers whose command of the L3 is (very) good

The widespread low command of the L3 amongst preservice teachers in the different contexts under analysis coincides with the results obtained by Beetsma (2002) in a study undertaken under the auspices of the European Commission and in which Mercator-Education[1] was asked to conduct a report on trilingual education in the European Union. Beetsma concludes that teachers' L3 proficiency can be termed as moderate or low, a situation that could be remedied by hiring native-speaking teachers, a theoretically easy chore taking advantage of the single labour market. However, and as Mettewie and Janssens argue, this is just unfeasible in Belgium and very complicated to achieve in the rest of the bilingual contexts, as in general the native speaker of a foreign language should also be capable of speaking the minority and the majority languages concerned. In Spanish state schools, moreover, teachers have to be civil servants, which complicates matters even further. Thus, it seems that the most reasonable course of action may be to boost foreign-language learning amongst preservice teachers by taking advantage of the student-exchange agreements set up within the Socrates/Erasmus programme, an option that has not been fully exploited so far and which could bear many linguistic fruits.

The Role of Teachers in this Multilingual Europe

It seems evident that teachers have a role of paramount importance to play in building a multilingual Europe, as their attitudes and everyday work should reflect a clear disposition towards tolerance of both linguistic and cultural diversity. Even more so if we consider that, according to the Eurobarometer Report 54, in the majority of European countries foreign languages are taught in primary education by general teachers, who are qualified to teach all (or almost all) subjects in the curriculum. Yet this is not the case in countries such as Spain or Malta, where specialist teachers of foreign languages usually work in secondary education. The European Commission is also aware of the pivotal role of teachers and, as a matter of fact, in its Action Plan entitled *Language Learning and Linguistic Diversity* teachers are called upon to exemplify the European values of openness to others, tolerance of differences and willingness to communicate. Moreover, research studies (see, for example Dooley, 2005a) indicate that preservice teachers are those who are most likely to renegotiate their initial reluctance towards more positive understandings of linguistic diversity. These results suggest how important it is to work on this question with those who will be teaching the next generation.

Teachers' knowledge and beliefs exert a clear-cut influence on their professional practice (Dooley, 2005b; Ellis, 2004; Woods, 1996) and their attitudes during the learning process also affect students' attitude formation, change and maintenance (Sotés *et al.*, 2005), up to the point that they can be more influential than parents and the context (Lambert & Tucker, 1972). Educational researchers have shown that the attitudes and beliefs teachers hold can have a subsequent effect on their perceptions and their behaviour in the classroom, a reflection of the so-called *Pygmalion effect* (Dooley, 2005b), a term which in a general way denotes the effect of teachers' expectations on students' results, attitudes, behaviour, etc. According to this effect, if teachers' attitudes towards the language of a group of students are positive (or, conversely, somewhat negative), these attitudes will correlate with the performance level in that particular language of those students. In this respect, Clark and Trafford (1995) argue that both teachers and students consider that the teacher/ student relationship is the most influential variable when it comes to the students' attitudes towards the L2 (or LX) learning.

Despite the ever increasing spread of multilingualism in society in general and at school in particular (and the chapter on Brussels in this volume is a very good case in point), there is no questioning about the presence of many monolingual teachers teaching languages. As Ellis (2004: 104–105) points out, this leads to a paradox in which 'teachers are preparing students for multilinguality without having a very clear idea of what it is and what it might be like to achieve it. ... It is difficult to think of another case where teachers are authorised to teach students to do something – in this case, learn a second language – they cannot do themselves.' Although this is the case in places all over the world, it does not affect the European bilingual contexts under scrutiny in this volume, since most of the future-teachers/participants had knowledge of two, three or more languages (albeit to very different degrees). In this context it seems necessary to discover more about teachers' attitudes towards languages, as this information could provide us with a very valuable means for, firstly, detecting their possible interpretation and implementation of the different language policies at work in each bilingual context, and secondly, for professional empowerment (Stavans & Narkiss, 2004).

Therefore, the analysis of teachers' attitudes is a must, as it may shed some light on language issues, while at the same time making them reflect on their own ideas, beliefs and knowledge (in the case of preservice teachers, as all the participants in this volume) and practices (in the case of in-service teachers). If teachers' language awareness is raised, it seems reasonable to affirm that there is a better opportunity to spread this awareness and valorisation of linguistic diversity amongst their students. In this way they will play a role that goes beyond the teaching of language structures and school contents, becoming thus main players in the promotion of multilingualism and multiculturalism and the integration of different languages in the school culture. Those teachers who are more aware of the advantages of multilingualism are the ones who are also more liable to take on the role of cultural mediators and to create a positive learning environment. As Wright and Bolito (1993) put it, language awareness may become the missing link in language teacher education and provide an important connection between teachers' knowledge of language and their practices in language teaching.

A Comparison of the Results Obtained in Different European Bilingual Contexts

The main objective of this volume is to analyse the linguistic issue among preservice teachers in different bilingual contexts where there are at least three languages in contact, as there is a dire need to examine this issue in multilingual school contexts, since, as Hoffmann and Ytsma (2004: 2) point out, the research studies on trilingualism completed so far mainly approach this issue from an educational, developmental or pycholinguistic angle (Cenoz *et al.*, 2001a;b), whereas those taking a sociolinguistic perspective are in the minority. We totally agree with Bernaus *et al.* (2004: 87–88) when they state the following:

> Multilingualism and the development of multilingual education programmes aiming to promote language proficiency in more than two languages are becoming increasingly widespread due to historical, political and economic factors. Future research should continue to examine students' (and teachers') attitudes towards and motivation to learn languages in this (they are referring to Catalonia) and other multilingual education contexts. By identifying the attitudinal and motivational elements related to learning languages in general and those that play a language-specific role, we can gain a better understanding of how these affective components function within multilingual communities. Furthermore, studies should continue to investigate the influence of language learning contexts, along with the use of the languages, and the role of relative language status on the attitudes, motivation and multilingual competence of students. (the comments in brackets are ours)

In this section we will proceed to compare the language competence, the language use, the importance attached to the minority language and the language attitudes shown by the participants in the nine European bilingual contexts put forward in the previous chapters. This is a rather complex task, as the comparison of some contexts is anything but straightforward. Hence, whereas the four Spanish bilingual contexts may be easier to compare due to obvious historical and political parallelisms (although there are also differences among them), the sociolinguistic situation in Brussels or Malta is very different, which contributes to complicating this task. However, we do believe that, bearing in mind the particular sociolinguistic features of each context, some tentative resemblances can be drawn.

Language competence

When the students' competence in the minority language is analysed (see Figure 10.2), the percentages of those with a (very) good command are fairly high. As a matter of fact, in all the contexts more than 70% of the respondents would be included in this category, and in French-medium Brussels, Catalonia, Ireland, Malta and Galicia these percentages are above 90%. Thus, it can be concluded that the language revival boosted in Europe after the Second World War is having a clear-cut impact on the recovery of minority languages and, thus, two out of three would-be teachers are already trained to teach in/through these languages. These results seem to confirm that the efforts made so far to include the different minority languages in the educational system are working out.

As far as the majority language is concerned, the trend is very similar to that observed in the case of the minority language, as percentages are close to 100% in all cases. The only exception would be Brussels, but as stated before (see Mettewie and Janssens, this volume), this is a rather peculiar context, which makes it difficult to compare its results with those of the other eight bilingual areas. The linguistic situation in Malta is also worth remembering (see Caruana, this volume), as it is hard to say which of the two languages, Maltese and English, represents the minority or the majority language.

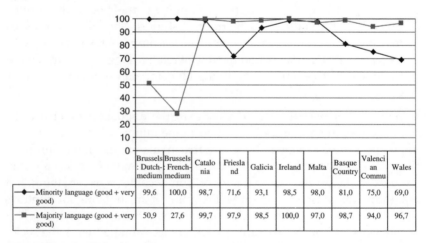

	Brussels: Dutch-medium	Brussels French-medium	Catalonia	Friesland	Galicia	Ireland	Malta	Basque Country	Valencian Commu	Wales
◆ Minority language (good + very good)	99,6	100,0	98,7	71,6	93,1	98,5	98,0	81,0	75,0	69,0
■ Majority language (good + very good)	50,9	27,6	99,7	97,9	98,5	100,0	97,0	98,7	94,0	96,7

Figure 10.2 Percentage of preservice teachers with a good command of the minority/majority language

It can therefore be concluded that there is a relative balance in the competence of the languages in contact, as the percentages of both minority and majority languages are quite close. The bilingual communities of Catalonia and Galicia in Spain, and Ireland and Malta are very good cases in point, as there are no differences between the minority and the majority languages. There is still some way to go in Friesland, the Valencian Community, the Basque Country and Wales where around a quarter of their would-be teachers need to improve their command of the minority language, in order to ensure that both the majority and the minority languages are given the same opportunities in schools.

Language use

In order to compare the language use of each bilingual context, three of the eleven items in the questionnaire were selected. These three items were chosen due to the fact that they represent the three more significant linguistic spheres to which an individual is exposed: the family (the selected item has to do with the language used with the mother), the school (the item concerning the language used with friends in the classroom) and the means of communication (centred on the item analysing the language used to watch TV). In the following text the answers given to each of these items will be examined.

As can be observed in Figure 10.3, French-medium Brussels, Dutch-medium Brussels, Malta, Catalonia and Friesland are the bilingual settings where a higher use of the minority language when addressing the mother is found: in all cases above 70%. In this sense, it has to be said

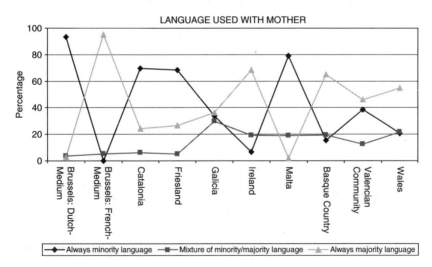

Figure 10.3 Language used with the mother

that Belgium is once again a rather exceptional context, provoking the most outstanding differences in both French-medium and Dutch-medium schools, as both languages are clearly separated in the home environment (the other language is hardly ever used). Malta is another context where there is a sharp contrast between Maltese and English due to the aforementioned sociolinguistic peculiarities of the country.

Contrastingly, in two Spanish bilingual communities, Galicia and the Valencian Community, there exists a balanced use of both languages when talking to the mother, although the mixture of both is more typical in the former. In Friesland and Catalonia the use of the minority language is much more habitual, whereas in the Basque Country and Ireland the majority language reigns supreme. The mixture of both languages is not the main option in any case (Galicia is as near as we come to an exception) and, therefore, it can be concluded that this linguistic practice is not in the least in vogue in these settings, which allows us to speak of some sort of *linguistic loyalty* in the home environment.

With regards to the language used with friends in the classroom (see Figure 10.4), once again Brussels follows a rather different pattern, where the home language is firmly preferred and, consequently, a mixture of Dutch and French is a very unusual choice. In the rest of the contexts, only in Catalonia is the minority language (if Maltese can be considered so) the predominant language, whereas in Ireland the majority language is used by three out of four subjects.

In contrast to the family context and the language used with the mother, in the rest of the contexts (Friesland, Galicia, Malta, the Basque Country, the Valencian Community and Wales) the most habitual

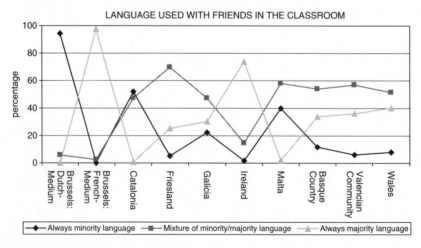

Figure 10.4 Language used with friends in the classroom

practice is to mix both the majority and the minority languages. This is also done by almost half of the Catalan sample. Therefore, the linguistic loyalty observed in the family context is not maintained when it comes to speaking with classmates, where it is much more fashionable to mix both languages.

When it comes to watching TV (see Figure 10.5), Brussels is once again the exception, as the family language is kept as the main language. However, the percentages of mixture of both languages is close to 40% in both the French and Dutch communities, a percentage of use much higher than in any of the other situations under analysis in the Belgian context. In the other contexts, the alternate use of both the majority and the minority languages is the most popular option. As could be expected, the viewing of channels which broadcast only in the minority language is minimum, except in Wales, where almost a third of the participants say they watch TV only in Welsh (Laugharne points out the outstanding impact of the Welsh channel S4C). Also in Friesland nearly 20% disclosed that they watch TV only in Frisian, but these two contexts represent the exceptions to the norm.

The percentages of those who watch TV always in the majority language are higher, but it has to remembered that majority-language channels are more widespread and habitual than minority-language channels in all contexts. In fact, Catalonia is the only bilingual community where those who watch TV only in the minority language surpass those who watch it in Spanish, although the vast majority of Catalan respondents alternate between them.

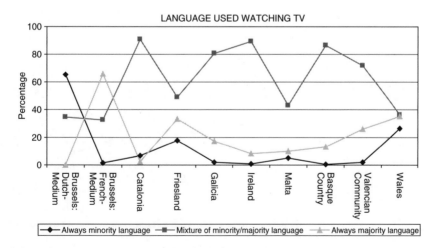

Figure 10.5 Language used to watch TV

Importance attached to the minority language

As we did in the case of language use, in this section we will also select three out the 15 items that were put forward in the questionnaire with a view to examining the importance attached to the different minority languages to do different activities, the three items being the following: importance attached to the minority language to make friends, to get a job and to be accepted in the community.

Figure 10.6, Figure 10.7 and Figure 10.8 reflect that there is no clear trend as a result of the different and diverse sociolinguistic contexts under study, which makes it difficult to reach conclusions. Maltese and Welsh are seen as *important* by more than 60% of the subjects to make friends (see Figure 10.6), but in the rest of the contexts those who support this idea are the minority. The *so so* option reaches high percentages in Dutch-medium and French-medium Brussels, Friesland and the Basque Country, but nowhere does the minority language seem to limit the possibility of making friends. This would allow us to conclude that the linguistic factor does not appear as discriminatory concerning the making of new acquaintances.

In the case of getting a job (see Figure 10.7), the minority language is regarded as important in the Basque Country, Wales and Ireland. These are bilingual settings where the minority language is not as widely spoken as in Catalonia or Galicia, where a good command of Catalan or Galician seems not to provide more job opportunities. The exception to this trend (less widespread use equals greater employment advantages) is represented by Malta. While Maltese is virtually universally under-stood (see Caruana's chapter), it is still considered an asset in the job market.

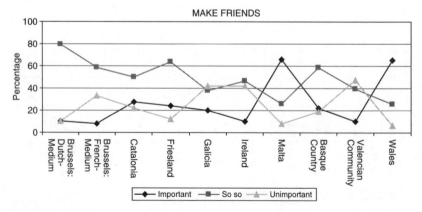

Figure 10.6 Importance attached to the minority language to make friends

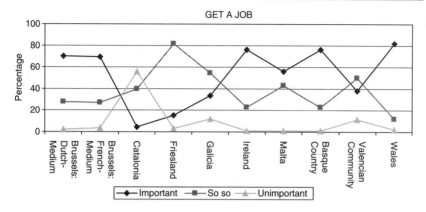

Figure 10.7 Importance attached to the minority language to get a job

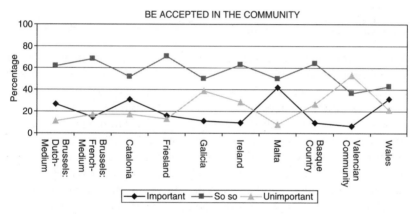

Figure 10.8 Importance attached to the minority language to be accepted in the community

Figure 10.8 indicates that the minority language does not play a discriminatory role when it comes to being accepted in the community. The highest percentages are found once again in Malta (where there is a strong identification with Maltese), together with Catalonia and Wales. In the other contexts the percentages are very low.

Language attitudes

One of the main novelties of this volume lies in the fact that it is focused on language attitudes towards three languages in different contexts, an issue hardly examined so far (Lasagabaster, 2003; 2004). Any language policy and planning to be implemented in multilingual contexts requires a deep understanding of the underlying attitudinal trends in order to

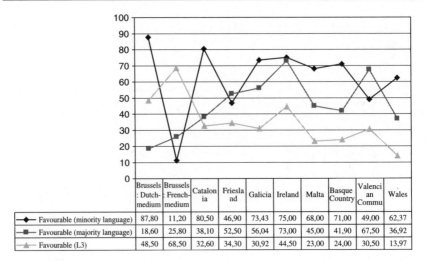

	Brussels: Dutch-medium	Brussels: French-medium	Catalonia	Friesland	Galicia	Ireland	Malta	Basque Country	Valencian Commu	Wales
Favourable (minority language)	87,80	11,20	80,50	46,90	73,43	75,00	68,00	71,00	49,00	62,37
Favourable (majority language)	18,60	25,80	38,10	52,50	56,04	73,00	45,00	41,90	67,50	36,92
Favourable (L3)	48,50	68,50	32,60	34,30	30,92	44,50	23,00	24,00	30,50	13,97

Figure 10.9 Favourable attitudes towards the L1, L2 and L3 in each context

avoid probable negative consequences such as tensions, disillusion and little willingness to accept it on the part of those who have to *suffer* the language policy concerned. Thus, it is really important to understand that language attitudes are deeply influenced by the context, which may result in not so favourable attitudes towards a given language even if it is very important worldwide (as is the case of English).

In our different samples, the favourable attitudes are much more pre-eminent than the neutral or unfavourable ones (see Figure 10.9). What is more, only in Friesland and the Valencian Community is the percentage of favourable attitudes towards the majority language higher than that of favourable attitudes towards the minority language and, in any case, only marginally so. As could be expected, the favourable attitudes towards the L3 or foreign language are not as high as those towards the L1/L2, except in the case of Brussels, where Mettewie and Janssens stress that the attitudes towards English as a foreign language are more positive than the attitudes towards French or Dutch as L2.

Another remarkable feature is the very low presence of negative attitudes towards any of the three languages, and also the high percentage of neutral attitudes in many cases towards the majority language, in particular the L3.

The family language and the linguistic model (more or less presence of the minority language) followed at school emerge as the most influential variables on language attitudes in all nine contexts under study. Other variables, such as socioprofessional status, gender, size of hometown or dominant language in the hometown, play a significant role in particular contexts.

The key unresolved question is therefore the existing relationship between the aforementioned two key factors, namely school and family, and the formation of language attitudes. Some researchers affirm that the language attitudes generated within the family context are more influential than those formed under the influence of the educational setting. Others believe that the curriculum plays a paramount role and that its influence on language attitudes through language learning at school is a key factor. A third standpoint, ever more popular, highlights that language learning and attitudes determine each other and therefore they both become cause and effect (Baker, 1992; 1996). The majority of theoretical models put forward in the last decades have been based on this last idea, although each of them puts the stress on different variables (Clément & Gardner, 2001; Gardner & Clément, 1990).

Evidently, as Huguet (in press) points out, and irrespective of which of the three postures outlined above is preferred, the complexity of the individual's linguistic context and the difficulties inherent in the analysis of family–school interaction are highlighted by all those interested in this field of study, which makes research on this question fundamental not only for the individual themselves, but also for the society they live in.

Conclusions

Competence in the minority language amongst European preservice teachers in the contexts here described is higher than ever before. The development of the linguistic situation in the Basque Country serves as a meaningful example of this process: in 1977, that is to say, less than three decades ago, only 5% of state primary teachers could speak Basque (Basque Government, 1990) and they were not generally proficient in its use in writing or for academic purposes. Basque was not even heard in teacher-training colleges, so there was little chance for training teachers to be able to teach in and through Basque. Nowadays, it is estimated that about 65% of practising teachers are qualified to teach in Basque, and amongst the Basque participants in this volume (see Lasagabaster's chapter) this percentage is even higher, at 81%, and these are future teachers who consider their command to be (very) good. There is no doubt that this improvement in such a short time is outstanding. And there are contexts such as Catalonia, Galicia, Ireland or Malta where minority language competence among teachers is even more widespread.

The picture regarding the command of foreign languages is, however, dimmer, especially in the four Spanish bilingual communities. This, together with the preponderance of neutral attitudes towards the L3 seem to indicate that there is a dire need to work on language attitudes towards foreign languages in the different educational systems. If the European Commission's objective of spreading the knowledge of a second foreign language is to succeed, language attitudes have to be considered. Some of the authors of this volume have proposed the inclusion of didactic units in the curriculum in which this issue is dealt with in order to erase linguistic parochialism and to make students aware of the richness inherent in linguistic and cultural diversity. Consequently, a reasonable way of improving the learning of foreign languages could be the inclusion of language awareness courses in all European curricula (Carter, 1992; Hawkins, 1984; van Lier, 1995). Much is said from a theoretical point of view, but now might be a good time to start implementing specific language policies in this respect.

Our results also corroborate those of different studies in which it was found that access to foreign language mass media does have a significant influence on the development not only of the foreign language concerned, but also on the attitudes towards it (Caruana, 2003; Dewaele, 2002; Lasagabaster, 2001; Sjöholm, 2004). Other factors to be borne in mind include exchange programmes between different European countries and also using the foreign language to teach content. The increasing popularity of the early teaching of the foreign language seems by itself insufficient, and may need to go hand in hand with its vehicular use.

The widespread favourable attitudes towards the different minority languages reflect how the linguistic situation has changed in the last few decades. Most of the minority languages examined in this volume have had no legal (and in some cases little social) support throughout the 20th century, which is why the results obtained in these nine European bilingual contexts are encouraging and seem to confirm the positive effect of the linguistic policies undertaken in order to protect them and boost their use. Most second-language learning models grant a main role to language attitudes in the success of the L2 learning process and, therefore, it can be said that this key element (a positive attitudinal stance) has been achieved. This will undoubtedly help to improve the situation of the different minority languages even more and strengthen and underpin the recovery process. In most contexts there is still a large margin for improvement (as the data on language use demonstrates), but the efforts made so far seem to be on the right track.

Trilingual education, understood as the presence of three languages in the curriculum, is becoming more and more commonplace and there is a dire need to take measures at the European level to make the most of this educational experience. Thus, we would like to round off this final chapter by quoting a series of recommendations put forward by Beetsma (2002: 122–123) that we consider to be worthwhile remembering:

- A guidance service should be organised on a European level for offering advice and providing stimuli to the regions with and without trilingual primary education.
- The European Commission should support pilot projects and experiments in the area of trilingual primary education.
- Special attention should be paid to the issue of trilingual primary education within the supply of study visits and exchange programmes offered by the European institutions.
- In order for trilingual primary education to become better known, an information programme is needed at European level. The programme should be aimed mainly at parents of school-age children as well as at schools in the minority-language communities.
- The exchange on an international level of knowledge and experiences will have a positive effect on the development of trilingual primary education in different regions.
- Data collection regarding trilingual provisions should be promoted in every region.
- Legislation regarding the teaching of and in a third and/or foreign language should be promoted, whereby the use of a foreign language as medium of instruction is formally allowed in every grade of primary education.
- To encourage the development in the realms of trilingual (primary and secondary) education with the member states of the European Union, it is important to set up a new network of researchers, policy makers and practitioners involved in trilingual schooling.

The consideration of these questions, together with the analysis of language attitudes and their formation, will undoubtedly help to understand the challenging European multilingual context. This volume is an attempt to break some ground in this direction.

Notes

1. Mercator-Education is an organisation whose main objective is to gather, store and distribute information on minority language education in European regions so that this information is at hand for policy makers, researchers, teachers, students and journalists. Mercator-Education has published several regional dossiers to meet this objective, which are also available on-line (www.mercator-education.org).

References

Baker, C. (1992) *Attitudes and Language.* Clevedon: Multilingual Matters.
Baker, C. (1996) *Foundations of Bilingual Education and Bilingualism* (2nd edn). Clevedon: Multilingual Matters.
Basque Government (1990) *10 años de enseñanza vasca.* Vitoria-Gasteiz: Servicio de Publicaciones del Gobierno Vasco.

Beetsma, D. (2002) _Trilingual Primary Education in Europe. Inventory of the Provisions for Trilingual Primary Education in Minority Language Communities of the European Union_. Ljouwert/Leeuwarden: Fryske Akademy/Mercator Education.

Bernaus, M., Masgoret, A.-M., Gardner, R.C. and Reyes, E. (2004) Motivation and attitudes towards learning languages in multicultural classrooms. _International Journal of Multilingualism_ 1, 75–89.

Carter, R. (ed.) (1992) _Knowledge about Language and the Curriculum: The LINC Reader_. London: Hodder & Stoughton.

Caruana, S. (2003) _Mezzi di comunicazione e input linguistico. L'acquisizione dell'italiano L2 a Malta_. Milano: Francoangeli.

Cenoz, J. and Jessner, U. (eds) (2000) _English in Europe: the Acquisition of a Third Language_. Clevedon: Multilingual Matters.

Cenoz, J., Hufeisen, U. and Jessner, U. (eds) (2001a) _Looking beyond Second Language Acquisition. Studies in Tri- and Multilingualism_. Tübingen: Stauffenburg Verlag.

Cenoz, J., Hufeisen, U. and Jessner, U. (eds) (2001b) _Cross-linguistic Influence in Third Language Acquisition: Psycholinguistic Perspectives_. Clevedon: Multilingual Matters.

Clark, A. and Trafford, J. (1995) Boys into modern languages: An investigation of the discrepancy in attitudes and performance between boys and girls in modern languages. _Gender and Education_ 7, 315–325.

Clément, R. and Gardner, R.C. (2001) Second language mastery. In W.P. Robinson and H. Giles (eds) _The New Handbook of Language and Social Psychology_ (pp. 489–504). New York: John Wiley & Sons.

Dewaele, J.-M. (2002) Psychological and sociodemographic correlates of communicative anxiety in L2 and L3 production. _The International Journal of Bilingualism_ 6, 23–38.

Dooley, M. (2005a) How aware are they? Research into teachers' attitudes about linguistic diversity. _Language Awareness_ 14, 97–111.

Dooley, M. (2005b) Linguistic diversity: A qualitative analysis of foreign language teachers' category assembly. Unpublished PhD dissertation. Barcelona: Universitat Autónoma de Barcelona.

Ellis, E.M. (2004) The invisible multilingual teacher: The contribution of language background to Australian ESL teachers' professional knowledge and beliefs. _International Journal of Multilingualism_ 1, 90–108.

Eurobarometer Report 54 (2001) _Europeans and Languages_. On WWW at http://europa.eu.int/comm/education/policies/lang/languages/barolang_ en.pdf. Access date: October 2004.

Eurydice (2001) _Key Data on Teaching Languages at School in Europe_. On WWW at http://www.eurydice.org. Access date: October 2004.

Extra, G. and Yagmur, K. (2004) _Urban Multilingualism in Europe. Immigrant Minority Languages at Home and School_. Clevedon: Multilingual Matters.

Gardner, R.C. and Clément, R. (1990) Social psychological perspectives on second language acquisition. In H. Giles and W.P. Robinson (eds) _Handbook of Language and Social Psychology_ (pp. 495–517). New York: John Wiley & Sons.

Hawkins, E.W. (1994) _Awareness of Language: An Introduction_. Cambridge: Cambridge University Press.

Hoffmann, C. and Ytsma, J. (eds) (2004) _Trilingualism in Family, School and Community_. Clevedon: Multilingual Matters.

Huguet, Á. (in press) Attitudes and motivation versus language achievement in cross-linguistic settings. What is cause and what effect? *Journal of Multilingual and Multicultural Development*.

Lambert, W.E. and Tucker, G.R. (1972) *Bilingual Education of Children. The St. Lambert Experiment*. Rowley, MA: Newbury House.

Lasagabaster, D. (2001) The learning of English in Finland. *Interface, Journal of Applied Linguistics* 16, 27–44.

Lasagabaster, D. (2003) *Trilingüismo en la enseñanza. Actitudes hacia la lengua minoritaria, la mayoritaria y la extranjera*. Lleida: Milenio.

Lasagabaster, D. (2004) Attitudes towards English in the Basque Autonomous Community. *World Englishes* 23, 211–224.

Sjöholm, K. (2004) English as a third language in bilingual Finland: Basic communication or academic language? In C. Hoffmann and J. Ytsma (eds) *Trilingualism in Family, School and Community* (pp. 219–238). Clevedon: Multilingual Matters.

Sotés, P., Oroz, N. and Vilches, C. (2005) Nafarroako irakaskuntza elebiduna: irakasleen jarrerak eta sinesmenak. In J. Cenoz and D. Lasagabaster (eds) Monograph of the Journal *Bat Soziolinguistika Aldizkaria*.

Stavans, A. and Narkiss, D. (2004) Creating and implementing a language policy in the Israeli educational system. In C. Hoffmann and J. Ytsma (eds) *Trilingualism in Family, School and Community* (pp. 139–165). Clevedon: Multilingual Matters.

van Lier, L. (1995) *Introducing Language Awareness*. London: Penguin.

Woods, D. (1996) *Teacher Cognition in Language Teaching*. Cambridge: Cambridge University Press.

Wright, T. and Bolito, R. (1993) Language awareness: A missing link in language teacher education? *ELT Journal* 47, 292–304.